TRADING FREE

Patrick Low

TRADING FREE

The GATT and
U.S. Trade Policy

A Twentieth Century Fund Book

The Twentieth Century Fund Press ◆ New York ◆ 1993

The Twentieth Century Fund is a research foundation undertaking timely analyses of economic, political, and social issues. Not-for-profit and non-partisan, the Fund was founded in 1919 and endowed by Edward A. Filene.

Library of Congress Cataloging-in-Publication Data

Low, Patrick, 1949-
    Trading free:the GATT and U.S. trade policy/by Patrick Low.
        p.   cm.
    Includes bibliographical references and index.
    ISBN 0-87078-352-1   ISBN 0-87078-351-3 (pbk)
        1. United States--Commercial policy.   2. Free trade--United States.   3. General Agreement on Tariffs and Trade (Organization)   4. Uruguay Round (1987-) I. Title.
    HF1455.L67   1993
    382'.92'0973--dc20   93-12630
                                                                CIP

Cover Design and Illustration: Claude Goodwin
Manufactured in the United States of America.

For Gloria

FOREWORD

A generation ago, the teaching of macroeconomics in many American classrooms did not involve any analysis of international flows of goods and services. The reasoning behind this approach was straightforward: the amounts involved were statistically trivial compared to the immense gross domestic product of the United States. Although Americans had the largest part of total global commerce, it was relatively unimportant to the prosperity of the United States.

Today, students of our economy are obsessed with America's place in global commerce. Indeed, in what is still by far the world's largest economy, concern and even anger about international competition is becoming an increasingly powerful political force. One would be hard put to find in Congress the optimistic consensus that animated the largely American-designed postwar economic order, the Bretton Woods system. Then, of course, the American giant—sole possessor of the atomic bomb and producer of 40 percent of the world's wealth—believed that free trade and Western-style business, under American leadership, would modernize the world.

This belief in the blessings that would come from American economic supremacy has been shaken as international competitors claim ever-larger slices of the global economic pie. Even the apparent demise of communism has failed to restore American confidence in its economic future. As international competition has increased, so too has the debate in this country between free traders and protectionists. The possibility of a global paradise seems as far away as ever.

Perhaps not surprisingly, as more jobs and businesses are affected, political resistance to further trade liberalization has hardened. Even so, the globalization of markets is proceeding rapidly, increasing international competition and driving nations to play catch-up on economic policy and the rules governing trade. In the United States, the debate about adjusting to the inevitable currently is focused on the proposed North American Free Trade Agreement (NAFTA). But, of course, as Patrick Low points out in the pages that follow, the main event for trade policy is the future fate of the GATT.

Advocates of further agreements argue that the benefits of freer trade will be far greater than the costs to those displaced by the relocation of production. They insist that, as cross-border trade increases, American consumers will pay lower prices for a wide range of goods. Countries will specialize and produce more efficiently, and the ability of American companies to compete with their international counterparts will be enhanced. And the result will be that the United States will experience a net gain in jobs.

Critics of the GATT, on the other hand, predict a continuing loss of U.S. jobs as companies switch to lower-cost workers abroad. Skeptics also are concerned about the elimination of trade barriers in Europe, Japan, and even Mexico. So far, the Clinton administration has been talking tough about protecting U.S. interests, implying that the past negotiations were not sufficiently advantageous to the nation.

The Twentieth Century Fund has been examining the many issues involved in this debate. We have supported examinations of the thinking behind NAFTA—Gilbert Winham's *Trading with Canada*, Earl Fry's *Canada's Unity Crisis*, and Robert Pastor's *Integration with Mexico*—as well as more general studies of trade issues, including Otis Graham's *Losing Time* and the second edition of I.M. Destler's *American Trade Politics*, and *The Free Trade Debate: The Report of the Twentieth Century Fund Task Force on the Future of American Trade Policy*.

In *Trading Free*, Patrick Low, who worked in the GATT secretariat in Geneva for eight years and is currently with the World Bank, makes a strong case against too much emphasis on trade negotiations as a zero-sum game, with winners and losers. He believes that the reductions in barriers to trade that have been accomplished since World War II have contributed to the high standard of living in this country and to desirable economic progress among our allies. In this thoughtful and provocative study, he sets out the background and clarifies the issues that will be debated by policymakers today, and classes tomorrow.

Richard C. Leone, *President*
The Twentieth Century Fund
March 1993

PREFACE

Writing about United States trade policy and the General Agreement on Tariffs and Trade (GATT) has been like trying to hit a moving target. For many months, the progress of this study was slowed by the seeming imminence of an event critical to the future of the international trading system—the termination of the Uruguay Round of multilateral trade negotiations. But repeated failure to complete the negotiations has laid bare the flagging commitment of nations to open trade, and ushered in a period of instability and uncertainty in international trade relations. In tracing how this has come to pass, the study argues that policy failure, and not a change of circumstance, is the root cause of the problem, and that there is no realistic alternative to a GATT-based trading system built on non-discrimination and open markets.

I am grateful to several members of the staff of Twentieth Century Fund, past and present, and to its president, Richard C. Leone, for the continued and patient support they have shown for this project. In particular, I should like to thank Nina Massen, John Samples, and Beverly Goldberg, all of whom have spent considerable time providing guidance and suggestions in a highly professional manner, even if they have not always shared the views expressed in the study. I should also like to thank Kathleen Lynch for editing the manuscript.

Many other people have been generous with their time, including Clem Boonekamp, Robert Eastwood, Richard Eglin, J. Michael Finger, Michael Hart, David Hartridge, Robert Hudec, Alejandro Jara, Mark Koulen, Sam Laird, Adrian Otten, Amelia Porges, Nick Smart, Arvind Subramanian, David Wall, and John Whalley. Most of the persons mentioned above have provided detailed comments on large parts of earlier drafts, and all of them are absolved from any responsibility for the final product.

Also absolved from any association with the views expressed in the study is my current employer, the World Bank, as well as its member countries, board of directors, and management. This book was conceived and largely completed before I joined the Bank. Much of the work was undertaken while I was a visiting researcher at El Colegio de México in Mexico City, from 1988–90. I am very grateful to El Colegio de México for the congenial and stimulating atmosphere in which I was permitted to work, and particularly to Adalberto García Rocha, Eduardo Pérez Motta, Alvaro Baillet, and José Romero for the many kindnesses they showed me.

I am greatly indebted to my wife, Gloria, for her support and encouragement, especially at times when I wondered if I was ever going to complete the work. Finally, I am grateful for the patience shown by our children, Ana and Maria, whose interminable, uncomprehending questions about the "book" kept me good-humored (most of the time).

Washington, D.C.
February 1993

CONTENTS

INTRODUCTION

A t their July 1990 Houston Summit, the leaders of the world's seven largest industrial democracies (the G-7) stated that:

> The successful outcome of the Uruguay Round has the highest priority on the international economic agenda. Consequently, we stress our determination to take the difficult political decisions necessary to achieve far-reaching, substantial results in all areas of the Uruguay Round by the end of this year.

Launched under the auspices of the General Agreement on Tariffs and Trade (GATT) in 1986, the Uruguay Round of trade negotiations represented a major multilateral effort by over one hundred countries to liberalize world trade and address a series of problems facing the trading system. The negotiations were to be completed at a GATT ministerial meeting in Brussels in December 1990, five months after the Houston summit. The GATT meeting ended in a bitter public squabble, failing to produce any results at all.

Seemingly unabashed by the gap between their words and deeds, the G-7 leaders declared at their London Summit in July 1991 that:

> No issue has more far-reaching implications for the future prospects of the world economy than the successful conclusion of the Uruguay Round. . . . We therefore commit ourselves to an ambitious, global and balanced package of results from the Round . . . The aim . . . should be to complete the Round before the end of 1991.

1

Having failed a second time to act upon their commitments, the G-7 leaders yet again declared at their July 1992 summit in Munich that they expected "an agreement [could] be reached before the end of 1992." Three times the G-7 heads of state set a target for completing the Uruguay Round, and three times they failed to meet their objective. Inability to reach agreement on an Uruguay Round package has turned primarily on differences between the United States and the European Community (EC), while dozens of other countries that participated actively in the Uruguay Round have looked on with growing frustration. Although trade in agriculture has ostensibly been the source of the problem, several other difficult issues have been set aside. Whether any package of results that might be finally put together will come near to meeting the ambitious agenda set in 1986 has become increasingly doubtful. The bold political declarations of recent economic summits look increasingly like ritualistic incantation. Is it simply collective hypocrisy at work? Why has the postwar multilateral trading system been allowed to decline, and how much does it matter?

These are some of the questions that this book addresses. The focus of the analysis is upon U.S. trade policy and the United States in the trading system. The study concentrates on the period from the early 1980s onward, although prior developments in U.S. trade policy and in the international trading system are taken up where they bear on this period. The attitude of the United States to the multilateral trading system has changed quite markedly over the last decade or two, and at the same time international trading relations have come under severe strain. The study traces these changes. A series of arguments are developed about the evolution of U.S. trade policy. The analysis then shifts to the GATT multilateral trading system and to a consideration of how well the system has functioned. At first sight, U.S. trade policy and the multilateral trading system may seem to be separate subjects of study. This is not, however, the way they have been treated. The preeminence of the United States in world affairs has left an indelible mark on the GATT system. This influence is as important to the evolution of the trading system and its future prospects as it was to its original design.

A basic contention in this study is that the trade policymaking process in the United States is failing. The advantages and strengths of the division of power between the legislative and executive branches of government, so carefully crafted in the Constitution, have been allowed to become something of a liability in the trade policy field. After the bitter lessons of unbridled protectionism and trade war in the 1930s, Congress delegated the exercise of its trade policy powers to the president as a way of insulating itself from sectoral protectionist interests. This aimed to provide the president, guardian of the welfare of the population at large, with authority to run trade policy in the national interest. The arrangements worked well for over three decades, and the United States was able to exercise its dominion and full leadership authority over stable and generally harmonious international trading relations. Although there were weak points and trouble spots, these arrangements were associated with a prolonged period of continuing growth and significant trade liberalization.

As world economic conditions have become more difficult, and as the demands of increased economic interdependency have made themselves felt against a background of relative decline in the economic power and influence of the United States, those constructive arrangements worked out in the 1930s between Congress and the president have fallen apart. More accurately, they have served an altogether different objective. They have accommodated an increasingly protectionist trade policy orientation, while at the same time allowing decisionmakers to avoid responsibility for policy outcomes. Much of the first part of this study explores the rhetoric, the statutes, the policies, the processes, and the procedures that have allowed the Congress, and to a lesser extent the executive branch, to create the illusion of accountable government while pursuing an expedient but ultimately destructive course of least resistance in trade policy matters. The strong over-emphasis of fair trade arguments, the protectionist subversion of fair trade remedies, reliance on the use of export restraints by trading partners, and populist posturing in Congress have all been used to give comfort to protectionist interests in the most opaque manner possible.

The pressures on the Clinton administration to persist with a trade policy stance orchestrated by fair trade rhetoric and manipulated through the politics of responsibility avoidance are strong. Even though President Clinton's declared aims of strengthening the competitiveness of American industry, improving physical infrastructure, raising productivity, enhancing technological capability, and investing in training and education all imply greater government intervention, none of these objectives are well served by trade restrictions. The challenge facing the administration is to refrain from the politically seductive, but costly and ultimately self-defeating, expedient of trade protection to achieve competitiveness objectives.

The consequences of current tendencies in trade policy only take hold gradually, and the United States remains a substantially open economy in trade policy terms. The risk, however, is that over time, the weakening of countervailing power and influence that has resulted from the pursuit of the politics of responsibility avoidance could lead to runaway growth in protection. Alternatively, the damage could be done quite rapidly in economic conditions such as those in the first half of the 1980s and the early 1990s. The United States has armed itself with potent policy weapons that could choke off trade and isolate the domestic economy. As a mode of political behavior, responsibility avoidance courts decline, prejudicing the attainment of important national objectives and debilitating the United States in its global leadership role.

What does all this mean for the multilateral trading system embodied in GATT? Seriously buffeted by multiple challenges to its authority and integrity, the system has proven less and less capable of mediating trade relations among countries. As demands made on it have grown in an increasingly complex world, the early shortcomings and limitations of the system have become apparent. At the same time, certain protectionist-minded governments or branches of government have too frequently regarded the GATT's disciplines and obligations as an inconvenience rather than an effective line of defense against the narrowly focused demands of special interest lobbies. Thus, the gap has widened between rhetoric and respect for the rules.

The United States—at least the executive branch of the U.S. government, has not been indifferent to this state of affairs. The GATT has served for many years as a valuable instrument of policy. Apart from the broad strategic objectives that may have induced the United States to promote multilateral, nondiscriminatory trading arrangements, especially in the immediate postwar period, the GATT has been used from the beginning by the executive branch as a lever to contain protectionist sentiment in Congress. The numerous initiatives taken by successive administrations to sustain and strengthen the GATT must be seen in this light. Moreover, as protectionist pressures have intensified, and the range of trade and trade-related issues subject to policy decisions has expanded, so too has the level of ambition of U.S. objectives in the GATT. The GATT agenda has multiplied accordingly, culminating in the vast and unwieldy enterprise that was the Uruguay Round.

But with doubts about the completion of the Uruguay Round and the quality of some of its results if the negotiations are completed, and with GATT credibility severely dented, this kind of strategy is no longer viable. A number of things have changed, some to do with U.S. trade policy itself and others with broader underlying trends. Within the latter category are the end of the cold war, changes in power relationships, and shifts in relative international competitiveness.

What of the way that U.S. trade policy itself has rendered the GATT less effective as an instrument for restraining protectionism? There are four main arguments. One is that by withdrawing delegated authority, Congress has reduced the flexibility that the executive branch once used to promote open trading arrangements through the GATT. Second, certain U.S. trade statutes have become more protectionist in intent, driving a wedge between GATT norms and their domestic counterparts. Third, Congress has increasingly obliged the executive branch to use the GATT as an instrument for pursuing a unilaterally defined trade policy agenda, where threats of retaliatory actions, including some of a GATT-illegal nature, back up demands for GATT reforms that are not necessarily perceived by other countries as being in the common interest. Fourth, the executive branch itself has increasingly compromised positions of principle that were supportive of the GATT system. The most notable instance of this is increased reliance on GATT-illegal voluntary export restraint agreements. This is one policy area where the administration may be said to have dabbled freely in the politics of responsibility avoidance.

The conclusions of the study argue for rethinking both in the approach of the United States to trade policy formulation and implementation, and in policies and attitudes toward the multilateral trading system. There are no viable long-term alternatives to multilateralism in trade policy, if the benefits from specialization through trade are to be preserved. Some of the alternatives that have been suggested to the GATT way of mediating trade relations involve systematic government intervention and permanent negotiations around market-sharing deals. These are inherently unstable and unlikely to lead to satisfactory outcomes. Other approaches, such as regionalism, may enjoy partial success or serve as temporary palliatives, but ultimately they are an inadequate substitute for a system based on nondiscrimination.

A caveat about this study is necessary at the outset, lest it be seen as a one-sided and unbalanced critique of the trade policies of a single country, the United States. The analysis should not be taken to imply that similar criticisms are not applicable to other countries that make up the multilateral trading system, especially the large ones. On the contrary, if this study focused on the EC, it would have had a lot to say about how multilateral commitments had been undermined or even sacrificed on the altar of European integration, and it would have argued that this neglect of multilateralism was myopic. Had the focus been upon Japan, it would have been argued that U.S. and European concerns about access to the Japanese market were not groundless, if sometimes exaggerated, and that Japan had been less than diligent in ensuring that its trade-liberalization commitments were commensurate with its increased export dependency and economic power. United States leadership is necessary to the multilateral trading system, but the responsibility for preserving its viability is a shared one.

I THE INTERNATIONAL TRADING ENVIRONMENT

CHAPTER 1

THE INTERNATIONAL TRADING SYSTEM: CHANGE AND TENSION

The traditional commitment of the United States to a liberal trade policy has come under pressure. The distribution of economic power among countries has shifted in the last two or three decades, and a relative decline in the U.S. position seems to be associated with a weaker commitment to the multilateral trading system. Strategic and geopolitical motivations for defending multilateralism have given way to economic priorities. This has made Congress and the executive branch more susceptible to protectionist demands.

The macroeconomic imbalances of the 1980s, especially the strong dollar, set off a protectionist clamor. The competitive difficulties of U.S. industry fed fears of the deindustrialization of America. Defense of national industries against imports was increasingly portrayed as a patriotic duty and equated to the national interest.

The trouble on the trade front will not go away. At home, government and business are asking basic questions about the future of the international trading system and the position of the United States in it. Maintaining an open and nondiscriminatory multilateral trading system has become a weaker and more contestable objective. Doubts about the system are nothing new— it has always had its supporters and detractors. But it is probably fair to say that the system has been found more wanting in the last few years than ever before.

The broad and ambitious agenda of the Uruguay Round was an attempt to address this problem. The view that the General Agreement on Tariffs and Trade has failed to rise to the modern challenges of trade policy, and to control protectionist pressures, was reinforced by governments' failure to complete the Uruguay Round on schedule at the end of 1990. Confidence in the GATT ebbed further in 1991 and 1992, as governments declined to settle the outstanding issues that divided them.

Much of the recent multilateral agenda has attempted to deal with historic failures of the GATT, with unresolved issues that have undermined its systemic integrity. This point is often overlooked in discussions about GATT tribulations. Understanding that many of the system's current difficulties are rooted in past failures and shortcomings erodes the facile assumption that multilateralism is outmoded. It was never properly tried in key respects. But the current problems are not only about old weaknesses; new challenges have emerged. Now so much more is being demanded of the trading system. Trade in services, trade-investment links, and intellectual property rights are all part of the new GATT agenda. Links between trade and the environment promise to be so soon.

As protectionism has built, it has also taken on more menacing forms (see chapter 4). The "industrial policy debate" of the early 1980s has given way to more subtle arguments about why the U.S. government needs to intervene to help out particular firms or industries. Today, much of the U.S. policy debate turns on demands for fair trade and reciprocity. This silences discussion about whether governments are justified in overriding markets. "Fairness" has become the war cry of protection-seekers, and trade policy has been defined predominantly in terms of defending domestic interests from alleged unfair foreign trade practices.

A CHANGING WORLD

Economic Changes

Trade plays an increasingly important role in most countries' economies, and the United States is no exception. In the twenty-eight years from 1960 to 1988, for example, the share of imports in U.S. gross domestic product (GDP) rose from 4.7 percent to 9.7 percent (in constant dollars). Over the same period, the export share in U.S. GDP rose from 5.2 percent to 11.4 percent.[1] The increased economic dependence among countries implied by numbers like these is what makes governments so much more concerned about each others' economic policies than they used to be. This change has been particularly stark for the United States, after decades of largely unchallenged leadership and economic primacy on the global scene, and more limited reliance than other economies on world markets.

Apart from increased trade flows, liberalized financial and capital markets have also led to greater integration of the world economy. These developments explain the interest in international policy coordination and the rise in tensions when consensus is lacking on basic policies and ground rules. Economic relations between countries can no longer be satisfactorily mediated by a few rules on border measures and exchange rates. Monetary policy, fiscal policy, subsidy policy, and a vast array of domestic regulations are all of direct international interest. No major country can act in any economic policy area today without pausing to consider the effect on other countries and their likely reactions. Moreover, the traditional institutional separation of trade, money, and investment at the international level is no longer useful, if it ever was.

Tension and disagreement have built up among countries since the beginning of the 1970s, as worldwide growth has faltered. Real annual average world growth amounted to 5.0 percent between 1950 and 1973, as compared to 2.9 percent between 1973 and 1990.[2] The numbers for the United States are 3.6 percent between 1950 and 1973, and 2.6 percent from 1973 to 1990.[3] World trade figures show similar, but more marked trends. Average annual export growth was 7.9 percent between 1950 and 1973, but only 3.7 percent between 1974 and 1990.

The oil price explosion of 1973 marked the beginning of the slowdown in the world economy, but other factors also contributed. After years of high growth and low inflation in the 1950s and 1960s, the first signs of accelerating inflation appeared just before the oil crisis. Faced with falling reserves, rising prices, and speculative capital movements, in 1971 the United States cut the long-standing fixed relationship between gold and the U.S. dollar. This was the end of the Bretton Woods system of fixed exchange rates. In a world of floating currencies, macroeconomic management assumed new and more complex dimensions. International capital movements became much freer and larger. Structural factors contributed to slower growth. The period of rapid productivity growth during the first two decades of the postwar period ended. A good deal of this productivity growth had been associated with recovery and renewal and could not be expected to continue indefinitely.

On the policy front, the intellectual challenge to Keynesianism and demand management, and the rise of monetarism, marked the beginning of this new period. As inflation spiraled out of control toward the end of the 1970s, the primary focus of macroeconomic policy became the control of rising prices. Employment and growth objectives took a back seat.

How adverse economic circumstances can provoke protectionist demands is easy to see. In recessionary conditions, or where growth is sluggish, resources displaced by competition will likely stay idle instead of being harnessed to alternative uses. This sort of adjustment hurts, and people want to stop it. As far as trade is concerned, governments sometimes seem to think they face a choice between sacrificing jobs and reducing imports. But the choice is only apparent: saving jobs in one sector involves costs for the economy as a whole.[4]

The strains imposed by sluggish growth on countries like the United States have been compounded by large differences in relative growth particularly in relation to exports. While the United States only registered an annual average rate of export volume growth of less than 2 percent between 1973 and 1986, many of the country's trading partners were expanding their exports much faster.[5] In such circumstances, the United States has felt squeezed between its own export growth and the incomparably higher levels of several of its major trading partners.

Another important source of adjustment pressure is technical progress and its effects on production and the organization of the economy. Technological advances facilitate all manner of transactions among countries. The main areas where technological advances have significantly lowered costs, and seemingly shortened distance and time, include informatics, transportation, the development of new materials, and the introduction of new production and processing techniques. These advances contribute to changing trading relations and the process of economic integration among countries, frequently referred to as "globalization."[6]

The Macroeconomic Quandary of the 1980s

A particular problem for the United States, one with global repercussions, has been the macroeconomic situation in the 1980s. The U.S. economy outperformed those of many other industrial countries after the recession of the early 1980s in terms of growth and, until more recently, job creation. Yet the United States achieved that relative success against a background of severe economic disequilibria. Those economic difficulties provoked protectionist pressures in the United States, with significant implications for the international trading system.[7]

Ronald Reagan, in his 1980 election campaign, committed his administration to controlling inflation (by then running at almost 14 percent a year).[8] At the same time, he said he would "reduce government," by cutting down on regulation and restoring private incentives, beginning with big tax cuts. The virtue of yielding to the magic of the marketplace appeared doubly attractive, because the conventional wisdom of "supply-side" economics also argued that tax cuts would raise government revenue by boosting economic growth. As the 1980s wore on and the fiscal deficit swelled, it became obvious that this relationship did not hold.

Tight monetary policy, responding to nervousness about inflation led to high interest rates. In mid-1981 the prime rate was almost 20 percent.[9] Inevitably, tight money and high interest rates led to a squeeze and the most severe recession since the 1930s. For the industrial world as a whole, real GDP growth was a negative 0.6 percent in 1982. The United States was harder hit, with a 2.6 percent shrinkage of the economy.[10]

Recovery from the 1982 recession was remarkably fast—real GDP growth was almost 4 percent in 1983 and over 7 percent in 1984.[11] A number of factors contributed to the recovery, and to sustained growth for the rest of the 1980s. By 1982, inflation was down from double digits to just 3.3 percent.[12] Monetary policy was relaxed to allow for expansion, tax cuts started to take effect, and government spending started to rise, especially on defense. In addition, oil prices were falling. All these factors combined to give a major stimulus to the economy.

A rising U.S. fiscal deficit paid for this growth. It is somewhat ironical that in effect, if not by design, the Reagan administration gave the economy a Keynesian fiscal stimulus. It was demand management in all but name. The strategy had its flaws. First, much of government spending went on consumption and not investment. Government was not using the borrowed resources in a way that would generate future income to repay the debt.

Second, government demand for financial resources meant that less was available for private investment. This translated into higher interest rates and an increase in the cost of funds. Most commentators believe that this competition for funds between the public and private sectors partly explains the disappointing pace of domestic private investment in the 1980s. Gross private domestic investment, just above 18 percent of GDP in 1979, was under 15 percent in 1982 and 1983, and at 16 percent or less in every year from 1985 to 1991.[13] Despite the favorable short-term growth effects of deficit spending, longer term costs are likely to be associated with low levels of investment. And persistent deficits eventually feed inflation as the economy approaches full capacity.

Third, there is the question of how the public deficit is being financed. Things might have turned out differently had private domestic savings financed the budget deficit but, already low by international standards, they fell between 1979 and 1987.[14] The fact is that government spending in the 1980s was very substantially financed by inflows of foreign capital. Something had to fill the gap between domestic income and expenditure.

So much foreign capital flowed in that the United States moved from being the world's largest creditor to the world's largest debtor in the 1980s. What were the mechanics of this process? Because domestic interest rates rose as the public and private sectors competed for credit, U.S. assets attracted more and more foreign investors. This triggered the increased capital inflows that financed excess domestic consumption. The increased foreign demand for U.S. assets put pressure on the dollar and provoked a very strong appreciation of the currency. Between 1980 and 1985, the dollar appreciated by about 40 percent.[15] This made U.S. exports more expensive for foreigners and U.S. imports cheaper for Americans.

In the process, it was harder and harder for U.S. producers to compete against imports at home and to sell in foreign markets. This reality was starkly reflected in the trade figures. Between 1980 and 1985, imports of goods and services increased by an average of 6.6 percent a year (current prices). The corresponding figure for exports was 0.6 percent. The U.S. trade account moved from approximate equilibrium in 1980 to a deficit of almost $120 billion in 1985.[16]

Caught in the strong-dollar squeeze, U.S. industries pressed hard for protection. Until 1985, the Reagan administration was mostly deaf to these claims[17] and unconvinced of the need for any macroeconomic measures aimed at moderating the fiscal deficit or bringing down the value of the dollar. The economy had recovered remarkably from the 1982 recession, and economic growth had been vigorous and noninflationary. If underlying macroeconomic conditions were not scrutinized, it was easy to conclude that all was well. The strong dollar and massive foreign capital inflows were trumpeted as signs of a strong and healthy economy. If foreigners were so keen to buy dollars and invest in the United States, the argument went, Americans should be proud, not concerned.

Not until the closing months of 1985 did the Reagan administration decide to moderate its policy of nonintervention. Domestic political demands that "something be done" had finally become irresistible. The Plaza Agreement of September 1985, between the monetary authorities of the United States and the other major industrial countries, was a belated recognition that something had to be done about domestic economic imbalances. Specifically, concerted action to reduce the value of the dollar was agreed. By 1987–88, the dollar was more or less back to its 1980 real value.[18] But the trade deficit continued to swell, reaching over $140 billion in 1987.[19]

Since 1987, the trade balance has improved, but doubts remain about whether this progress will be sustained.[20] Why the trade deficit did not follow the dollar down has been much discussed. A favored explanation turns on time lags (the so-called J-curve effect). Perhaps the single most important reason for the dollar depreciation's lack of positive impact on the trade deficit is simply that the trade deficit largely reflects the budget deficit. Only action on the deficit will produce the desired effect on the trade account.[21] If domestic consumption exceeds domestic production, the difference has to be accommodated by foreign capital inflows, which in turn are reflected in the current account deficit.

Of particular interest here is the effect of the trade deficit on public views about foreign competition, and government policy responses to the pressures that these views generated. As noted, the strong dollar had a severe effect on the tradable sector and gave a hefty boost to protectionist sentiment. The absence of a coherent package of economic policies made it impossible for trade flows to respond more vigorously to the depreciation of the dollar, because this encouraged the notion that exchange rates were of no consequence. Protectionist lobbies quickly seized the argument that the only way to stem a foreign economic invasion was through restrictive trade policy. It was convenient to be able to serve sectoral protectionist interests, while at the same time arguing that the national interest, as represented by the overall trade situation, was at stake. That trade barriers cannot be expected to have any lasting effect on the trade balance is quietly ignored by protectionist lobbies and their political representatives.[22]

Macroeconomic conditions in the United States in the 1990s have been no more favorable from a trade policy perspective than in the recent past. The persistence of recessionary conditions has militated against trade liberalization, and government has proved unable or unwilling to control the budget deficit. This big deficit has severely circumscribed the option of a fiscal stimulus as a means of "jump starting" the economy, despite President Clinton's election promise to do so. High unemployment and sluggish growth continue to dominate the economic scene, and low interest rates appear to have had limited effect as an investment stimulus. While there were clearly signs of economic recovery in early 1993, the pace of the recovery is unlikely to match that of the early 1980s. Economic growth for 1993 was forecast by the outgoing Bush administration at some 3 percent. Moreover, the slowdown in the Japanese and German economies will mean sluggish demand for U.S. exports in the immediate future.

Changes in the Global Power Structure

The position of the United States in the world economy today, as compared with two decades ago, is like that of a political party that loses its absolute majority in a multiparty system. When a party has an absolute majority, it has little need to consult or to worry about the votes of the other parties when making decisions. But when the opposition parties can muster enough votes jointly to override a ruling party decision, then power relationships change. In the immediate postwar period and for a decade or two afterward, the United States had its absolute majority. Today, it risks being outvoted by the opposition acting in coalition. Some commentators characterize the U.S. position today as being "first among equals."[23] Bhagwati has called relative U.S. decline the "diminished giant" syndrome.[24] In effect, using the same analogy from party politics, there is little likelihood that the United States could in practice be "outvoted." The United States is still too large and powerful relative to other countries for such a vote to lead to any U.S.-opposed action, particularly if the United States itself was required to give effect to such a decision.

In economic terms, the manifestations of reduced U.S. power and influence on the world stage are seen in its smaller shares of global trade, production, and foreign equity investment, its trade deficit and external debt, and its diminished technological lead. In 1950, for example, the United States accounted for about 40 percent of world GDP and 17 percent of world exports. By 1980, the relevant numbers were 22 percent and 11 percent.[25] Japan, Western Europe, and certain developing countries in Asia, by one or more of the above indicators, have gained in relation to the United States. The U.S. decline is relative, however, not absolute—in terms of absolute size measured by GDP, the economy of the United States is still over twice as big as Japan's and much larger than the European Community's (EC).[26]

As far as the trade deficit and external debt are concerned, a sudden loss of appetite on the part of foreigners for dollars could cause the U.S. economy some difficulties. That is symbolic of a loss of hegemony, but the rest of the story is that if the U.S. economy continues in recession or the situation deteriorates, the rest of the world will feel it. Relative decline would have to persist for many years before other countries could view economic shocks emanating from the United States with equanimity.

The loss of U.S. technological preeminence is difficult to quantify or demonstrate precisely. According to one study of twelve high-technology areas of research, the United States had the leading edge over Japan on basic research and advanced development in most, but not all, twelve areas. In manufacturing and engineering, however, Japan was significantly ahead.[27] A congressional study published in 1986 estimated that the trade surplus of the United States in high-technology goods had fallen from $27 billion in 1980 to $5 billion in 1985.[28] International comparisons of educational attainment are also relevant to this kind of discussion. Although the United States spends more per head on education than any other nation, attainment levels in mathematics, science, and reasoning skills are behind those of all other major countries.[29]

Nothing conclusive can be said about why the United States is in relative decline, even though causes have been exhaustively debated, not just in the context of the modern-day United States but over the course of human history. The work of Mancur Olson is particularly interesting in this regard.[30] He seeks to demonstrate how, over time, stable and prosperous societies fall into decline as special interest groups capture government and inhibit change and adaptability. Among the more direct and popular explanations put forward for the loss of hegemony by the United States are low levels of savings, investment, and research and development (R&D) expenditure, poor management skills, and an increased liking for leisure. The difficulty in establishing anything conclusive about these kinds of considerations makes discussions of them subjective.

Adjustment to relative decline is often thought about primarily in economic policy terms, but an important political and social component of adjustment must be taken into account. To quote Vernon and Spar:

> With the United States having been both strong and independent for so many decades, the nation's leaders have found it especially hard to contemplate the possibility that they might need the cooperation of other countries in order to achieve the most basic national objectives.[31]

The former President of Tanzania, Julius Nyerere, used to say that when America sneezed, the world caught a cold. The imagery probably still applies, but it is also true that in its foreign economic dealings, the United States now has to persuade others, and not just make demands on them.[32]

In the trade policy sphere, certain domestic statutes were designed and deployed in the 1980s to persuade countries to adopt particular policies, unilaterally defined as desirable objectives by the United States. As discussed more fully in later chapters, however, the administration has used its unilateral retaliatory powers sparingly, to the annoyance of many legislators, but doubtless in realization that threats should be issued only if credible and that their credibility rests in part on the pliability of threatened parties. Adjustment to a world in which economic power is more diffuse is made doubly difficult, not only because the United States has seen its relative position decline, but because it has also seen its dependence on the international economy increase as trade-related activity accounts for a growing share of national income.[33]

Two separate issues are raised by this shift in relative economic power. One relates to the consequences of this kind of change for U.S. trade policy. Although no causal links can be formally established between relative decline and changes in trade policy, a good part of this study is about those changes and how they have influenced the multilateral trading system. The other issue concerns the effects a redistribution of power, or the demise of a hegemon, will have on the kind of system of international economic relations that it is realistic to try to defend. Political scientists have debated the question with some vigor,[34] and a branch of theory known as regime theory has developed around this debate. A starting point is Kindleberger's writings on the Great Depression.[35] Kindleberger argues that the maintenance of an open, liberal international regime requires the presence of a hegemonic power, more powerful than its partners, and prepared to assume the costs of maintaining a regime in times of difficulty. These costs arise because a liberal international regime functions on the basis of what economists call public goods.[36] The hegemon takes responsibility for producing the public goods, while the weaker members of the regime can free ride. If the hegemon ceases to be, or stops paying for public goods, the international regime collapses.

For international trade, this implies that without a hegemonic power an open trading system is no longer possible, and nations retreat into traditional interactions based less on cooperation than on defense against undesirable action on the part of trading partners. In such circumstances, the multilateral trading system represented by the GATT cannot be sustained. Adequate incentives for cooperation do not exist. Thus, the argument goes, with the relative decline of the United States since the mid-1960s, the GATT system has become less and less viable, because no hegemon has replaced the United States. From a policy perspective, therefore, it is at best unwise, and perhaps dangerous, to promote a liberal world trading order in the absence of the required underlying relative power relationships. Under this scenario, espoused by the "realists," past GATT success in mediating trade relations only reflects relative power relationships existing at a particular historical juncture. If those relationships cease to exist, the GATT is dead.

A rival view is taken by the "liberals." Keohane, a leading liberal,[37] argues that an open international regime can exist independently of the configuration of power among members of the regime. From this perspective, countries can cooperate without the presence of a single world government, first cousin to a hegemon, provided that cooperation can be organized around a set of mutual interests and mediated by a regime or system of rules. This kind of cooperation can be characterized as the product of enlightened governance, or as a balance of terror, where the consequences of noncooperation are so unattractive as to guarantee continuing cooperation. It may not be easy under this scenario to identify the necessary conditions for stability or the binding constraints on noncooperative behavior. From observation of the GATT system over the years, however, the idea that a viable regime can exist under varying configurations of more or less asymmetric power is more persuasive than the notion that an unchallenged hegemon must preside.

Empirical evidence to test hegemonic stability theory is taken mostly from twentieth-century experience, and the consequences for world order of the behavior of Britain and the United States when faced with the decline of their power and influence. None of the evidence is entirely persuasive, not least because of the absence of a precise specification of what hegemony is, and therefore of how its rise and decline should be measured. On a more practical note, the GATT system has clearly been under great strain in recent years, and discipline has slipped. On the other hand, efforts to sustain the system such as the Tokyo Round have continued, and considerable efforts were made to launch the Uruguay Round. Although the fate of the Uruguay Round might raise doubts, governments seem unwilling to discard the multilateral model,[38] and they still struggle, with mixed success, to define and maintain a system of rules that secures cooperation in the pursuit of mutually beneficial outcomes.

The weakness of the empirical evidence to sustain the theory of hegemonic stability is not the only problem. The simplicity of the model makes it attractive, but it lacks explanatory power at any significant level of specificity. More important, by failing to look at internal group processes and the dynamics of the interaction between different interest groups, the theory has nothing to say about how governments respond to these internal pressures. Obviously, such responses feed into the behavior of governments in international regimes. The growing literature on the political economy of trade policy analyzes these issues. This literature, to which public choice theory has made a major contribution, tends to focus on such matters as imperfections in the market for political influence and the effects of the domestic distribution of losses and gains from trade policy on the behavior of governments within international regimes.[39]

WEAKNESSES IN THE GATT TRADING SYSTEM

The claim is widely accepted that the GATT has made a valuable contribution to postwar economic growth, by stabilizing trade relations and promoting trade liberalization. Indeed, the gloomy pronouncements so frequently made about the GATT's current difficulties and failures, and the impossibility of the challenges it faces, are almost always prefaced by these consolatory and nostalgic sentiments. What the GATT was designed to achieve and what may be expected of international trading arrangements based on the GATT in the future will be taken up in detail later on. This introductory chapter is intended to highlight some key aspects of the trading system, and the way it has functioned, insofar as these are relevant to understanding current tensions and difficulties besetting trade relations among nations.

There are many ways of conceptualizing the objectives and functions of the GATT. At the most fundamental level, the GATT defines a framework for the mediation of international trade relations, such that conflicts about trade can be avoided and trade can take place in a stable and predictable environment. The GATT was designed to offer opportunities for mutually beneficial cooperative behavior, where the alternative was mutually destructive defensive behavior. A persuasive argument can also be constructed for seeing the GATT as a mechanism for mediating domestic conflicts between competing interest groups. What better mechanism does a government have than a series of international obligations that allow it to avoid a partisan posture on domestic issues or decisions that make for good politics but bad economics? In other words, for both internal and external reasons, the GATT was intended as a system of rules.

The dispute-settlement function of the GATT supplements its rule-setting and policing role. Two separate aspects of the GATT as a legal system are mirrored in its successes and failures. First is the willingness of countries to abide by defined disciplines and second is the quality of the norms adjudicated. In successful dispute-settlement cases, countries accept multilateral rulings on the GATT-consistency of their policies and make any necessary policy adjustments to conform. But attempts to finesse different views and objectives in designing rules have often postponed interpretative difficulties and stored up trouble for later. What at a certain point has been allowed to pass as constructive ambiguity has in reality been a refusal to face up to issues. Such examples abound in GATT history: the use of subsidies, agricultural protection, and the definition of unfair trading practices. As the Uruguay Round difficulties demonstrate, some of these issues are coming home to roost.

The other major function of the GATT, besides being a system of rules, is to provide a forum for negotiating trade liberalization. In the immediate postwar period, when trade flows were heavily influenced by quantitative restrictions and high tariffs, the GATT was very successful in promoting trade liberalization. Trade barriers were easy to see and measure, countries were disposed to dismantle them, and successive rounds of GATT multilateral trade negotiations provided the setting for doing it. Most of today's trade barriers are less visible, and the GATT has been less successful in pushing them back.

The nature of the GATT system may be analyzed at two levels. One involves its economic objectives; the other, the relation between its economic and noneconomic objectives. The GATT has often been characterized as a free trade charter, but the original conception was much less pure than that. The objective has always been the promotion of freer trade over time. Toward this end, the GATT sponsors negotiations for lowering trade barriers, by "binding" attained levels of liberalization against future increases in protection, and by requiring protection levels to be expressed and maintained as tariffs. The principle of nondiscrimination plays a central disciplinary role by prohibiting a selective retreat from open-market commitments. Not only does the GATT's gradual approach suggest that freer—not free—trade is the objective, but temporary or occasionally permanent exceptions to the general disciplines of the GATT are also sanctioned on a number of different grounds (chapter 7).

Undoubtedly, the GATT would be more effective if it only had to worry about the economics of trade relations. If its only function was global welfare maximization, an exclusively technical focus could be adopted to evaluate the design and application of legal disciplines. Judgments on the adequacy of the GATT could be made accordingly. If economic efficiency was the only yardstick, however, the GATT would be bound to fail, and so would any other set of arrangements. Politics intrude. Robert Baldwin puts the case for regarding the GATT as a political entity this way:

> Maximizing the collective economic welfare of individuals making up either a country or the world is . . . , not the main policy objective of the GATT. The GATT is an international legal document whose primary purpose is to promote or protect certain political goals of nation-states. . . . In the GATT, as in such other postwar economic organizations as the International Monetary Fund (IMF) and the World Bank, the broad objective is to help maintain international political stability by establishing rules of "good behavior" as well as mechanisms for settling disputes.[40]

Though undoubtedly legitimate, these observations border on the atheoretical, if taken too literally. It is one thing to say that the law and practice of the GATT are conditioned by political interests or goals, but quite another to argue that there is no system, only realpolitik. An adequate understanding of the GATT, and the difficulties it faces, requires an appreciation of the political realities that intervene to shape the system, but this does not render naïve an attempt to specify a trading system in terms of rules that are insensitive to the shifting sands of political events and power relationships.

Is the GATT a Mercantilist Institution?

Observers of the GATT exclusively in terms of its economic functions are often moved to characterize it as a mercantilistic institution. In other words, governments appear to behave as if imports are intrinsically undesirable, economically costly and welfare-reducing, while exports are virtuous. The behavior of countries in the GATT often gives every indication of being motivated by this faulty economic reasoning, but both political and economic arguments suggest why seemingly irrational mercantilistic attitudes may on occasion make sense. To take the political argument first, in a democratic society it is easier to secure trade liberalization over the opposition of affected domestic producers if a government can show that additional foreign market opportunities will result from its own trade-liberalizing actions. Much of the literature on the political economy of trade policy[41] focuses on the asymmetry between producers and consumers that makes consumers a far weaker domestic political lobby, even though the trade-liberalizing outcome preferred by consumers is generally welfare-superior for the country as a whole.[42] In short, reciprocal bargaining on trade liberalization may be able to secure more open markets than the economically rational course of unilateral trade liberalization.

Three main economic arguments are sometimes used for insisting on reciprocity and eschewing unilateral trade liberalization. First, unilateral trade liberalization may lead to terms-of-trade losses.[43] In other words, by reducing its trade barriers, a country might induce higher import prices and have to sell more exports to acquire the same volume of imports. In effect, this can occur only where a country is large enough to affect the world price of a good. In practice, this argument could be shown to be valid in a limited number of instances. Second, although from an economic perspective it can be shown that if trade liberalization is worth undertaking at all, it is worth undertaking unilaterally, it is also true that such action benefits trading partners. Therefore, if a government can exchange its own trade liberalization for comparable action by a trading partner, it can augment national welfare. This argument is limited because it only makes sense in the short term. A point is reached where the cost of delaying trade liberalization exceeds the benefits that would accrue from reciprocal action by a trading partner. At that point, there is no case for waiting. Moreover, for this strategy to be economically valid, some rather restrictive assumptions are required about the information available to trading partners and their behavior patterns.

The third argument turns on the existence of market imperfections, where it can be shown that particular market conditions require reciprocal action for welfare gains to be realized, or may even argue either for no liberalization at all or for increased protection. Models that produce these kinds of results are sensitive to very specific assumptions about market conditions, which are generally difficult to identify with any certainty, or to create. This kind of analysis and economic modeling opens up interesting avenues of investigation but provides little useful policy guidance.[44]

In sum, the economic arguments for seeking reciprocity, or for needing negotiations to reduce barriers to trade, are at best special case arguments. This leaves the political arguments, which cannot be wished away. Nonetheless, there is much that suggests that, far from being a political expedient to facilitate trade liberalization, reciprocity arguments have become an excuse for avoiding it (chapter 3). The idea has become so entrenched that reduced import barriers are a concession, or a sacrifice that cannot go unrequited, that governments are forced into an apparently schizophrenic posture in the GATT. If trade liberalization can be made into a welfare gain only if reciprocated, then presumably governments should prefer to do nothing rather than expend the effort and live the frustrations and difficulties of multilateral trade negotiations. In this scheme of things, trade liberalization offers no greater economic gains than doing nothing. The truth is that governments usually know benefits are to be had from trade liberalization, including the unilateral kind, but are held hostage by domestic protectionist groups that prefer inaction.

Much current U.S. trade policy is predicated upon the reciprocity imperative. In practice, demands for reciprocity have become so strong as to inhibit trade liberalization and to protect special interests. Moreover, the form taken by demands for reciprocity seriously threatens the proper functioning of the multilateral trading system, and maybe its very survival. This issue will be taken up in due course. For present purposes, it is sufficient to note that reciprocity arguments have too often served to arrest rather than promote trade liberalization.

The Incomplete Coverage of the System

The assumption is too easily made that at its creation the GATT was a complete and coherent system and that recent tensions have arisen because countries no longer respect that system as they once did. The GATT was never complete in three ways that shed light on some of today's difficulties. First, for all practical purposes, certain key sectors were excluded from GATT disciplines. For agriculture, looser rules were written into the agreement at the outset, but even these were rendered largely irrelevant as country after country found ways of avoiding GATT disciplines on agriculture. The United States secured a GATT waiver for its support programs in 1955. Shortly afterward, the new European Community resorted to variable levies as the centerpiece of protection against imports for its common agricultural policy (CAP), and claimed that nothing in the GATT prohibited or controlled these levies. Switzerland exempted its agricultural sector through special arrangements in its Protocol of GATT Accession. Japan has consistently applied various restrictive measures to its agricultural sector without any clear GATT authority.

After years of mutual indulgence, some countries find this situation no longer acceptable.[45] The United States, and a number of agricultural exporting countries, pressed hard for agricultural reform in the Uruguay Round. The reasons for this turn of events are not immediately relevant here. What is important is that the early omission of agriculture from established trade discipline gave way to one of the most contentious and potentially explosive negotiations in the entire Uruguay Round. The system did not break down; it had never been applied.

Trade in textiles and clothing is another case in point. The situation is a little different from agriculture, in that problems only emerged when Japan joined the GATT in 1955.[46] Many countries thereupon invoked the nonapplication provisions of the GATT in the belief that Japan's dynamism was more than their domestic industries could cope with. The United States, having sponsored Japanese accession to GATT, could hardly refuse to apply the GATT principles and disciplines in its own trade relations with that country. Under strong pressure from the U.S. textiles and clothing industry, fearful of Japanese competition, the two countries agreed on restraining Japan's textiles and clothing exports to the United States. By 1961, this arrangement had been formalized and extended to other importing and exporting countries.

The modern incarnation of textile and clothing restrictions, the Multi-Fiber Arrangement (MFA), was introduced in 1974. All major developing-country textile exporters and most industrial-country importers subscribe to it. The MFA has become more and more restrictive with each renewal. There was never any pretense that the MFA was consistent with the GATT. It was simply regarded as a negotiated departure. The MFA was another flash point in the Uruguay Round.

The second instance of incompleteness relates to particular policy areas and activities. The most notable of these is subsidies. It took until 1960 for the major industrial countries, and until 1979 for all industrial countries, to agree to eliminate export subsidies on manufactured exports. Developing countries are still permitted to use these subsidies, although individually, several developing countries are moving to eradicate them. Subsidies on exports of primary products, and domestic subsidies, are still subject to very weak disciplines. Attempts have been made over the years to rectify the situation, and subsidies were once again an issue in the Uruguay Round. The lack of adequate subsidy disciplines has been a source of friction in the system, including with respect to countervailing-duty law.

In another sense, a notion of incompleteness about the system has presented new challenges, but with no serious history of attempting to deal with the issues concerned prior to the Uruguay Round. The issues, all introduced onto the international agenda by the United States, are trade in services, the protection of intellectual property rights, and trade-related investment measures. Each of these has proved highly contentious.

A significant omission from the GATT system of disciplines yet to be addressed is competition policy. Proposals have been made from time to time to examine restrictive business practices in the GATT, but the major trading nations have never been enthusiastic. Although these countries have found domestic rules on competition necessary, they have traditionally excluded enterprises from antitrust strictures in their international operations. The ability of a firm to extract an economic rent from a monopolistic advantage in another country has not been regarded as a matter of domestic concern, or as something on which negotiated international commitments are required. As countries become increasingly reliant on foreign investment and international capital flows, however, views on the matter may change. In a similar vein, what started out in the antidumping field, at least in the United States, as a competition-policy approach to predatory pricing developed into a remedy based on import restrictions. Antidumping measures have been applied with increasing frequency in recent years (chapter 4), and concerns over the protectionist abuse of these measures have led to renewed interest in the idea of addressing predatory pricing behavior through competition law rather than trade measures.[47]

Finally, incompleteness of country coverage has generated a series of problems, as more and more countries have joined the GATT system. For one reason or another, most GATT members today could not have joined the GATT at its inception in 1948, and their subsequent incorporation has raised difficulties that the trading system now has to confront. Mention has already been made of the Japanese case, which continues to be a source of considerable friction. In addition, as more and more developing countries have joined the GATT, pressure has increased to modify its rules to deal with what the developing countries have seen as their special development needs. For the most part, rules have been modified or reinterpreted to give developing countries greater flexibility in applying GATT disciplines. This process has gone hand-in-hand with discriminatory actions against developing-country exports, where industrial countries have been unwilling to absorb the adjustment costs necessary to allow these exports GATT-consistent access to their markets. Textiles, agriculture, and steel are all a part of this story, although textiles is the only sector where discrimination is practiced exclusively against developing countries. Increasingly, also, the trading system has to respond to industrial country demands for enhanced developing-country trade policy discipline.

Another looming issue is how the GATT system will accommodate the former members of the Soviet Union and the East European countries that are currently undergoing an economic and political transformation. The status of China in GATT is also subject to negotiation. The GATT has had to deal with these kinds of questions before: Slovakia, the Czech Republic, Poland, Hungary, and Romania are all long-standing GATT members. In one way or another, special arrangements were made for these countries. The arrangements generally involved discrimination against them and some rather ineffectual mechanisms that were supposed to be proxies for guaranteed and growing access to their domestic markets.[48] In many ways, the socialist countries of Eastern Europe were marginalized in the GATT system. As Poland, Hungary, Romania, and the new Czech and Slovak republics seek a renegotiation of their GATT status, as China seeks to redefine its GATT membership (which lapsed in the early 1950s), and as new nation-states emerging from the former Soviet Union and Yugoslavia show growing signs of wishing to join the GATT,[49] the challenges and difficulties for the system are mounting.

A "Conspiracy" of Noncompliance?

Thus, significant difficulties facing the GATT trading system today involve issues that have never been adequately addressed. Countries that have tolerated less than satisfactory legal situations find them unacceptable today. It is as if in the past there existed a "conspiracy" of noncompliance. The United States is the major *demandeur* in many of these matters,[50] and the new situation has placed a significant strain on the system.

There is a second element to this idea of a conspiracy of noncompliance. It involves the role of the United States in building up and defending the GATT system in the early years. From its predominant position during the postwar years, the United States saw the development of a strong multilateral trading system as the most satisfactory means for defending its strategic interests and exercising political and economic leadership. The United States therefore overlooked what then seemed mere legal niceties. Examples of this can be seen most clearly in the apparent U.S. indulgence with regard to various aspects of European Community arrangements. In particular, agreement was never reached on the GATT-compatibility of the EC customs union. The same was true of EC arrangements with Mediterranean states and former European colonies or territories in Africa, the Caribbean, and the Pacific (the ACP states).[51]

With the gradual dilution of the position of the United States as the dominant world power, U.S. strategic interests have been superseded by more directly economic interests. As a result, the trade policy posture of the United States has shifted from indulgence to reclamation. As with the arguments set out above in relation to the incomplete coverage of the GATT system at its inception, the weakening of the conspiracy of noncompliance also has important implications for an understanding of the nature of the trading system and the challenges it faces. This line of argument calls into question the popular conception of the Golden Age of GATT. There never was such a time, and many of today's challenges are yesterday's failures or indulgences.

THE SYMPTOMS OF TENSION

So far, an attempt has been made to identify the main agents of change in international trading relations and the way that these changes have created uncertainty and difficulty in the trading system. This situation has been reflected in the economic and trade policy debate, particularly in the United States, and in heightened protectionist pressures. The evidence of increased protectionism in the 1970s and most of the 1980s is strong. The precise effects of rising protectionism on economic performance in general, and trade flows in particular, is impossible to measure. Available measurement techniques yield only approximate results, and a good deal of the evidence is qualitative. Aspects of increased protectionism will be touched on in varying degrees of detail in this study.

Fair Trade

One of the clearest manifestations of current difficulties in the trading system, and of disquiet in the United States, has been the attempts to replace the objectives of "free" or "freer" trade with demands for "fair" trade. Fair trade, an altogether more subjective concept, is increasingly employed to justify government actions aimed at protecting domestic industry or pressing for foreign trade liberalization. Together with reciprocity, it has become the foundation upon which the case for interventionist policy is built. This is the rhetoric that has partly displaced the call for industrial policy. Unlike industrial policy, it has the added attraction of appealing to a notion of natural justice. This is what demands that the government act in order to "level the playing field" are all about.

The clamor for fair trade has shifted the ground of the trade-policy debate in two ways, often leading to new policy directions and threatening the integrity of the multilateral trading system. First, the suggestion that fair trade must be pursued as an explicit policy objective has forced the U.S. government into bilateral and unilateral actions in the trade field, going beyond or simply ignoring GATT rules. This implies that multilateral provisions and processes have been unable to produce equitable outcomes, and all that is left is self-help. The policy actions thus provoked blend increased protection in the domestic market and ever more strident demands for trade liberalization by trading partners. The threat of increased protection backs up the demands for trade liberalization.

Second, the conclusion may also be drawn that the absence of "fairness" in trade relations bespeaks the need for greater intervention and planning in the domestic economy to avoid the privations that will follow from foreign foul play. This kind of response leads to the inconsistency of practicing planning at home and pillorying it abroad. If the emphasis on fairness in trade leads in this direction, the only sensible basis on which governments may be expected to cooperate is in administratively dividing out market shares, sector by sector. The alternative is an escalating war of subsidization and retaliation. The case for market sharing must be based on the belief that markets systematically fail or that governments are systematically nefarious. Either or both conditions would make a market-oriented, rules-based system for mediating trade relations inviable.

Accusations of unfair foreign trade practices are much more palatable from the point of view of domestic industries struggling against rising imports than the admission of an inability to compete. This has been reflected in the U.S. use of the trade statutes. It is not a coincidence that no safeguard action under Section 201 of the 1974 Trade Act has been taken since 1986, while the Section 301 cases continue to mount (chapter 4). Section 201 deals with relief from "overly competitive," but fairly traded imports, whereas Section 301 provides remedies for unfair trade practices. At face value, this deployment of the statutes suggests that the only need for action against imports arises from the miscreant behavior of foreigners. American producers can compete as long as such behavior is controlled or neutralized. At the heart of this issue is the relationship between fair trade and protectionism.

"Reciprocity"

The notions of reciprocity and fair trade have become closely linked. While reciprocity has always had a mercantilist flavor, in the early days it was associated with a drive for freer trade, not with leveling playing fields. Over the years the meaning of reciprocity has changed and the system has been less and less able to cope with the concept.[52]

In GATT tariff negotiations, it has been standard practice to seek reciprocity in terms of exchanges measured by trade coverage. Rough estimates are made to determine how far equivalent trade expansion opportunities are being offered, and then a bargain is struck. Governments have not always sought full reciprocity from each other in these negotiations, but the notion of reciprocity has always been important. In the early days of the GATT, harmony was maintained between the principles of reciprocity and nondiscrimination, although it is easy to see how they may clash. Any suggestion of free-riding creates an incentive to discriminate against the culprits.

For four main reasons nondiscrimination and reciprocity were compatible early on. First, only a few countries were involved in multilateral trade negotiations, and they shared similar objectives. Second, the United States was willing, in its role as prime mover and inspiring force behind the multilateral trading system, to cut its tariffs by more than its trading partners did.[53] This gave the multilateral process momentum. Third, because negotiations were only about tariffs and not rules, they avoided all the complications that have since bedeviled GATT negotiations on norms. Finally, some de facto discrimination was possible through the selection of products for tariff-reduction offers. In practice, because principal suppliers were the ones with which tariff reductions were negotiated, any free-riding behavior would have been considered of minor consequence.

The simplicity and convenience of this situation began to break down in the 1970s (chapter 8). In the Tokyo Round negotiations involving nontariff measures, no built-in mechanisms were left to protect the principle of nondiscrimination. Negotiators were concerned lest, if new rules were applied in a nondiscriminatory fashion, countries would have a positive incentive not to subscribe to them. Although discriminatory trade policy only emerged in isolated areas as a result of the Tokyo Round nontariff negotiations,[54] an important principle of the system had been called into question in the name of reciprocity. This was also the first time, since the founding of GATT, that the United States explicitly contemplated the conditional application of the most-favored-nation (MFN) principle. The MFN principle is the cornerstone of the GATT system, since it is the basic provision that guarantees nondiscrimination.

Since the end of the Tokyo Round in 1979, trade policies based on reciprocity have increasingly intruded upon the GATT's original nondiscriminatory conception. Moreover, continuing insistence upon reciprocity-based policy in negotiations involving substantive norms has created pressures toward the standardization of laws at the international level. Slowly, with the strengthening of protectionist attitudes in the 1970s and 1980s, and with the extension of trade negotiations into more and more areas of trade and trade-related policy, a new feature of reciprocity has emerged. This is the notion that reciprocity is about equal market access in terms of outcomes rather than equality of opportunities. The term "effective" market access springs to mind in this context. The expression is heard with increasing frequency in multilateral trade negotiations.

What does this new meaning of reciprocity imply for international trading arrangements? First, it requires a much more sectoral and country-specific focus on trade policy than has traditionally been the case. Ideas such as the forced balancing of bilateral trade flows have been mentioned in this connection. Reciprocity becomes hard to measure except in terms of precise, probably quantitative, commitments. Second, it creates the need for some kind of ex post reckoning of whether effective market access has been reciprocally achieved as a result of negotiated policy changes. In short, this kind of reciprocity is about the search for "fair" trade, about discrimination, and about market sharing. It is not about operating in open, competitive markets, according to predetermined rules and disciplines. The increasingly restricted and literal meaning given to reciprocity in trade negotiations is, in effect, fully consistent with a system of managed trade.

This helps to explain the strident unilateral approaches that have been adopted in recent legislation aimed at forcing other countries into trade liberalization (and other) measures that will contribute toward a reciprocal balance of rights and obligations in the system. This approach relies on unilateral definitions of what is reciprocal and equitable, it defines the subject areas that are negotiable, and it may lead to actions that are incompatible with international obligations (chapter 4).

Regional Approaches to Trade Policy

Interest in establishing regional trading arrangements has grown strongly in the 1980s, both in the United States and elsewhere.[55] The United States did not seriously contemplate such arrangements until its 1987 free trade agreement (FTA) with Israel, followed by the 1989 Canada-U.S. FTA. With the subsequent inclusion of Mexico in the latter arrangement, the United States was poised in 1992 to join the North American Free Trade Agreement

(NAFTA). These agreements marked an important policy change. While the United States has maintained that regional arrangements complement its multilateral trade interests, the policy change is doubtless a reflection of frustration with GATT and uncertainty about its future. The GATT has often been criticized for its inability to secure agreement among many countries with diverse interests, its slowness to act, its limited agenda, and its inability to enforce established disciplines. Moreover, in the face of similar trends elsewhere, particularly in Europe, the establishment of a sphere of influence in trade takes on a certain appeal.

The GATT permits member countries to enter into free trade areas or customs unions, but lays down conditions aimed at ensuring that trade creation predominates over trade diversion (chapter 7). These rules have been subject to competing interpretations and have not been effectively applied. Regional arrangements may be seen as a positive development if they create trade and are open-ended and nonexclusive, but they can also fragment the trading system and become punitive to outsiders. As free trade areas and customs unions become more pervasive, their impact on the multilateral trading system also increases.

Trade and the Environment

Newly revived concerns about environmental quality and the depletion of natural resources further complicate the picture.[56] Many environmental groups have long been calling public attention to environmental degradation and lobbying for remedial action, but only in 1991 did the issue move to center stage in the United States. This occurred in the context of the public debate on whether or not Congress would accept the administration's request for "fast-track" negotiating authority, as foreseen in 1988 trade legislation.[57] Following the failure to complete the Uruguay Round on schedule at the end of 1990, and in view of the administration's intention to negotiate a free trade area with Mexico (and possibly with other countries), President George Bush sought an extension of his delegated negotiating authority in 1991. The authority was extended until May 31, 1993.

From the trade policy point of view, renewed attention to environmental issues was significant in that they had become firmly linked to the question of whether the president should be permitted to negotiate trade agreements under preexisting arrangements. The focus of the debate was upon the proposed FTA with Mexico, where environmental issues were of more direct concern, and not upon the Uruguay Round. To understand the relationship between trade and the environment,[58] the following three-fold distinction among issues may be helpful: (1) the effects of trade policy on environmental quality; (2) the use of trade policy to attain environmental objectives; and (3) concern over the differential costs between countries of meeting environmental standards under open trading conditions.

There are two broad concerns about the trade policy implications for environmental quality. One is that, as trade liberalization leads to specialization and growth, it results in more pollution and more resource degradation. This view rests partly on the belief that growth is bad for the environment. It ignores the reality that a zero-growth scenario in a world where population growth is positive would lead to impoverishment, particularly in developing countries, even in the highly unlikely event of a massive redistribution of income and wealth to address existing poverty. A growing body of work shows no intrinsic conflict between economic development and environmental quality; on the contrary, they can be complementary.[59] Poverty itself may be a recipe for environmental degradation if environmental quality is seen as a luxury good, ever-more in demand as income goes up. On the other hand, trade liberalization might, through its effects on relative prices, accelerate environmental degradation. Whether this happens is an empirical issue, but for the reasons given above, environmental degradation should be addressed through appropriate environmental policies and not through growth-inhibiting interventions such as trade protection.

The other concern about trade liberalization is that it will generate pressures for competitive deregulation and thereby compromise the environment. Once again, trade restrictions are not an appropriate environmental policy. Differences are bound to exist between countries in relation to environmental quality and standards, reflecting differing environmental absorptive capacities and social priorities. In economics, the "state of the environment" is often treated as an additional factor of production or as a country-specific resource endowment and as part of what determines comparative advantage.[60] Competitive deregulation occurs if governments allow it to happen, not because opening up to trade forces a defined set of standards upon a country. If a country has a comparative advantage over another on environmental grounds, it will tend to specialize accordingly. The same logic applies to differences in wage levels between countries, which influence the labor intensity of traded goods.

The second category of issues, relating to the use of trade policy to achieve environmental objectives, is largely about enforcement. Trade measures may be required to give force to domestic environmental standards. When the United States, for example, establishes standards for automobile exhaust emissions that apply to domestic auto manufacturers, it will not wish to allow the importation of cars that do not meet these standards. This (potential) use of trade restrictions is fully accepted in the normal course of international commerce, provided that the standards themselves are not set or applied so as to act as a disguised barrier to trade.

Less straightforward uses of trade restrictions, however justified on environmental grounds, can disrupt international trade relations. Problems arise when a country uses the threat of trade restrictions to impose its own views about acceptable environmental standards or appropriate production and process methods upon another country, where the restrictions have nothing to do with the enforcement of standards set domestically for domestic producers. It is easy to see how intrusive, not to mention anticompetitive, such an approach could prove to be. Where trade policy is turned to environmental ends in this fashion, it becomes disruptive, in just the same way as do the unilateral determinations of "fairness," discussed earlier.

The third issue involves the capture of environmental arguments by protectionist interests. In much of the debate surrounding the extension of fast-track negotiating authority in early 1991, an alliance seemed to exist between environmentalists and certain labor/industry groups whose opposition to an FTA with Mexico was undifferentiated. Only as the debate developed, and the administration responded in writing to some of the issues raised,[61] did distinctions start to become more explicit between trade policy and environmental policy. As noted above, the grounds for seeking uniform environmental standards are weak, particularly among countries facing very different environmental conditions and levels of development. Even weaker are arguments for uniformity of costs of pollution abatement and control among countries,[62] which in essence are no different from an argument that the wage rate should be uniform across countries, or simply that specialization through trade is a bad idea. From an environmental standpoint, also, a focus on competitive considerations, rather than environmental quality as such, could easily lead to a situation in which trade intervention in the name of the environment does nothing, or even does harm, to environmental quality.

In sum, trade policy and environment policy can easily become entangled, in part because of direct links between trade and environmental quality, but also because of the ease with which trade policy comes to hand as an enforcement mechanism. The risks of confused and unhelpful entanglements are manifest and could be costly in terms of both trade and the environment. Demands on governments to do something about the environment via trade policy are likely to increase, in both the multilateral and the regional contexts.[63] A judicious and nonprotectionist response to these demands will be one of the major trade policy challenges of the 1990s.

CHAPTER 2

THE UNITED STATES IN THE TRADING SYSTEM

T he General Agreement on Tariffs and Trade (GATT) emerged as a stop-gap arrangement in the immediate postwar period after the International Trade Organization (ITO), a much more comprehensive and ambitious international undertaking, failed to materialize. Thus, the GATT received a longevity and role for which it had not been designed. Some of the features that made the GATT incomplete had to do with systemic weaknesses and its less than full coverage of certain sectors and policy areas (chapter 1). By default, the GATT's provisional constitutional status became a permanent feature of the system and undermined the legal authority of the institution.

An understanding of the precise status of the GATT and related international agreements in the domestic law of the United States is basic to the analysis of U.S. trade policy behavior in relation to GATT commitments. Here, two questions arise. First, does an infringement of GATT law imply an infringement of U.S. domestic law? The answer is, "Not necessarily." The second question follows from this answer. If the president can infringe the GATT without breaking domestic law, how far does domestic law impose an obligation upon the president to obey GATT law? Such protection is only guaranteed when domestic law and GATT law coincide. GATT law is not incorporated directly into U.S. domestic law.

U.S. TRADE POLICY AND THE ORIGINS OF GATT

The Lessons of the 1930s

The costly policy failures of the interwar years explain in large part the major industrial countries' efforts from the early 1940s onward to construct a durable and stable system of multilateral trade and monetary arrangements.[1] In the trade field, cooperation among countries prior to the 1940s had been essentially bilateral, although a most-favored-nation (MFN) clause had appeared in some bilateral agreements at various points in history, having the practical effect of creating a network of interrelated commitments among countries. While some commercial treaties in the nineteenth century contained MFN clauses, in the interwar period this feature was largely absent from bilateral arrangements.[2]

Protectionism had been growing in the early part of the twentieth century, but a much stronger trend became apparent after World War I, when highly discriminatory and restrictive trade regimes were in place in most countries. Unlike the period after World War II, there was no drive from 1918 onward to remove obstacles to trade that had grown up during the conflict. Instead, trade barriers became more and more restrictive, reaching their zenith in the early 1930s, in the context of the 1929–32 recession. Some progress had, however, been made by a few countries in removing quantitative restrictions from 1919 to the late 1920s, but it was quickly reversed after the United States enacted the Smoot-Hawley tariff in 1930. Moreover, throughout the entire post-1918 period, most tariffs had been moving inexorably upward.

The Smoot-Hawley tariff and its immediate aftermath amounted to trade war. It was the climax to many years of policy madness. The introduction of massive tariff increases by the United States provoked dismay among its trading partners, which would not only encounter greater difficulty in meeting war debt payments to the United States but also considered that raising tariffs already much higher than those of most other countries was unjustified. Retaliatory action was swift and far-reaching. Tariffs were increased in Europe, Canada, Australia, New Zealand, and some Latin American countries. By the end of 1931, twenty-six countries had imposed quantitative import restrictions, exchange controls,[3] and any number of less official administrative barriers to trade. Britain abandoned its free trade doctrine in 1932 and established preferential regional trade and monetary arrangements with the Commonwealth countries. The collapse of the gold standard gave way to competitive devaluations and uncertain exchange relations. International liquidity dried up, cutting off both credit availability and investment flows. Domestic investment suffered a major downturn in most countries. The effect of all this on international trade flows was devastating. The total imports of seventy-five countries in 1932 were only 39 percent of what they had been in 1929.[4]

When President Roosevelt took office in early 1933, signs of economic recovery were already in evidence. The new administration was more interested in building on this upturn, and in dealing with pressing domestic issues than in confronting a highly charged and difficult situation in international economic relations, in both the trade and monetary fields. The search for solutions on the international front would not, therefore, capture much immediate attention.[5] However, President Roosevelt's Secretary of State Cordell Hull was committed to lowering import tariffs and stimulating exports as a means of assisting U.S. economic recovery. The fruits of Hull's efforts—the Reciprocal Trade Agreement Act of 1934—set the scene for tariff reductions. According to Kindleberger, the government acquiesced in the initiative as an "act of piety in which the Roosevelt administration had little faith but which it undertook out of tradition and to appease the secretary of state."[6] Hull sold the program basically as a means of prizing open protected foreign markets, which explains the emphasis on reciprocity. Improved foreign market access was to stimulate production, and above all, put people back to work.

Congress authorized the president to enter into bilateral executive trade agreements. The agreements generally followed a standard model, including an unconditional MFN clause, and were the centerpiece of U.S. tariff policy up to and including World War II. By the outbreak of war, twenty agreements had been signed, reducing unweighted average U.S. tariffs on dutiable products to 35 percent, from the Smoot-Hawley rate of 52 percent.[7] During the war years, a further twelve trade agreements were signed.[8] The negotiating authority under the Reciprocal Trade Agreements program lasted only about three years, after which it had to be renewed. Between 1934 and 1945, the authority was renewed four times. Similar legislation was passed on seven more occasions, up until the early 1960s.[9]

Whatever interpretation is given to the circumstances under which the Reciprocal Trade Agreements program came into being, this program indisputably signaled the end of a sixty-year pattern in which U.S. tariff rates were unilaterally and unpredictably adjusted by Congress, acting solely on the basis of the Treasury's demand for revenues and producers' demands for protection. Decisions about tariff rates would thereafter be tempered by economic diplomacy and be controlled primarily by the executive branch. Perhaps more significantly, though in part fortuitously, the Reciprocal Trade Agreements program was the intellectual, and for the United States, the legislative, progenitor of the GATT.

Negotiations for an International Trade Organization

Two basic considerations influenced attitudes in the U.S. administration toward international economic relations in the 1940s. First, experience with the Reciprocal Trade Agreements program had been encouraging and led many to believe that similar arrangements could be incorporated within some kind of multilateral design. Second, there was a growing realization that postwar international economic arrangements and institutions would have to be established if the chaos of the 1930s was not again to prevail. Other countries shared the latter view, particularly Britain, with which the United States discussed the early proposals for an international trade organization. Also, in the early 1940s parallel but more advanced negotiations were taking place on other economic issues, and the International Monetary Fund (IMF) and International Bank for Reconstruction and Development (World Bank) emerged from the 1944 Bretton Woods conference.

The Atlantic Charter, drawn up by Britain and the United States in 1941, was the starting point for postwar institutional arrangements. This document had strong internationalist connotations, emphasizing the need for close cooperation and equitable arrangements in international economic affairs.[10] It was clear from meetings in 1943 that Britain and the United States were thinking along similar lines as regards an international trade organization, but with certain important differences. Perhaps the major one was the British desire to maintain Imperial Preferences, which had been established in the early 1930s, and the policy of the United States to secure fully nondiscriminatory arrangements.[11] In 1946 the discussions became more openly multilateralized, with the convening of a United Nations Conference on Trade and Employment. This followed agreement that negotiations should begin on the establishment of an International Trade Organization (ITO). The conference appointed a preparatory committee, consisting of eighteen governments, charged with drawing up a proposed charter for the ITO. The preparatory committee began its work on the basis of a "Suggested Charter" submitted by the United States.

Drafting the charter took about a year and a half, involving meetings in London (October–November 1946), New York (January–February 1947), Geneva (April–August 1947) and Havana (November 1947–March 1948). Much of the trade aspect of the U.S. Suggested Charter was based on elements contained in the bilateral executive agreements which the United States had been drawing up with its trading partners since the 1934 Reciprocal Trade Agreements Act. However, as Hudec notes, the Suggested Charter reflected U.S. interests, which did not coincide in all respects with those of the other protagonists.[12] For example, while opting for rigor with respect to national treatment[13] and balance-of-payments safeguards,[14] which were not difficult issues for the United States, the attitude was rather different with respect to the sensitive problems of protection for agriculture, safeguards for weak industries, and subsidies. The Europeans, on the other hand, wanted to maintain the right to use trade controls to protect their balance-of-payments, but at the same time wanted firmer subsidy rules and greater discipline in the use of safeguard measures for troubled industries. The Europeans also wanted an exception for customs unions and free trade areas. Compromise was made on both sides, but essentially each indulged the other's wishes for less international discipline in their respective areas of interest. For Hudec, the conduct of governments suggested they "were of the view that the charter had almost no chance of prevailing over any important domestic interest which was then receiving more protection than a desired rule would have allowed." Hudec also noted, however, that where policy changes were not immediately required, countries were ready to accept firm legal obligations.[15]

The General Agreement on Tariffs and Trade

At the meetings of the preparatory committee in Geneva in 1947, the GATT was created, but not for the purpose it subsequently came to serve. In 1946 the United States had suggested that a multilateral tariff negotiation be undertaken, parallel to, but independently of, the ITO negotiations. Some twenty-three governments participated in the tariff-cutting exercise, whose results were to be embodied in the General Agreement on Tariffs and Trade and subsequently incorporated into the trade chapter of the ITO. The negotiations were completed in August and the GATT went into force on January 1, 1948.

Having secured the tariff results, an option would have been to hold them in abeyance, pending the finalization of the ITO Charter. It was decided instead to implement the results forthwith for two main reasons. First, there was concern that unless the tariff cuts were implemented rapidly, they might be jeopardized should political opposition to the liberalization become organized. Second, the president's negotiating authority under the 1945 extension of the Reciprocal Trade Agreements Program was to expire in June 1948, making subsequent implementation problematic. As a practical matter, the existing drafts of certain trade policy disciplines from the ITO Charter were written into the GATT to protect the value of tariff commitments. This entire document was intended later to find its way back into the ITO Charter.

Two peculiar features of the GATT may be explained both by the way the agreement came into force and by the fact that the ITO was never ratified. First, when a decision had to be made in the latter half of 1947 about how to give the GATT legal force, it became clear that, while many governments could implement agreed tariff reductions, they could not bring other aspects of their commercial policy into conformity with the agreement without legislative authority. The solution agreed upon was for governments to sign a Protocol of Provisional Application, under which all substantive policy commitments other than adherence to the MFN principle, the maintenance of tariff bindings, and the rules on customs unions and free trade areas would be respected to the fullest extent not inconsistent with existing legislation.[16] It was assumed at the time that the provisional status of the GATT and the exemption from its disciplines for preexisting legislation would disappear once the ITO Charter came into force. These were supposed to be mere holding operations. No particular legal significance seems to attach to GATT's provisional status.[17] The key difficulty, which has weakened the system over the years, is its allowing contracting parties to maintain GATT-inconsistent mandatory legislation if it predates their signature of the agreement. Any attempt to establish the definitive application of the GATT would have to confront that problem.

The second notable feature of GATT relates to its status as an organization. The problem here arose from congressional limitations on U.S. executive branch authority: it could enter into trade agreements but could not join organizations without an affirmative act of Congress. When it became clear that the GATT would enter into force before the ITO had been fully negotiated, its text was modified to remove any suggestion that the GATT was an organization. This was why the "Contracting Parties acting jointly" became the highest GATT authority.[18] Many members of Congress were not pleased with this arrangement, believing that indeed the GATT was an organization and that the president had exceeded his authority by sleight-of-hand. This is an important part of the reason for congressional ambivalence, and sometimes hostility, toward the GATT.

Congressional displeasure with GATT has manifested itself in various ways. In extensions of negotiating authority under the Reciprocal Trade Agreements program, for example, such language as the following has been written in:

> The enactment of this Act shall not be construed to determine or indicate the approval or disapproval by the Congress of the executive agreement known as the General Agreement on Tariffs and Trade.[19]

This kind of reference to the GATT has generally been expressed in softer language as the years have passed, and today is no longer a customary addendum to new trade laws. Moreover, since the Kennedy Round, there has been specific congressional authority for the executive branch to negotiate, and, since the Tokyo Round, a new procedure that involves Congress much more directly in multilateral trade negotiations.[20] However, this has not prevented Congress from explicitly directing the executive branch to breach the GATT in certain cases.[21] Additionally, ample discretionary authority has been vested in the president, allowing him to violate international commitments negotiated in GATT or under its auspices.

The Failure of the ITO

The ITO negotiations were completed in March 1948. Most governments deferred their decisions on ratification until they saw what the United States was going to do. The executive branch submitted the charter for congressional approval in April 1949. About a year later, the House Committee on Foreign Affairs held hearings on President Truman's request for a joint resolution permitting U.S. participation in the ITO. The committee never reported, and the issue never reached the floor of the House. At the end of 1950, the State Department announced that the charter would not be resubmitted for congressional consideration.[22] Like the League of Nations before it, the ITO had little chance of survival as an institution without the active participation of the United States. Any doubts about congressional attitudes toward the ITO or anything resembling it were dispelled in 1956, when the Organization for Trade Cooperation (OTC) was submitted for congressional consideration, and met with a fate similar to that of the ITO. The OTC had been drafted in the context of a GATT review session in 1955, which had been convened mainly to take stock of the situation in the light of the ITO's demise.[23]

Many different explanations have been offered for why Congress so clearly rejected the ITO. By the time it was submitted, the political situation had changed. International cooperation seemed less imperative than a few years earlier. Even at this early stage there was some disappointment, and skepticism, about what international organizations could do for the world. The ITO could no longer be sold as a universal effort of cooperation, which would promote peace. The cold war had been engaged, and trouble was brewing in the Far East. In short, the ITO lacked urgency—and relevance. The government's commitment to promoting the ITO, which may have always been open to some doubt, had waned. Unceremonious rejection of the charter by Congress did not run the risk of confrontation with the executive branch. Indeed, the executive branch at least tacitly acquiesced in rejection by not resubmitting the charter.

Much as in any other country, some protectionist sentiment in the United States had always been apt to oppose outright initiatives such as the ITO. Opposition from this quarter may well have applied without distinction to the GATT. The interests here, then as now, probably involved a mixture of economic and nationalistic considerations. An additional contributory fac- tor, which should not be ruled out, was the uneasiness between Congress and the executive branch over the separation of powers. The U.S. Constitution gives prime authority in trade policy matters to the Congress, but the Congress has delegated some of this authority to the president. The issue with respect to GATT, therefore, was whether the executive branch was committing the United States to an ITO in all but name, thereby exceeding its delegated authority. This became a more sensitive issue once the ITO failed, but the essential point is that Congress has never been well-disposed to making firm commitments to international organizations that it cannot fully control.

Pure protectionist sentiment may have been influential, but not decisive as regards rejection of the ITO. Other sources of opposition[24] had to do with both the detailed content of the ITO and with what seemed to be its under- lying ethos and policy predilections. First, the liberals were dismayed by the lack of strong, clear rules in the charter. They found loose, exhortatory, lan- guage in too many places and considered it useless. Second, some felt that this soft approach to discipline might not only fail to improve market access for U.S. exports but also facilitate increased protection, which, through the ITO, would have been sanctioned multilaterally. Third, non-trade policy elements in the ITO caused great concern. The ITO charter had chapters on "Employment and Economic Activity," "Economic Development and Reconstruction," "Restrictive Business Practices," and "Inter-Governmental Commodity Agreements." Many of these were dear to the developing coun- tries that had participated in negotiating the charter, but they were anathema to liberals and neoclassical economists who believed that the degree of state intervention implied by the proposed international commitments on subjects like these was bad policy. For these critics, the ITO was a retreat from markets and an investiture of power in bureaucrats and politicians.[25] Diebold has char- acterized the defeat of the ITO Charter as the product of an alliance between "protectionists" and "perfectionists."[26]

U.S. TRADE LAW AND GATT LAW

To clarify the relationship between GATT and U.S. trade law, a slightly technical diversion is required at this point. Conflict between the United States and its trading partners frequently cannot be settled by reference to law.

The law itself is often unclear, and as international law GATT is enforceable through voluntary compliance and rarely through trade action. More important, by itself, the law cannot address underlying political and economic interests that shape attitudes to interpretation and obedience. Thinking in terms of clarifying the law is, therefore, not enough.

To explain the legal reality underlying attitudes and behavior toward the GATT in the United States, four questions must be addressed. First, what validity does the GATT have as an international agreement as far as the United States is concerned? Second, is the GATT a part of U.S. domestic law? Third, if it is, by what legal authority? Finally, in view of the nature of the legal authority, what is the standing of the GATT in U.S. domestic law?

The answers to these questions define what, under U.S. domestic law, the executive and legislative branches can and cannot do that is inconsistent with GATT. Thus, when Congress passes a law, is there any domestic requirement that it should be GATT-consistent? Or, when the president takes action on GATT matters, does U.S. law require him to abide by U.S. obligations in the GATT? Can U.S. domestic courts invalidate government action that violates GATT obligations? If the answers to these questions were unequivocally affirmative or negative, there would be no need to go any further. Unfortunately, the situation turns out to be surprisingly complex, and on some points, not fully defined. Moreover, the discussion here is not only about the General Agreement, but about the nontariff measure agreements and arrangements negotiated in the Tokyo Round as well.[27]

The Basic Concepts

Along the lines of Hudec's analysis,[28] certain concepts and issues need clarification before proceeding to the substance of the issues. The first question is definitional, relating to the difference between "self-executing" and "non-self-executing" agreements. An international obligation is self-executing if it becomes directly applicable upon ratification. It is non-self-executing if it requires some additional act of domestic law-making to become applicable.

The next point relates to the hierarchy of these different kinds of agreements in U.S. domestic law. A self-executing international agreement could be a "treaty," on which the Senate must give "advice and consent," meaning approval by a two-thirds majority vote of the Senate membership. Second, a self-executing international agreement could be an Executive Agreement approved by both Houses of Congress. Finally, the president could enter into an Executive Agreement pursuant to his constitutional powers to conduct foreign affairs. The first two agreements would have the equivalent legal force of all federal law overriding all state law, past and future, and all past federal law.

Existing federal law can obviously be supplanted by new federal law. As far as the third kind of self-executing international agreement is concerned, that is, one entered into by the president but not approved by Congress, the legal status has not been fully determined. However, Hudec argues persuasively that, while such agreements would be superior to all past and future state law, they would be inferior to all past and future federal law. The basic reason he gives is that it is difficult to imagine Congress allowing the president to change federal law on the basis of his own powers, without congressional participation in the decision. Moreover, if the president attempted to do so, Congress could always pass legislation nullifying any supposed effects.

Before looking at the hierarchy of non-self-executing international agreements in U.S. law, the disposition of constitutional powers in this area merits some mention. The Constitution of the United States gives Congress exclusive power "to regulate commerce with foreign nations" and "to lay and collect . . . duties." The Constitution also gives certain foreign policy powers to the president. Over the years, Congress has delegated significant trade policy powers to the executive branch. This situation has led to confusion at times about whether the president is exercising delegated authority or his own constitutional rights in trade policy dealings with other nations. In particular, in the early days, lawyers in the executive branch suggested that the General Agreement may in part have been entered into under the president's foreign policy powers. However, the famous Capps case of 1953[29] ruled that an Executive Agreement with Canada, dealing with certain trade matters, was invalid. This was because the Congress has power over the regulation of foreign commerce and had not delegated this power to the president. This precedent would therefore suggest severe limitations to any idea that agreements like GATT could be validly entered into without approval of the Congress by one means or another.

Returning to non-self-executing international agreements, their status depends entirely upon the nature of the legal authority under which a non-self-executing agreement has been entered into. If the non-self-executing agreement is implemented through a law of Congress, it will have the same force as federal law. However, where non-self-executing agreements result from executive action such as a regulation, an Executive Order, or a Proclamation, legal status depends on the source of legislative authority behind the executive action. While the president would not normally have the authority to change federal law, the Congress could grant him such authority. In addition, the president has constitutional authority to take executive action that overrides state law, even in instances where there is no concurrent or parallel authority to change existing federal law.

The third clarification relates to the extent to which the executive branch is legally bound to abide by international agreements.[30] Constitutionally, the president is required to implement the laws of the land. Thus, if international obligations form part of those laws, the president must abide by them. Examples of the latter would be treaties, self-executing Executive Agreements approved by Congress, and non-self-executing agreements whose execution depends on a law of Congress. However, in some circumstances it is not clear that the executive branch is required to observe international agreements. First, the implementing legislation for international obligations may be mandatory, or it may simply empower but not oblige the president to act. In this situation, the president is free to decide whether or not to observe an international agreement. This is the case for much trade legislation. Second, the president has powers permitting him to denounce self-executing international obligations, thereby nullifying their domestic legal effects. Third, the president has certain constitutional powers as commander-in-chief and head of state, whose limits are not entirely clear.

A final clarification relates to whether the GATT was a valid international agreement as far as the United States is concerned. Under international law, the GATT is binding on the United States, since the GATT was validly entered into. However, from what has been said, in practical terms this may not be highly significant, since it does not automatically mean that the GATT has domestic legal force. Indeed, in the case of the United States, the GATT is not part of U.S. law by virtue of being a valid international agreement.

GATT, the Tokyo Round Agreements, and U.S. Law

Over the years, the General Agreement has been supplemented by a number of side agreements, which elaborate upon or extend GATT obligations. Most of these agreements were drawn up in the Tokyo Round of multilateral trade negotiations (Part III, this study). The domestic law status of both the GATT and the side agreements is considered briefly here. Taking the GATT first, it is convenient to treat tariff commitments separately from the commercial policy provisions of the General Agreement in the context of a comparison between GATT law and U.S. law. The authorization for the original GATT tariff commitments is the 1945 renewal of the Reciprocal Trade Agreements Act of 1934. Specifically, the president was authorized to:

(1) enter into foreign trade agreements . . .

(2) proclaim such modifications of existing duties and other import restrictions, or such additional import restrictions, or such

continuance . . . of existing customs or excise treatment of any article covered by foreign trade agreements, as are required or appropriate to carry out any foreign trade agreement that the president
has entered into hereunder.[31]

This authority applied for subsequent GATT trade negotiations, up until
the Trade Expansion Act of 1962, which provided authority for the Kennedy
Round.[32] Since the language of Section 350 of the Reciprocal Trade
Agreements Act of 1934 requires the Proclamation of the negotiated results
of trade agreements, it is not a self-executing statute. The Proclamation is the
instrument that enters negotiated duty changes into domestic law. Moreover,
in this case, the proclamation authority does permit the president to change
duties, thereby changing federal law.

A second question is whether, once a GATT-bound rate of duty has been
proclaimed, the president has the authority in domestic law to infringe the
GATT binding. The answer is that he does. An important 1975 court decision[33]
made it clear that a GATT tariff binding had no force in domestic law, since the
president was empowered, but not obliged, to proclaim tariff reductions.

The relationship between the rest of the General Agreement, excluding
tariff commitments, and U.S. trade law is a little more complex. It is also a
good deal less clear, since neither the law nor court precedents give adequate
guidance on all points. Jackson[34] and Hudec both agree, on the basis of
available evidence, that the General Agreement is a non-self-executing
agreement. This means that the General Agreement itself never entered
domestic law, and it is therefore necessary to determine by what mechanism
the General Agreement was given domestic law authority. Once again, both
Jackson and Hudec agree that the domestic law authority for the GATT
derives from a presidential Proclamation.

The question remains, however, as to what was the authority for the
Proclamation. Based on his analysis, Hudec identifies Section 350(1) as giving the force of domestic law to the GATT. Under this section, the president
is authorized to "enter into foreign trade agreements," and Hudec identifies
the proclamation power as either being implicit or deriving from the president's inherent foreign affairs power. The practical implication of all this is
that the commercial policy rules of the General Agreement entered domestic
law with a status inferior to federal law, both past and future, since this is the
legal status of a presidential proclamation that does not contain explicit
authority to override existing federal law.

As far as state law is concerned, however, a validly proclaimed international agreement appears to be superior to all conflicting state law, past or

future. GATT rules are thus superior to state law to the extent the two are in conflict. Whether state actions conflict with GATT obligations is not a simple question, however, because the GATT obligation regarding local governments is a rule that merely requires that the central government take such reasonable means as may be available to it to secure local government compliance. Hudec concludes that this ambiguity does not dilute GATT obligations for local units of government within the United States, because under the U.S. Constitution the federal government has plenary power over state actions affecting international commerce. In short, he says, state governments are fully bound by GATT rules. But the issue has not been authoritatively settled.

The situation of the 1979 Tokyo Round Agreements and Arrangements (also known as codes) in regard to GATT law is quite distinct from that of the General Agreement.[35] This is because the results of the Tokyo Round were taken on board through the Trade Agreements Act of 1979, which in turn was the product of the fast-track approval mechanism contained in the Trade Act of 1974, whereby Congress authorized the negotiation of the Tokyo Round Codes in return for substantial congressional participation in the process.

What is fundamental about the relationship between the codes and U.S. domestic law, however, is that the whole negotiation and adoption process within the United States was designed to ensure that the codes would themselves not be part of U.S. domestic law. Therefore, in each case separate domestic legislation was written, and this is the operative domestic law expression of the international commitments.[36] In other words, the codes are non-self-executing in U.S. domestic law. To leave no doubt about the supremacy of U.S. federal law over the GATT Codes, the implementing legislation in the Trade Agreements Act of 1979 states explicitly that domestic law has priority over the codes in case of conflict, and that U.S. membership in the codes does not create any private right of action or remedy under the codes in U.S. domestic courts.[37] Apart from the absence of domestic legal recourse with respect to the international obligations of the United States, a number of problems arise from key differences between certain code provisions and what was written into U.S. domestic law. These will be discussed elsewhere in this study.

Finally, on the question of executive discretion, the distinction is clear between the mandatory character of some of the implementing statutes and the substantial executive leeway existing in others. For the antidumping, subsidies, and customs valuation codes, mandatory legislation was written. In the case of the first two codes, Congress considered that the antidumping and countervailing statutes had been applied too liberally in the past. The detailed mandatory language written into the 1979 Trade Agreements Act was intended to remedy this deficiency. In the case of customs valuation, the mandatory language was explained by preexisting practice.

As far as government procurement was concerned, the new law merely authorized the president to "waive" existing buy-American the provisions, which had supposedly been negotiated away in the Tokyo Round code. In part, this could be accounted for by the conditional MFN policy followed by the United States,[38] but that does not explain the fact that signatories to the code would also be subject to executive discretion in the application of the code. The standards code contains mandatory language to the effect that standards should not constitute unnecessary obstacles to trade, but for remedies the situation is different. Only signatories to the standards code are permitted to make representations about U.S. noncompliance, and the executive branch is required only to listen and consult. In short, the president can decide how far to comply with the procurement and standards codes.

To sum up the legal relationship, the GATT is a valid international agreement under U.S. law. It is also part of U.S. domestic law, but is a non-self-executing executive agreement, meaning that it cannot be made operative until an additional, essentially independent, act is undertaken. In other words, the GATT itself is not the operative instrument in U.S. law. The tariff commitments under GATT entered U.S. domestic law through presidential proclamation, and they have the effect of changing past federal law. Nothing in U.S. domestic law, however, prevents the president from subsequently violating U.S. tariff commitments under GATT. The commercial policy provisions of the GATT also entered U.S. domestic law by presidential Proclamation, but given the nature of the proclamation authority, they are inferior to all past and future federal law. They are superior to all past and future state law. The Tokyo Round Agreements and Arrangements entered U.S. domestic law through specific statutes or provisions written for the purpose (except import licensing) under the Trade Agreements Act of 1979. The Tokyo Round codes themselves are non-self-executing executive agreements.

In practice, this means that the status of the GATT and associated agreements under U.S. law gives virtually limitless potential in U.S. trade policy for noncompliance with GATT. To establish the actual extent to which U.S. trade policy has diverged from the international obligations of the United States under the GATT, it is necessary to identify: (1) where the executive branch is mandated to violate GATT commitments, and (2) where, through the exercise of vested discretionary power, the executive branch has opted to violate GATT commitments. Although it is not the purpose of this study to make a systematic analysis of this issue, these relationships are important to an understanding of the participation of the United States in the multilateral trading system. Reference will therefore be made to them in various parts of the study.

SUMMARY

From its uncertain origins, the GATT evolved into the central instrument for regulating international trade relations, filling in for the much more structured and far-reaching concept that was the ITO. The provisional status of the GATT may not have mattered much in purely legal terms, but it had important consequences for the way that Congress viewed and reacted toward the GATT. Since the Congress never approved the GATT as a treaty or empowered the president to take the United States into the GATT as an international organization, it jealously guarded its trade policy prerogatives and was sensitive to the risk that international commitments by the executive could usurp them. Congress has never shown a strong commitment to multilateralism in trade policy. It is a matter of conjecture whether a more propitious and official beginning for the GATT would have had any effect on congressional attitudes, or given rise to greater scope for limiting potential and actual trade policy departures from GATT law.

Another disadvantage of the GATT's continued provisional status is that it left intact the exemption granted for inconsistent legislation that preexisted the agreement (grandfather clause). If the GATT had been superseded by the ITO, the departures permitted under the rubric of the grandfather clause would have been modified. As it is, over the years the grandfather clause has been a source of weakened discipline, and on occasion, open dispute.

The Reciprocal Trade Agreements program was not defended in terms of the virtues of an open trading system and liberal trade. Rather, the program was made to seem attractive by emphasizing the economic benefits that would accrue to U.S. export interests from reduced trade barriers in foreign countries. The issue was not whether the domestic economy might also benefit from liberal trade through lower prices and a more efficient allocation of domestic resources. The language associated with this perspective has lived on, and a country's own trade liberalization moves are called a "concession" to extract improved foreign market access opportunities. The keen concern over reciprocity and fair trade, so central to modern U.S. trade policy, is hardly new although the emphasis given these matters has increased.

The original design of the GATT accommodated the different departures desired by countries from straightforward rules prohibiting discrimination in trade policy and the use of quantitative restrictions. Perhaps these departures were inevitable from a practical point of view, but they have been the vehicle for ever-growing neglect of the rules of the system. That the original design of the GATT contained the seeds of many of its subsequent difficulties is confirmed by examination of the less-than-sound legal status of the institution. The idea of the Golden Age of GATT is more an expression of distorted nostalgia than of reality.

II UNITED STATES TRADE POLICY

CHAPTER 3

THE EVOLUTION AND IMPLEMENTATION
OF TRADE LEGISLATION

E arly U.S. trade policy was basically about tariffs. Tariffs went up and down, depending on the exigencies and predominant interests of the time, and most of them were much higher than they have been since the end of World War II. From the end of the Civil War until the beginning of the twentieth century, tariffs averaged over 30 percent. The rises and falls in tariff levels depended in some measure upon which party was in power.[1] In those days, Democrats favored liberal trade and Republicans were more protectionist minded. The Democrats controlled the southern states and saw open-trading arrangements as serving their predominantly agricultural interests. The Republicans of the north, however, were much more concerned with import substitution and industrialization. From high rates at the beginning of the 1900s, the Underwood Tariff of 1913 brought the average rate down to less than 15 percent. By contrast, the Ford-McCumber Tariff of 1922 took average rates up to 40 percent and more by the early 1930s. The Smoot-Hawley Tariff Act of 1930 was the last and most protectionist of these legislative tariff exercises, resulting in an average tariff on dutiable imports of some 60 percent by 1932.

The Smoot-Hawley tariff considerably worsened the already disastrous economic circumstances of the early 1930s (chapter 2). The beginning of a historic trade policy reversal occurred with the enactment of the Reciprocal

Trade Agreements Act of 1934, which set the scene for negotiated tariff reductions. The Reciprocal Trade Agreements program marked the end of many decades of congressional tariff setting right down to the product line level. From 1934 onward, the main responsibility for setting tariffs fell to the executive branch. Congress legislated itself out of a process so imbued with log-rolling and pressure-group sensitivities as to make a coherent international trade policy impossible. As Destler puts it, Congress "opted to exercise a 'voluntary legislative restraint.'"[2]

The executive branch of government had not been entirely excluded from trade policy decisions prior to the delegation of tariff-negotiating authority in 1934. Negotiating authority had been delegated before, although the Senate had rejected several trade agreements negotiated by the executive with other governments pursuant to this authority.[3] In addition, the president had been given authority to impose countervailing and antidumping duties.[4] Other possibilities for executive action included the right to impose import duties or restrictions on foreign goods in retaliation for unreasonable or discriminatory import policies on the part of other governments[5] and the right to prohibit imports that benefit from unfair methods of competition or unfair acts.[6] These are the precursors of modern trade policy instruments.

POSTWAR LEGISLATIVE DEVELOPMENTS

Most important U.S. trade legislation in the postwar period has been concentrated in relatively few pieces of legislation, each becoming longer and more complex as the years have gone by. The relative acts are the Trade Expansion Act of 1962, the Trade Act of 1974, the Trade Agreements Act of 1979, the Trade and Tariff Act of 1984, and the Omnibus Trade and Competitiveness Act of 1988. In each case the salient features of the legislation and their main themes will be mentioned. This brief survey will be used to draw some general conclusions about the directions in which policy changes have pushed trade legislation over the last half century.

The Trade Expansion Act of 1962

The Reciprocal Trade Agreements Act of 1934 delegated tariff-negotiating authority to the executive branch. This authority was provided initially for three years and was renewed periodically by a joint resolution of both houses of Congress, until 1945. Then, a further three-year renewal was granted under the Trade Act of 1945. This was the legislative authority under which the president was able to participate in the 1947 multilateral tariff-cutting negotiations in Geneva, whose results were eventually formalized under the General Agreement of Tariffs and Trade (GATT). Over the next ten years, until 1958, seven more acts were passed, all but one entitled "Trade Agreement Extension Acts."[7] Renewals of negotiating authority during these years were shorter, reflecting doubts about the systematic delegation of negotiating authority to the president, and perhaps also a certain suspicion that the administration might make international commitments that Congress would not be comfortable with. Also, from around the mid-1950s onward, postwar financial generosity and openness with respect to trade issues were beginning to give way to more nationalistic and protectionist sentiments.

The Trade Expansion Act of 1962 was the first legislation explicitly to authorize U.S. participation in a round of multilateral trade negotiations in GATT.[8] In addition to specifying the precise nature of the executive branch's negotiating authority,[9] the 1962 legislation contained a number of interesting features. Among these were the introduction to the United States, of the concept of adjustment assistance for displaced workers, which was seen as an alternative to import restrictions. Also, a new statute appeared under Section 252 of the act, giving the president additional authority to react against unfair foreign trade practices in the sphere of agriculture. Comparable legislation existed prior to this, but the 1962 statute was the predecessor to Section 301 of the Trade Act of 1974, which has become one of the central instruments of U.S. "fair trade" policy. A further innovation in the 1962 act was its Section 232, still the basic authority to restrict imports on national security grounds.

Finally, under the 1962 act the Office of the Special Trade Representative (STR), attached to the executive office of the president, was created with responsibilities for dealing with trade issues. The establishment of the STR, a pressure point in the president's own office with which lawmakers and interest groups could deal directly on trade issues, was one of the earliest manifestations of the desire of Congress to dilute the powers of the president in trade policy matters. Congress had wanted to shift trade policy responsibilities away from the State Department, where they had resided since 1934, to the Commerce Department, where domestic producer interests were bound to receive a more sympathetic hearing. STR was a compromise, and over time the State Department's influence and importance in trade policy matters has shrunken.

The Trade Act of 1974

The next major legislation was the Trade Act of 1974. A significant feature of this legislation was the authority it provided for the president to introduce trade preferences for developing countries under the Generalized System of Preferences. Another important purpose of the 1974 act was to give the administration negotiating authority for the Tokyo Round. Much of what emerged in this legislation reflected a weakened presidency. This was the time when President Richard M. Nixon was confronting the Watergate scandal. Apart from providing negotiating authority for tariff reductions, the act also introduced a fast-track authority for nontariff measure negotiations. The 1962 adjustment assistance provisions were improved, and Section 406, permitting relief from disruptive imports from communist countries was strengthened. Some changes were made in the most-favored-nation provisions in the 1974 act (Sections 401 and 402), as a result of the Jackson-Vanik amendment. This amendment made MFN treatment for communist countries conditional on their emigration policies. What the 1974 legislation is best remembered for, however, is the reformulation of the basic instruments of protection against unfair imports (Section 301) and fairly traded but injurious imports (Section 201). The reformulation of these statutes made it easier than before for domestic producers to obtain protection from imports.

Section 301 is arguably the single most important piece of U.S. trade legislation insofar as relations between the United States and GATT are concerned. Although some of the intent behind Section 301 was reflected in earlier statutes, the 1974 act introduced for the first time what is, along with antidumping and countervailing-duty provisions and Section 337,[10] the legislative and regulatory backbone for unfair trade remedies. The basic idea behind Section 301 was to give the president broad authority to retaliate against other countries' "unreasonable" and "unjustifiable" trade practices affecting the commercial interests of the United States.

Section 301 gave the president leverage to deal with various foreign trade practices that were otherwise outside the reach of U.S. trade laws. Practices mentioned in the legislative history as unfair included discriminatory rules of origin, government procurement practices, licensing systems, quotas, exchange controls, restrictive business practices, discriminatory bilateral agreements, variable levies, border tax adjustments, discriminatory road taxes and other taxes discriminating against imports, certain product standards, and subsidies.[11]

The Section 301 provisions of the 1974 act were similar to those of Section 252 of the 1962 act, but they reflected the dissatisfaction of Congress with the modest use that the president had made of the earlier legislation. They introduced the right of private parties to initiate complaint proceedings, forcing the president to answer and explain if he did nothing. Section 301 was also a response to perceived inadequacies in the GATT rules and procedures for dispute settlement, although this became a more compelling reason later for reforming the statute. Most of the dissatisfaction with GATT dispute-settlement arrangements derived from the length of time the procedures took to work and the ease with which threatened parties could frustrate them. Section 301 was the first formal articulation of a willingness by the Congress to see the administration act independently in a manner potentially inconsistent with the GATT. Successive formulations of Section 301 have become increasingly restrictive of presidential discretion, increasingly demanding of action, and increasingly likely to lead to retaliatory trade actions.

Section 201 of the 1974 Act was the domestic equivalent of the GATT Article XIX safeguard mechanism, or escape clause.[12] The first escape clause provision to appear in the United States was in a 1942 trade agreement with Mexico,[13] and the GATT provisions were modeled on this arrangement. The escape clause was subsequently codified in the Trade Agreements Extension Act of 1951. Under these provisions, relief might be provided to a domestic industry if imports were entering the United States in such increased quantities as to cause or threaten serious injury to a domestic industry. The United States International Trade Commission (USITC) has to make an injury determination when a petition is filed, and if injury is found, a recommendation to the president concerning relief. In the early years, import relief was seldom granted.[14] The 1974 amendments to the escape clause, through the new Section 201, responded to the feeling that existing arrangements were inadequate. From the perspective of Congress, they did not provide domestic industries with sufficient protection. Important changes in the safeguards provisions in 1974 included a relaxation of the criteria for establishing injury[15] and language intended to persuade the president to grant relief more readily than in the past. Although the success rate for relief petitions accelerated after 1974,[16] the feeling persisted that the administration was not sensitive enough to the needs of troubled industries.

Despite subsequent modifications to Section 201 in the Trade Act of 1984 (see below), the statute has fallen into disuse. By historical standards, few cases were filed in the 1980s. No Section 201 petition has been successful since the one on wood shakes and shingles in 1986. The latest petition to be filed, one on cameras in 1990, was rejected at the stage of injury investigation by the USITC. The last case before that one was the 1988 knives case, which met the same fate as the 1990 petition. A variety of substitute policies have been developed and more widely used (chapter 4). Among these are voluntary export restraints, Section 301 actions, and antidumping and countervailing duties. The feeling that these different arrangements, statutory or otherwise, have grown up in parallel but become increasingly substitutable, is reinforced by a remark by Senator Ernest F. Hollings (D.-S.C.), reported by Derrick,[17] to the effect that "going the 201 route is for suckers."

The 1974 Act also modified some antidumping and countervailing-duty provisions. The modifications were in the same, restrictive direction as the new Sections 201 and 301. However, the president was authorized to waive the application of countervailing duties for four years, in the context of negotiations on this issue in the Tokyo Round. This waiver authority was necessary to enable U.S. trading partners to feel that the United States was negotiating with them in good faith. Pressure had been growing over several years for action to enhance remedies against dumping and subsidization. On the subsidies side, this came from evidence of growing subsidization in most countries[18] and the conviction that the United States was being out-subsidized by its trading partners.[19] One part of the response was a drive in the Tokyo Round for improved international subsidy disciplines.[20] The other was to tighten the antidumping and countervailing-duty laws. This was done by establishing more rigid time limits for processing petitions, by establishing judicial review procedures, and by making several other technical changes that enhanced the likelihood that action would be taken against imports after filing a petition.

A number of institutional changes were made in the 1974 legislation, involving the renaming of the Tariff Commission as the International Trade Commission, and the Special Trade Representative (STR) as the United States Trade Representative (USTR). Both bodies acquired enhanced power, inhibiting the exercise of presidential discretion a little more. In addition, private-sector advisory organs were formally established in the law. The idea behind these advisory groups was to ensure that the administration was sufficiently responsive to private-sector concerns. Finally, the 1974 act contained details on what U.S. negotiating objectives should be in the Tokyo Round.

The Trade Agreements Act of 1979

The Trade Agreements Act of 1979 implemented the results of the Tokyo Round negotiations. It was the first time the new fast-track method of granting negotiating authority and approving results, introduced in the Trade Act of 1974, was used by Congress. Under the fast-track method, the executive branch must consult with Congress prior to and during the negotiations. Provided that the executive branch gives advance notice of its intention to sign an international agreement, and Congress does not disapprove at that stage, implementing legislation may be submitted for expedited approval. The House and Senate must then vote on the agreement within ninety days, with no possibility of moving amendments.[21] It is an up or down vote. The fast-track procedure gave negotiators more credibility with their foreign counterparts because it lessened the likelihood that Congress would unravel a deal, once struck. On the other hand, Congress was also given a greater opportunity to influence and control the administration during the negotiations.

The 1979 legislation made substantial changes in antidumping and countervailing-duty law, reflecting the Tokyo Round results. However, the domestic statute did not incorporate the Tokyo Round codes themselves. It was parallel, and not always fully consistent with the international obligations of the United States. Moreover, it was different in many areas of detail, as well as more elaborate, thus giving ample scope for different interpretations from those of the GATT agreement at the implementation level. In other words, as in most areas of U.S. trade policy, the president could be on the wrong side of GATT law without infringing U.S. law. Respect for GATT is often a matter of presidential discretion.

The most important change was the introduction of the injury test in countervailing-duty investigations.[22] This might have made duties less likely to be applied on subsidized imports, but other modifications were to have at least a partially offsetting effect. Among these changes, applying in both dumping and subsidy cases, stricter and more precise time limits were set for investigations and decisions, and the time period was reduced from twelve to three months within which deposits were payable following a positive preliminary finding. Perhaps most significant of all, both the Tokyo Round codes and the mirror U.S. legislation introduced the concept of an "undertaking" in antidumping and countervailing-duty cases. This meant that exporters could arrest antidumping or countervailing-duty procedures against them by agreeing to raise their prices. In subsidy cases, quantitative export restraints could also be accepted. In contrast to the European Community, the United States has not made frequent use of undertakings via the antidumping and countervailing-duty statutes,[23] but these arrangements reinforced already growing tendencies toward "voluntary" trade restraints and market sharing.[24]

The Trade Agreements Act of 1979 also modified Section 301 of the Trade Act of 1974, reflecting congressional dissatisfaction with the way the USTR had been using the remedy. The idea that the USTR, and for that matter the president, have been too "soft" on foreigners in trade matters has exerted a powerful influence in the U.S. Congress for nearly two decades. The 1979 changes mainly involved placing time limits on the handling of petitions and the decisionmaking process. Petitioners were also to be kept more fully informed throughout the proceedings. Compared to the later Section 301 modifications, the 1979 changes were quite mild. In 1984 and more especially in 1988, important changes were made to Section 301, designed to ensure its more frequent and aggressive use, and to broaden its scope.

Finally, the president was required to reorganize departmental functions to promote a more sympathetic attitude toward domestic producer interests. As a result, responsibility for managing aspects of the antidumping and countervailing-duty statutes, as well as certain national security provisions, was transferred from the Treasury Department to the Department of Commerce.

The Trade and Tariff Act of 1984

The next important trade legislation was the Trade and Tariff Act of 1984.[25] Unlike the 1974 act and the subsequent 1988 act, the 1984 act did not involve a grant of generalized, multilateral negotiating authority and, unlike the 1979 act, it did not involve ratification of multilaterally negotiated commitments. The Tokyo Round tariff cuts were still being implemented, and nontariff barrier negotiating authority ran until 1988. Instead, the 1984 act cobbled together action on a range of disparate issues.

In one important respect, the 1984 legislation signaled a new trade policy departure, the authority to negotiate a free trade agreement (FTA) with Israel. This was the first significant breach in the postwar tradition of maintaining MFN trading relationships.[26] This authority covered other possible bilateral trade arrangements and was later used for the FTA negotiations with Canada.

The 1984 act included the first detailed provisions on the new issues that the United States has emphasized so strongly in recent years—services, trade-related investment measures, intellectual property rights, and trade in high-technology goods. When these were raised by the administration in the early 1980s as areas where clearer and more extensive international disciplines were needed, the reaction of Congress was favorable. The 1984 Trade and Tariff Act established negotiating objectives for services, foreign direct investment, and high-technology products. The new issues were included in FTA negotiations. The act also foresaw the imposition of conditionality with respect to some of the new issues in the essentially unilateral process of determining GSP benefits for developing countries.

Services and investment were brought explicitly within the purview of Section 301. Trade-related services had been included under the definition of trade in the 1979 legislation. For the first time, however, direct foreign investment was included in the definition of "commerce." Related to this is a provision in the 1984 legislation giving the USTR authority to retaliate against export performance requirements. Such requirements are sometimes imposed as a condition of foreign investment. This is one aspect of the wider issue of trade-related investment performance requirements, which became a prominent issue in the Uruguay Round. These modifications enormously expanded the areas where Section 301 can be applied.

Among other important changes in Section 301, explicit statutory definitions were given for the first time for the terms "unreasonable," "unjustifiable," and "discriminatory."[27] "Unreasonable" is defined to include acts, policies, or practices that might not be in violation of or inconsistent with the international legal rights of the United States, but which in any case are deemed to be unfair or inequitable. Unreasonable practices may include the denial of fair and equitable market opportunities, opportunities to establish an enterprise, or adequate protection of intellectual property rights. Since established legal rights are not involved where unreasonable acts are identified, this is a step toward a unilateral interpretation of what an international trading system should be. The term "unjustifiable" is an act, policy, or practice that is in violation of or inconsistent with the international legal rights of the United States. Such violations may include the denial of MFN, national treatment, the right of establishment, and intellectual property rights. The term "discriminatory" is defined as including, as appropriate, any act, policy, or practice that denies MFN treatment to U.S. goods, services, or investments. The executive branch was directed actively to seek out foreign trade barriers, or in other words to self-initiate cases and negotiate for their removal or reduction. Section 301 procedures themselves were also tightened, and a system of annual reporting by the USTR to Congress was mandated.

The rules and regulations relating to antidumping and countervailing duties were revised extensively. In general, the changes favored claimants over respondents. The likelihood of successful petitions was increased through an expansion of the definition of legal standing—who had the legal right to bring a case. There were also changes relating to the alleged practice of "persistent" dumping that made the self-initiation of cases by the Commerce Department more likely. Some clarifications were introduced in relation to the concept of the "threat" of injury. In addition, the new rules for calculating injury required that exports from all sources must be taken into account. The obligation to "cumulate" meant that even very small exporters could be considered to cause injury to domestic industries. In the countervailing-duty area, "upstream" subsidies were included in the definition of prohibited subsidies.

On the question of import relief for products threatened by fairly traded imports (Section 201), the "serious injury" criterion was amended in an effort to make it less likely that the absence or presence of particular factors in an injury investigation would lead to a negative finding by the USITC. In addition, procedures by which Congress could override a presidential refusal to follow a recommendation for relief were modified. This arose from a legal finding that concurrent resolutions by both houses overriding a presidential decision (the legislative veto) was unconstitutional. This arrangement had been enacted in the Trade Act of 1974 as a means of permitting Congress to autho-rize import relief recommended by the USITC in Section 201 cases even where the president had not approved the relief. Concurrent resolutions were replaced by joint resolutions and the presidential veto was restored.

During House debate of the legislation for the Trade and Tariff Act of 1984, several congressmen attempted to make special protectionist arrange-ments for particular industries. While this is hardly a novel feature of U.S. lawmaking processes, the pressure was particularly intense in 1983 and 1984. At different stages special provisions were included in draft legislation for steel, footwear, copper, ferroalloys, wine, textiles, bromine, and dairy products. Most of these provisions, except for the steel-sector arrangements and the wine reciprocity provisions,[28] were finally dropped or made into sense-of-the-Congress resolutions.

The Omnibus Trade and Competitiveness Act of 1988

The Omnibus Trade and Competitiveness act of 1988 is the largest trade legislation initiative to date in the United States. The act provided tariff-negotiating authority to the executive and envisioned the possibility of fast-track approval for nontariff barrier measure negotiations. Objectives were carefully spelled out in every area of the negotiation, but the authority is more circumscribed than before, and reversible. In this context, the functions of the private-sector advisory committees established under the 1974 act were fur-ther strengthened. The 1988 act dealt with much more than trade issues. It also contained provisions on international financial policy, foreign corrupt practices, technology competitiveness, and education and training.

Apart from its trade provisions, this legislation attempted to address a range of issues affecting relations between the United States and its main eco-nomic partners, especially how to respond to a relative decline in economic power and influence internationally. To deal with a widely perceived decline in U.S. competitiveness, emphasis was placed on developing and commer-cializing technology and on improving educational standards. The contrast was striking between the act's competitiveness provisions, which diagnosed solutions to problems through domestic action, and its trade provisions, which were largely predicated upon the level playing field imperative or the need for more fairness and reciprocity in the trading system. In the trade sphere, it might be tempting to argue that this act was less about preparing the United States to participate in the Uruguay Round,[29] and more about unilateral armament to make demands for reciprocity effective and decisively influence the shape of the future international trading system. This legislation was a culmination of severe pressure from Congress on the administration to "do something" about trade. In 1985 alone, over three hundred trade bills were introduced into Congress, the bulk of which, in one way or another, harbored a protectionist intent.

Section 301 of the Trade Act of 1974 was substantially modified in the 1988 act. This has been described as the "heart" of the act.[30] As part of a continuing trend to dilute the discretionary power of the president, the act transferred section 301 authority from the president to the USTR for (1) determining whether foreign practices are "unjustifiable," "unreasonable," or "discriminatory"; (2) deciding whether and what action is appropriate; and (3) implementing such action. Executive discretion was further reduced by making retaliatory action mandatory in the case where "unjustifiable" (illegal) practices are identified.[31] However, some discretion was retained. Exceptions were permitted when: (1) the practice was not GATT-inconsistent; (2) the foreign country was eliminating the practice; (3) the foreign country offered compensation; (4) the adverse impact of retaliation on the U.S. economy would outweigh the benefits thereof; or (5) retaliation would cause serious harm to the national security of the United States. The USTR maintained discretionary authority to retaliate with respect to "unreasonable" or "discriminatory" practices, that burden or restrict the commerce of the United States.

The 1988 act reduced various time limits within which the USTR must take a decision or action following the initiation of an investigation. As soon as an investigation was initiated, the USTR was required to request consultations with the foreign country concerned. If consultations were inconclusive after 150 days, the USTR was required to begin formal GATT dispute-settlement procedures, if appropriate. In cases that went through GATT dispute-settlement proceedings, retaliation might be required under U.S. law before the GATT case was settled, although recent efforts to improve the GATT dispute-settlement procedures may have the effect of making that less likely. The 1988 act sets a minimum time limit of 30 days for retaliatory action, but it can be extended up to as much as 180 days in certain circumstances.

A number of new practices were specified in the legislation as being actionable under Section 301. Their mention was more for emphasis than as a means of extending the reach of Section 301, whose coverage was already vast. Each practice mentioned could almost certainly have triggered 301 action before the 1988 act. The practices were the persistent denial of workers' rights, export targeting, and toleration by foreign governments of anticompetitive behavior among firms that adversely affected U.S. firms. These practices all fell into the category of "unreasonable" actions, and so must be shown to be burdensome or restrictive, and retaliation remains discretionary.

The transfer of Section 301 authority from the president to the USTR, which on the face of it may appear a somewhat inconsequential shuffling of functions within the Executive Office of the President, was in effect a move of some significance. The point is that cabinet officers are more exposed than the president to pressure from outside. Despite the inherent power of the presidency to control decisions of cabinet officers, presidents do not usually step in unless very important interests are at stake.

The 1988 Act also introduced "Super" 301, whereby the USTR had to identify in 1989 and in 1990 "U.S. trade liberalization priorities," including both priority practices whose elimination would have the "most significant potential to increase U.S. exports," and priority foreign countries. The USTR had to initiate Section 301 investigations with respect to the priorities identified and seek to negotiate an agreement with the countries concerned that provided either for the elimination of, or compensation for, the practices in question at the end of a three-year period, or the reduction of the practices over the same period. In the latter case, there was an expectation that U.S. exports to the foreign country would, as a result of the reduction of the practices, increase incrementally during each year of the period. The USTR had to submit a report annually to Congress on evidence of substantial progress toward eliminating the priority practices, whether or not through bilateral negotiations. Where such evidence was lacking, the USTR had to indicate any other actions taken under Section 301 with respect to the priority practices. Super 301 caused a good deal of controversy because it forced the USTR to name countries and was seen by U.S. trading partners as little more than aggressive unilateralism, whose effects on trade are highly uncertain (chapter 4).

Two other sectoral provisions in the Omnibus Trade and Competitiveness Act of 1988 operate in a similar fashion to Super 301. They involve intellectual property rights and telecommunications. The provisions on intellectual property rights have become known as "Special 301." Section 1303 of the Omnibus Trade and Competitiveness Act of 1988 provides the sense of Congress that international protection of intellectual property rights is vital to the international competitiveness of the United States and that the absence of adequate and effective protection of U.S. intellectual property rights has harmed U.S. economic interests. It requires the USTR to identify foreign countries that "deny adequate and effective protection of intellectual property rights, or deny fair and equitable market access to U.S. persons that rely upon intellectual property protection." The USTR must only identify countries that "have the most onerous or egregious practices," with "the greatest adverse impact" on U.S. products, and which are not (1) "entering into good faith negotiations" or (2) "making significant progress in bilateral or multilateral negotiations, to provide adequate and effective protection of intellectual property rights." The protection of intellectual property rights is being denied if there are not "adequate and effective means under the laws of the foreign country to secure, exercise, and enforce rights relating to patents, process patents, registered trademarks, copyrights, and mask works." The absence of "fair and equitable market access" is defined as the denial of

> access to a market for a product protected by a copyright, patent, or process patent through the use of laws, procedures, practices, or regulations which: (A) violate provisions of international law or international agreements to which both the United States and the foreign country are parties, or (B) constitute discriminatory nontariff trade barriers.

Concerning telecommunications, Section 1374 of the 1988 act requires the USTR to identify priority countries with which negotiations were to be carried out with a view to increasing market opportunities for telecommunications products and services. Such identification was to take place within five months of the act's coming into force, and negotiations should be completed within eighteen months of the same date. In identifying priority countries, factors to be taken into account included the nature of barriers to U.S. sales of telecommunications products and services and the potential benefits that would accrue from removal of the barriers. Upon identification of priority countries, the president had to specify negotiating objectives for each country. If no agreement was secured within the time limits, the president was authorized to take a wide range of actions in relation to any priority foreign country, including any actions envisaged under Section 301.

The above provisions have received the most attention, but there have been important changes in other areas of trade policy as well. Provisions relating to Section 201 tighten deadlines that apply to the president and USITC and extend the period for which relief may be made available. At the same time, a new emphasis is placed on positive adjustment, and specific provisions are made on adjustment assistance.

Numerous changes were made in the antidumping and countervailing-duty statutes, relating to definitions, criteria, and the circumstances of permitted or required action. As with previous legislative modifications, these changes raised the likelihood that in one way or another, petitioners would succeed in insulating themselves further from import competition. Among the changes is a provision that all direct and indirect subsidies in all countries that participate in an international consortium be included in determining the amount of subsidization.[32] New provisions were introduced to deal with multiple dumping involving short life-cycle products. Certain arrangements were also introduced to prevent the circumvention of U.S antidumping or countervailing duties through shipments via third countries or the importation of component parts for assembly. New provisions are also made for monitoring imports of "downstream" products, that is, products that contain components previously found to be subsidized or dumped.

In addition to Special 301, changes in the field of intellectual property included the introduction of easier access to remedies under Section 337 of the Tariff Act of 1930. The national security provisions of Section 232 of the Trade Expansion Act of 1962 were modified by shortening or setting time limits for certain procedures, expanding the role of the secretary of defense, and improving the enforcement of restraint agreements reached under the statute, notably, the one on machine tools. A series of changes to the export control laws were intended to make them less obstructive for bona fide exporters, while at the same time tightening procedures for export controls. In regard to sectoral issues, various provisions were included for securing reciprocity in transport and financial services (in addition to telecommunications). Agricultural provisions allow for marketing loans and a rise in direct export subsidization, in case agricultural talks under the Uruguay Round fail. Also, specific sections were devoted to steel, wine exports, and meat inspections.

SUMMARY

In tracing major trade legislation since World War II, several themes have emerged. Legislative developments point to greater reliance on direct, administrative decisions to regulate trade flows, especially through the gradual adaptation of the trade-remedy statutes. By the same token, the United States has been arming itself legislatively over the years in a way likely to make policy more protectionist and more confrontational internationally.

Much of the history of trade policy in the postwar period turns on the struggle between Congress and the executive branch for primacy in trade policy matters. Having delegated considerable policymaking authority to the executive after the bitter experiences of the 1930s, centering on the Smoot-Hawley tariff and its aftermath, Congress has spent the last three decades circumscribing the administration's trade policy authority. The constraining pressures have involved nontariff measures much more than tariff-negotiating authority, which was the subject of the original delegation of powers. Congress has never delegated powers in the nontariff barrier field but rather has acted to narrow the scope of discretionary application and interpretation of the statutes by the administration. Congress has not been limiting the trade policy authority of the executive in order to exercise it itself on a day-to-day basis. Instead, Congress has sought indirectly to force the executive to promote, actively or passively, policy outcomes favorable to particular domestic constituencies.

The vehicle for achieving this has been to make trade-remedy statutes more and more likely to produce trade-restricting outcomes, and at the same time to ensure that the executive is less able to intervene to mitigate the restrictive effects of these policy changes. Congress has imposed new obligations on the executive both to act and to avoid action, in circumstances that essentially favor domestic production over trade.

Another vital ingredient to make the strategy workable has been to shift the emphasis of the entire policy debate toward the new rhetoric of fair trade. Few trade issues on the U.S. domestic agenda today do not have as their primary concern the unfair trade practices of other countries. Correspondingly, most trade actions are justified on the same grounds. This is the story behind the continuing modifications in Section 301 and the antidumping and countervailing-duty statutes. Closely linked to the fair trade emphasis are the growing demands for reciprocity, also reflected in the development of the relevant statutes. As Ahearn and Reifman put it:

> There is a growing rejection of the standard free-trade-versus-protectionism dichotomy among members of Congress. Reciprocity, newly defined as a comparison of how the United States treats its trading partners versus how our trading partners treat us, is the conceptual basis on which trade problems are now commonly approached. . . . The center of political gravity is now a willingness to limit access to the U.S. market as leverage in opening up foreign markets.[33]

CHAPTER 4

TRENDS IN TRADE POLICY

It is hazardous to make any precise statement about how far protectionism characterizes the policy of a country or how protectionist one country is compared to another. Even before considering measurement difficulties, significant problems of definition must be solved. Yet judgments on these matters are implicit, if not directly stated, in most trade policy discussions. The importance of "level playing field" rhetoric and reciprocity in U.S. trade policy illustrates this point.

Protection, at its simplest, is any policy intervention that lessens foreign competition for domestic producers. Such a straightforward approach poses obvious difficulties. First, it does not recognize the possibility that some interventions can increase national welfare and should not therefore be regarded simply as protectionist and "bad." Much of the academic debate on protection is concerned with the justification for different interventions.[1] Second, broad-based interventions to ease adjustment costs of changes in competitive conditions are commonly considered necessary to avoid more sectorally focused measures that retard trade. Third, some trade-policy interventions may be defensive and necessary to counter genuinely predatory behavior by trading partners. The widespread and growing use of antidumping and countervailing duties is the most obvious area where the distinction between legitimate self-defense and protection is relevant. Fourth, a series of noneconomic arguments has to be evaluated, relating to the equity concerns underpinning reciprocity arguments, national security, and foreign policy.

Arguments of this kind risk capture by special interests and use as thinly veiled excuses for protection. Some commentators see a serious protectionist threat deriving from economic arguments such as the infant-industry case or other instances of market failure, and noneconomic arguments such as the national interest, equity, and miscreant foreign behavior. These observers prefer an approach that relies on a strong presumption that no intervention is the best policy. This means that any intervention that reduces foreign competition should be eschewed, at least in the first instance, as protectionist. Politicians and bureaucrats face pressures that make a disciplined observance of such an approach difficult to manage. Moreover, the macroeconomic problems besetting the U.S. economy have made trade policy hostage to events and conditions entirely beyond its reach.

AGGREGATE INDICATORS OF PROTECTION

Assessments and estimates of the incidence of protection are only as good as the data and the methodological approaches used. A limited amount of work has been done on directly measuring the protectionist costs of different policy interventions mainly because results that often turn out to be intrinsically uncertain and easily subject to challenge take considerable effort to generate. The uncertainty derives both from inadequate data and from the existence of alternative, and often contested, methodological approaches to measurement. Four policy instruments to regulate protection are examined here: tariffs, nontariff measures, subsidies, and voluntary export restraints (VERs).[2]

Tariffs

The most significant success story for postwar trade policy and multilateral trade diplomacy is commonly viewed as the massive reduction in tariffs that has occurred. During the forty-year existence of the General Agreement on Tariffs and Trade, many tariffs have been reduced very substantially in the major trading countries. Weighted average tariffs were around 35 percent in nine principal industrial country markets before the establishment of the GATT in 1947, and less than 5 percent in the 1980s following the Tokyo Round.[3] The Tokyo Round of trade negotiations, the seventh GATT round, left the average tariffs of the United States, Japan and the European Community (EC) at 3.9 percent, 3.5 percent, and 4.2 percent, respectively (table 4.1).

TABLE 4.1
POST-TOKYO ROUND TARIFFS BY SECTOR
(PERCENTAGES)

	UNITED STATES	JAPAN	EC
All food items	4.1	9.7	3.7
Food and live animals	3.8	10.0	0.1
Oilseeds and nuts	1.4	5.6	10.3
Animal and vegetable oils	0.9	0.3	0.1
Agricultural raw materials	0.3	0.7	3.4
Ores and metals	1.9	2.5	2.8
Iron and steel	4.3	5.0	5.5
Nonferrous metals	0.7	5.5	3.2
Fuels	0.4	1.5	0.1
Chemicals	3.7	5.5	8.4
Manufactures excluding chemicals	5.6	5.7	8.1
Leather	4.2	11.9	10.2
Textiles, yarn, and fabrics	10.6	8.6	17.3
Clothing	20.3	15.0	19.9
Footwear	11.7	14.2	22.5
Other items	4.2	2.3	4.8
All products	3.9	3.5	4.2

EC: European Community
Source: Sam Laird and Alexander Yeats, *Quantitative Methods for Trade Barrier Analysis* (London: Macmillan, 1990).

The continuing reduction of tariffs under GATT auspices suggests at first glance that progress toward trade liberalization has been steady and marked. It would also seem that the process has occurred reciprocally, among major trading countries. Two reservations have to be registered about this picture. First, the tariff reductions have not been even for all products and sectors. Relatively high average tariffs continue to prevail in the textiles, clothing, and footwear industries, for example (table 4.1). The presence of tariff peaks like these casts doubt on the popular assertion that tariffs no longer matter as an instrument of trade policy. An uneven tariff structure, with some high nominal rates, can yield high levels of effective protection.

Second, lower tariffs have been accompanied by growth in other measures of protection of a nontariff variety. That this has occurred is undisputed, and it modifies the picture, at least for most of the last two decades, of steady trade liberalization among the major trading nations. One interesting question that arises as a result of counter-tendencies with respect to the use of tariffs and nontariff barriers (NTBs) to trade is how far NTBs have substituted for tariffs. In other words, has the success of GATT in reducing the use of a transparent and relatively efficient mechanism of protection led to a worse system of opaque and economically costly alternatives? Perhaps the GATT has served as a smokescreen for growing protectionism, by making hidden vice seem virtuous. No definitive answer to this question is available, but it is difficult to believe that there is no connection. If the premise is accepted that there is a link, this modifies the judgment about how constructive the traditional emphasis on tariff reductions has been, and it also has implications for the way trading arrangements should be worked out in the future.

A recent study on the United States by de Melo and Tarr[4] has estimated the tariff equivalent of nontariff barriers applied in the textiles and apparel, auto and steel sectors—which are among the most protected sectors in the U.S. economy. They found that a uniform tariff of 23.7 percent was required to replicate the distortionary effects of the nontariff barriers in all three sectors, and that a 49 percent tariff would produce the same welfare costs as the NTBs in these sectors. While these numbers do not prove that NTBs have been deliberately used to compensate for tariff reductions, they do emphasize the futility of looking at tariffs alone as a protection mechanism in some sectors.

Nontariff Barriers to Trade

The de Melo and Tarr study also offers estimates of the increase in U.S. income that might be expected to result from the removal of all quantitative restrictions (QRs) affecting imports into the United States. The authors calculate the income gain at between $25 billion and $29 billion, around 0.5 percent of national income. De Melo and Tarr use their general equilibrium model to estimate the cost per job protected by QRs in the textiles and apparel, auto, and steel sectors. They found that about 294,000 jobs were being protected at a cost of $72,000 per worker per year. These figures represent 5 times annual compensation in the textiles and clothing sector, and 1.7 times the compensation of workers in the steel and auto sectors.

The protection of these sectors implies that the government has decided that a job in one of these industries is worth more to society than jobs in unprotected industries. Setting aside the political process through which this outcome may have been decided upon, and the question whether it reflects the public will, the fact is that protection of these industries is being secured in a costly manner. To push the point home, de Melo and Tarr calculate that for every dollar of earnings lost by workers who would be displaced by the removal of QRs in the textile and apparel, auto and steel sectors, the economy at large gains $28. This clearly suggests that there is scope for a combination of trade liberalization and adjustment measures that leaves everybody better off.

Quite a few studies have been made of the trade coverage of NTBs. Though less useful as an indicator of the trade restrictiveness or real significance of measures than the analytical approach used by de Melo and Tarr, certain patterns are discernible. The trade coverage methodology also facilitates some cross-country comparison. Table 4.2 (see page 74)reports some results of trade coverage studies of NTBs in the United States, Japan, and the European Community, undertaken between 1984 and 1988.

These results are not easily comparable with each other except in terms of trends that they show. At greater levels of precision, comparisons fall apart, since the studies use different definitions of NTBs, refer to different years, and do not all measure trade coverage in the same manner. However, a shared conclusion of all five studies is that the trade coverage, and by implication the frequency of use, of NTBs increased in the United States and the EC in the 1980s, at least up to 1986.[5] The trend is more marked for the United States than the EC for all the studies where the comparison is made. The figures generally show a static situation with respect to Japan, but different definitions of NTBs give widely differing estimates of trade coverage in Japan.

In a more recent study by the World Bank and International Monetary Fund (IMF)[6] on the impact of the industrial countries' trade, agricultural and industrial policies on developing countries, it is argued that levels of protection have been static in the closing years of the 1980s and early 1990s. A few new measures were adopted by various industrial countries, but not on the scale witnessed in the 1970s and early 1980s. It is hard to know what accounts for the slowdown. That the Uruguay Round was in progress may have had an influence, and in the United States a reduction in the value of the dollar was helpful.

Despite the weaknesses of most approaches to estimating the trade restrictiveness of NTBs, the evidence from diverse sources uniformly points to two conclusions about recent U.S. trade policy. First, protection through NTBs has been increasingly granted. Second, this protectionist tendency has been more pronounced in the United States than in its major trading partners. For the three of the five studies that provide the necessary data, the United States seems to have been "catching up" with EC use of NTBs. Japan's trade

TABLE 4.2
ESTIMATES OF NONTARIFF BARRIER (NTB) PROTECTION

STUDY	YEAR	UNITED STATES	JAPAN	EC	OECD
BALASSA AND BALASSA (1984)[a]					
Share of imports covered by NTBs (%)	1980	6	7	11	n.a.
	1983	3	7	15	n.a.
HUFBAUER, BERLINER, AND ELLIOTT (1986)[b]					
Share of imports (%) covered by "special"	1975	8	n.a.	n.a.	n.a.
protection (based on 30 case studies)	1980	12	n.a.	n.a.	n.a.
	1984	21	n.a.	n.a.	n.a.
UNCTAD (1987)[c]					
Imports subject to certain NTBs	1982	106	99	106	n.a.
(import coverage index, 1981 = 100)	1983	106	99	111	n.a.
	1984	112	99	114	n.a.
	1985	119	99	121	n.a.
	1986	123	99	118	n.a.
WORLD BANK (1987)[d]					
Share of imports subject to "hard-core" NTBs (%)					
From industrial countries	1981	9	29	10	13
	1986	15	29	13	16
From developing countries	1981	14	22	22	19
	1983	14	24	16	17
LAIRD AND YEATS (1986)[e]					
Trade coverage of "hard-core" NTBs (%)	1981	11	24	13	15
	1983	14	24	16	17
	1986	17	24	16	18

EC: European Community; OECD: Organization for Economic Cooperation and Development; UNCTAD: United Nations Conference on Trade and Development; n.a.: not applicable
[a]   Bela and Carol Balassa, "Industrial Protection in Developed Countries," *World Economy*, vol. 6, no. 2 (June 1984). The definition of nontariff measures is quite narrow in this study.

coverage is estimated as both below and above those of the United States and the European Community. In any event, any margin by which the United States might have been able to assert that it was lagging in the use of NTBs has been eroded to the point of elimination, at least with respect to the European Community. These aggregate data cast some doubt, therefore, upon the justification for a U.S. trade policy predicated upon the need for unilateral action to level the playing field.

Subsidies

Table 4.3 (see page 76) presents some Organization for Economic Cooperation and Development (OECD) national accounts data on subsidies, where subsidies are expressed as a share of GDP in the United States, Japan, and the European Community. For these purposes, subsidies are defined as all government grants on current account to private industries and public corporations, and grants by public authorities to government enterprises in compensation for operating losses when these losses result from deliberate government pricing policy.

These data are an indirect indicator of protectionism because they do not distinguish clearly between targeted, sectoral protection and more generally available subsidies designed to meet social ends or influence domestic income distribution. Moreover, whether they fully cover subsidies granted at the local government and state levels is dubious. In any event, table 4.3 indicates that subsidy levels have been rising in all three over the past twenty years, which

---

[b]   Gary Clyde Hufbauer, Diane T. Berliner, and Kimberly Ann Elliott, *Trade Protection in the United States: 31 Case Studies* (Washington: Institute for International Economics, 1986). Among the items included in the case studies are book manufacturing, benzoid chemicals, glassware, rubber footwear, ceramic articles, orange juice, canned tuna, textiles and apparel, steel, ball bearings, color televisions, CB radios, bolts and nuts, prepared mushrooms, automobiles, motorcycles, dairy products, peanuts, meat, fish, petroleum, lead, and zinc. These are relief, not unfair trade cases, from 1953 to 1986.

[c]   UNCTAD, "Problems of Protectionism and Structural Adjustment: Restrictions on Trade," TD/B/1126 (Geneva: UNCTAD, 1987). The definition of NTBs include paratariff measures, quantitative restrictions, import surveillance, and price control measures.

[d]   World Bank, *World Development Report 1987* (New York: Oxford University Press, 1987). "Hard-core" NTBs include import prohibitions, quantitative restrictions, voluntary export restraints, variable levies, MFA restrictions, and non-automatic licensing.

[e]   Sam Laird and Alexander Yeats, *Quantitative Methods for Trade Barrier Analysis* (London: Macmillan, 1990). "Hard-core" NTBs include variable import levies and product-specific charges, quotas, prohibitions (including seasonal), non-automatic licensing, voluntary export restraints, and MFA restrictions. The figure for Japan is significantly higher than for other studies. This is attributable in part to restrictions on coal (25 percent of the total). By contrast, petroleum products are excluded.

TABLE 4.3
Subsidies Applied by Selected Countries, 1960–1988
(PERCENT OF GDP IN CURRENT PRICES)

	1960	1965	1970	1975	1980	1985	1986	1987	1988
United States	0.2	0.4	0.5	0.3	0.4	0.6	0.7	0.7	0.6
Japan	0.5	0.7	1.1	1.5	1.5	1.4	1.1	1.0	0.9
European Community	1.2	1.5	1.8	2.5	2.6	2.8	2.8	2.7	2.5

Source: Organization for Economic Cooperation and Development, National Accounts, 1960–1988, Paris.

might be taken as preliminary evidence of increased protection. The United States, however, appears to grant subsidies at more modest levels in relation to its national income than do Japan and the EC. The EC grants significantly higher relative levels of subsidy than the two other countries.

Voluntary Export Restraints

A widely observed feature of the "new protectionism" that has grown rapidly in the last two decades is its reliance on de facto market sharing or administered trade arrangements that lack transparency, and whose form often releases governments from direct accountability. Voluntary export restraints, and variants of VERs, have become an important policy instrument in uncompetitive sectors. Jan Tumlir describes VERs and similar export-restraining arrangements as the "core of what is called the new protectionism."[7]

One of the earliest surveys of the incidence of VERs was provided in 1987 by Michel Kostecki.[8] In a listing that the author describes as "not by any means exhaustive," 137 separate export restraint agreements are identified. A more complete 1989 listing by the GATT secretariat[9] identified some 236 measures, most of them put in place in the 1980s. The listing excluded bilateral export restraint agreements made under the Multi-Fiber Arrangement. The term VER is used loosely in this context, and the arrangements in the GATT listing involve a variety of mechanisms, including trade-flow monitoring, orderly marketing arrangements (OMA), export forecasts, basic price systems, discriminatory import systems, ad hoc requests for reduced shipments, consulting arrangements, and industry-to-industry agreements. The markets of the EC and its member states were protected by 127 of the arrangements, the U.S. market by 67, Canada and Japan by 12 each, Sweden by 6, Australia by 4, Norway and Finland by 3 each, and Switzerland and Austria by one each.

Countries restraining their exports under these arrangements were Japan (49 arrangements), all other high-income countries (67 arrangements), East European countries (35 arrangements), Korea (33 arrangements), and other developing countries (52 arrangements). Thus, Japan and Korea accounted for one third of the VERs reported. The EC and its member states were applying 16 of the restraint arrangements to their exports, all of them with respect to the United States and neighboring European markets, and the United States applied only 4 VERs. What should be concluded from the fact that the two major demandeurs for VERs are such thrifty users of the instrument themselves? A full answer to the question may require detailed analysis of specific industries. However, it is difficult to avoid the conclusion that the distribution of VERs is in significant part a reflection of relative political power, domestic protectionist pressures, and a willingness to use aggressive pressure tactics on trading partners. Perhaps VERs are essentially the hallmark of the politically strong but economically weakening members of the trading community.

In many instances, VERs are rearguard actions in industries that are losing their competitive edge in mature industrial economies, or which involve agricultural products.[10] They are always protectionist in effect, even where the justification for them is embellished by "fair trade" arguments. One of the difficulties with using fair trade rhetoric to justify VERs is that the requirements for establishing and monitoring unfair trade practices in many cases are simply set aside.[11]

For the most part, the industries covered in the GATT secretariat's sample bear out the assertion that the VER is the preferred instrument of protection for declining, uncompetitive industries, and for agriculture. In the sample of 236 VERs, the vast majority cover agriculture and food products (60 arrangements), steel and steel products (50 arrangements), electronic products (27 arrangements), non-MFA textiles and clothing restrictions (21 arrangements), automobiles and road transport equipment (17 arrangements), footwear (16 arrangements), machine tools (13 arrangements), and a range of other items (32 arrangements). These arrangements have created what is virtually a fully managed trading system for textiles and clothing (taking the MFA into account as well) and steel. Kostecki estimated that at least 10 percent of world trade was covered by export-restraint arrangements by the mid-1980s,[12] but because his listing of measures was significantly smaller than the GATT secretariat's listing, the trade coverage estimate may be on the modest side.

Finally, modifications in the antidumping and countervailing-duty statutes in the 1970s, also reflected in the Tokyo Round GATT agreements in these areas, provide for price or other undertakings[13] by exporters in lieu of the imposition of antidumping or countervailing duties. VERs may reflect some such undertakings. An independent source, however, the reports to the relevant GATT Committees,[14] indicates that the United States accepted five undertakings in relation to antidumping proceedings between 1981 and 1988, and ten relating to countervailing-duty proceedings between 1984 and 1988. The EC accepted many more price undertakings in antidumping cases, amounting to 105 between 1981 and 1988. Price undertakings are conceptually similar to quantitative undertakings, although they may distort competition less. These listings may be incomplete, as in other cases, more or less formal undertakings of one sort or another may have been exchanged against the cessation or threat of unfair trade proceedings.

TRENDS IN APPLYING THE STATUTES

Fair Trade: Section 201

Section 201 of the Trade Act of 1974 is designed to provide relief for industries facing problems from competitive but fairly traded imports (chapter 3). It is the domestic law equivalent of the safeguard provisions of GATT Article XIX. Section 201 has fallen into disuse in recent years, as illustrated in table 4.4, which records all Section 201 cases from 1975 to 1989. Apart from three unsuccessful petitions, in 1986, 1988, and 1990,[15] the statute has not been used since 1985. Moreover, of the sixty-one petitions filed since 1975, less than 30 percent of them were filed in the 1980s.

Of the sixty-one petitions, twenty-eight were subject to negative injury findings by the United States International Trade Commission (USITC), and a further twelve were subject to negative relief decisions by the president. In other words, only about one third of all Section 201 petitions have resulted in trade protection or some other kind of assistance.[16] In the circumstances, it would have been surprising if industries had persevered with Section 201 petitions while the unfair trade remedies were being sharpened year by year to facilitate favorable decisions for petitioners.

If the "fair" trade remedy of Section 201 has fallen into disuse, but the "unfair" trade remedies (Section 301, antidumping and countervailing duties, etc.) have not (see below), two conclusions are possible. One is that the difficulties faced by domestic industries on account of import competition arise

Table 4.4
Section 201 Cases, 1975–90

Year	Number of cases	Negative/ no relief	Affirmative or equally divided	Presidential action	Number of cases
1975	14	5	9	No relief	3
				Adjustment assistance	5
				OMA	1
1976	5	1	4	No relief	1
				Adjustment assistance	1
				Income support	1
				OMA	1
1977	12	7	5	No relief	4
				Tariff increase	1
1978	7	1	6	No relief	3
				Tariff increase	2
				Import quota	1
1979	4	2	2	No relief	1
				Tariff increase	1
1980	2	1	1	Tariff increase	1
1981	1	1	—	—	—
1982	3	1	2	Tariff increase	2
1983	1	1	—	—	—
1984	6	3	3	TAA coordination	2
				Ordered VRA	1
1985	4	3	1	Tariff increase	1
1986	1	1	—	—	—
1987	—	—	—	—	—
1988	1	1	—	—	—
1989	—	—	—	—	—
1990	1	1	—	—	—

OMA: orderly marketing arrangement; TAA: trade adjustment assistance; VRA: voluntary restraint agreement.
Source: United States International Tariff Commission, Annual Reports, various years.

from illegitimate trade practices in other countries, and that the appropriate response to this is recourse to the unfair trade remedies. In other words, unsustainable competitive pressures from imports, which prompt firms to petition the government, do not arise from the weaknesses of domestic industries.

The other conclusion that could be drawn is that the trade remedies have become increasingly substitutable, so that petitioners can go "forum shopping." If this is true, the distinction between fair and unfair trade is not operationally relevant, bringing to mind Senator Hollings' remark cited in the previous chapter, that Section 201 is the route for suckers. Petitioners naturally prefer to go for the remedies that are most likely to yield favorable results. Moreover, the unfair trade remedies have the additional attraction of shifting all blame for injury from imports onto foreigners.

Unfair Trade: Antidumping and Countervailing Duties

The antidumping and countervailing-duty statutes are the most technically complex and mystifying part of U.S. trade law. Laws, regulations, and procedures in this field are intricate.[17] Tables 4.5 and 4.6 (see pages 82–85) summarize, respectively, the number of antidumping and countervailing-duty (antisubsidy) actions taken by the countries that principally use the measures, between 1981 and 1991. The tables show that comparatively few countries resort to antidumping and countervailing-duty procedures on a regular basis. In the case of antidumping, the United States, European Community, Canada, and Australia account for the vast majority of the actions taken. In the antisubsidy area, the United States is by far the most regular user, accounting for over 90 percent of all cases.

The frequency with which these measures are used has increased over the years, but not uniformly. The number of cases initiated has varied from year to year, and seems to have peaked in the mid-1980s. A more relevant figure for assessing the trend, however, is provided in the final column of each table, showing the number of cases outstanding in a particular year. For antidumping, there has been a clear accumulation of current actions in the United States and Canada. The data are not sufficient to make a judgment in the case of the European Community, and the trend appears to have been downward in Australia since the mid-1980s. As regards countervailing duties, the picture of accumulation is again unmistakable, certainly for the United States and Canada.

These numbers cannot be taken as incontrovertible evidence that larger trade volumes are now covered by antidumping and countervailing-duty measures than previously because they are based on a count of actions, not on trade flow analysis. Nor, in the case of the United States, can it simply be asserted that increased resort to these measures has nothing to do with the degree of dumping and subsidizing that is occurring. Perhaps increased resort to these measures indeed reflects the changed behavior of foreigners. But when these figures are considered together with the legislative trends discussed in chapter 3, and the fate of Section 201, it is hard to believe that the count of antidumping and countervailing-duty cases does not indicate a greater degree of trade inhibition than has existed previously.

How far do antidumping and countervailing-duty actions reflect protectionism, rather than a legitimate defense against unfair trading practices?[18] There is no direct way of establishing this, but some aspects of the rules and the way they are applied provide a clue.[19] Perhaps the most important of these relates to the relationship between the two steps involved in making determinations, those of investigating dumping or subsidization on one hand, and injury on the other. As shown by Finger and Murray,[20] subsidization or dumping is found in the vast majority of cases brought in the United States.[21] The figure for positive findings was around 90 percent of all cases between 1980 and 1988. When it came to injury determinations, the numbers dropped markedly, to below 60 percent for antidumping cases and below 30 percent for countervailing-duty cases.[22]

The fact that nearly all petitions investigated led to subsidy or dumping findings[23] means that the injury finding is the decisive one as regards the decision whether or not to apply a duty. Injury determination procedures are altogether less precise than those for investigating the existence of subsidies or dumping because the concept is more multifaceted, requiring more data and more subjective judgments. In effect, a number of criticisms have been made in the past of USITC rules and procedures for investigating injury.[24] The main point, however, is that if it is the injury decision, not the definition of subsidization or antidumping, that determines the outcome, then in essence, the issue is the ability of domestic industry to compete, not the existence or otherwise of an unfair trading practice.

The regularity, or even near guarantee, of a subsidy or dumping finding follows from the way the law defines these concepts, not from administrative malpractice. The problem is definitional, and in some cases one of underspecification or lack of specificity. Some interesting recent studies by academics and U.S. government officials have analyzed current methodologies used by the Commerce Department to calculate dumping margins and subsidy rates.[25] A basic conclusion of a good part of this work is that the unfair trade laws have increasingly become an instrument for providing relief from both fairly and unfairly traded imports, precisely explaining the atrophy of Section 201. The extraordinarily complex nature of dumping margin and subsidy-rate

TABLE 4.5
ANTIDUMPING ACTIONS, 1981–91[a]

COUNTRY	YEAR	INVESTIGATIONS INITIATED	PROVISIONAL MEASURES	DEFINITIVE DUTIES	PRICE UNDER-TAKINGS	OUTSTANDING ANTIDUMPING ACTIONS
United States	1981	15	9	4	1	85
	1982	51	11	47	1	n.a.
	1983	19	25	9	1	52
	1984	46	36	33	—	104
	1985	61	37	28	—	112
	1986	63	43	25	—	122
	1987	41	55	38	2	151
	1988	31	13	22	—	167
	1989	25	36	29	—	198
	1990	24	20	17	—	196
	1991	52	30	17	—	209
European Community[b]	1981	22	8	5	8	n.a.
	1982	39	7	5	17	n.a.
	1983	26	18	8	25	n.a.
	1984	33	10	10	13	124
	1985	34	11	7	15	146
	1986	23	6	7	11	123
	1987	17	12	7	11	n.a.
	1988	30	10	4	5	n.a.
	1989	29	9	13	6	170
	1990	15	8	7	10	151
	1991	15	10	9	2	143

Table 4.5 (Continued)
Antidumping Actions, 1981–91[a]

Country	Year	Investigations Initiated	Provisional Measures	Definitive Duties	Price Under-takings	Outstanding Antidumping Actions
Canada	1981	29	20	15	—	123
	1982	64	23	8	—	159
	1983	34	48	37	—	152
	1984	26	40	13	—	155
	1985	35	31	16	1	132
	1986	27	23	25	2	152
	1987	24	12	8	2	150
	1988	20	20	18	5	159
	1989	14	13	4	1	143
	1990	15	7	6	—	103
	1991	12	12	4	1	71
Australia	1983	71	33	39	10	159
	1984	70	22	32	7	192
	1985	63	25	15	3	167
	1986	54	32	20	5	171
	1987	40	17	3	1	109
	1988	20	10	5	1	49
	1989	19	9	8	4	19
	1990	23	10	—	4	20
	1991	46	39	6	—	20

Source: GATT, Basic Instruments and Selected Documents, various years.
[a] Years end in June.   [b] The EC actions reported refer only to other signatories of the Antidumping Code

TABLE 4.6
COUNTERVAILING DUTY ACTIONS, 1981–91[a]

COUNTRY	YEAR	INVESTIGATIONS INITIATED	PROVISIONAL MEASURES	DEFINITIVE DUTIES	PRICE UNDER-TAKINGS	OUTSTANDING ANTIDUMPING ACTIONS
United States	1981	7	5	3	n.a.	48
	1982	75	46	9	n.a.	n.a.
	1983	35	34	23	n.a.	53
	1984	22	17	4	—	56
	1985	60	39	21	6	86
	1986	43	24	17	1	76
	1987	11	16	16	2	89
	1988	13	9	10	1	88
	1989	8	11	8	—	91
	1990	6	5	4	—	86
	1991	8	7	4	10	70
Canada	1981	3	3	—	n.a.	n.a.
	1983	2	1	—	n.a.	n.a.
	1984	3	3	—	n.a.	3
	1985	2	2	3	—	3
	1986	1	1	1	1	5
	1987	4	3	2	—	6
	1988	—	1	1	—	8
	1989	1	1	—	—	8
	1990	3	2	1	—	9
	1991	1	—	3	—	8

TABLE 4.6 (CONTINUED)
COUNTERVAILING DUTY ACTIONS, 1981-91 [a]

COUNTRY	YEAR	INVESTIGATIONS INITIATED	PROVISIONAL MEASURES	DEFINITIVE DUTIES	PRICE UNDER-TAKINGS	OUTSTANDING ANTIDUMPING ACTIONS
European Community	1982	1	n.a.	n.a.	n.a.	n.a.
	1983	3	n.a.	1	n.a.	n.a.
	1984	1	1	2	n.a.	n.a.
	1985	0	—	—	—	4
	1991	—	1	—	—	n.a.
Chile	1983	33	1	n.a.	n.a.	n.a.
	1984	20	—	—	—	n.a.
	1985	10	—	—	—	n.a.
	1986	11	1	—	—	n.a.
	1991	2	2	2	—	n.a.
Australia	1983	6	1	n.a.	n.a.	2
	1984	3	7	n.a.	n.a.	2
	1985	3	1	3	1	—
	1986	3	6	—	3	7
	1987	3	2	—	3	10
	1988	—	—	—	1	5
	1989	2	2	—	—	2
	1991	10	—	—	—	1
New Zealand	1987	1	—	—	—	—
	1988	4	1	—	—	n.a.
	1991	1	—	—	—	n.a.
Japan	1983	1	n.a.	n.a.	n.a.	n.a.

Source: GATT, Basic Instruments and Selected Documents, various years. n.a. : not available.
[a] Years end in June. [b] The EC actions reported refer only to other signatories of the Subsidies Code.

calculations, going far beyond a mechanistic accounting exercise, often leaves room for bias. Economic analysis is applied in the studies mentioned above to Commerce Department practices and procedures. It can even be shown that in some cases firms would have to charge higher prices in the United States than in other markets to be sure of avoiding a dumping finding.

This kind of analysis suggests that virtually any industry that considers itself adversely affected by foreign competition, and presents a competently assembled petition, stands a good chance of demonstrating through the antidumping or countervailing-duty statutes that it is under attack from unfair trade practices. The decision about a remedy then turns on the injury finding.[26] The injury investigation is exclusively oriented toward producer interests. The concept does not accommodate any notion of national interest or consider the injury to consumers that might follow from the imposition of a countervailing or antidumping duty.

The similarities of current antidumping and countervailing-duty law and practice with Section 201 safeguard provisions are instructive, as are the differences. The antidumping and countervailing-duty statutes have, through dozens of incremental modifications over time, moved closer and closer to the original conception of Section 201 as an instrument for providing protection for troubled industries. But in two vital respects antidumping and countervailing-duty processes are unlike Section 201. First, a presumption of foreign wrong-doing disguises any protection granted. Second, the procedures remove presidential discretion as it exists for safeguard provisions under Section 201, ensuring that a positive injury finding leads automatically[27] to the provision of a remedy, with no second thoughts about the national interest or consumer welfare. Domestic protectionist interests can be satisfied, without any protectionist decision seemingly having been taken.

Quite apart from the argument that developments in antidumping and countervailing-duty law and practice have converted these statutes into a safeguards clause for the United States, the provisions can in effect be easily used to create uncertainty and inhibit trade, and they can also "soften up" exporters to make them more amenable to some kind of trade-restricting accommodation.[28] Mere initiation of a case can have trade harassment effects. The presence of these effects is, of course, extremely difficult to document systematically, but it is hard to believe that petitioners do not see the potential benefits from such outcomes. The use of antidumping and countervailing-duty petitions as a precursor to the negotiation of export restraint agreements in the steel sector has been well documented (chapter 5).

Finally, the relationship between antidumping and antitrust or competition rules bears mention. Conceptually, they are close, since dumping may be seen as monopolistic pricing behavior of just the variety that antitrust regulators would wish to pursue in a domestic context.[29] Yet the differences in approach are striking. In making price comparisons, for example, marginal cost pricing is not generally regarded as an actionable pricing practice in an antitrust context, but for dumping cases a much higher standard is employed, such that pricing below average costs plus a margin for profit would be considered dumping. More fundamentally, while antitrust remedies are concerned with preserving competition, antidumping remedies seem increasingly designed to inhibit competition. The creation of the EC customs union, and the abolition of antidumping remedies among member states, has led to an increased emphasis on competition policy. A similar trend may eventually emerge in North America under free trade arrangements.

Unfair Trade: Section 301

Section 301 of the Trade Act of 1974 is the president's own retaliatory instrument, although presidential control of the instrument has been diminishing. To a certain extent, Section 301 was developed as a domestic counterpart to GATT dispute-settlement machinery, as frustration grew with the seeming incapacity of the GATT machinery to work adequately.[30] Considering these origins, not surprisingly the sole focus of Section 301 is the policies and practices of other countries. Circumstances in which retaliatory action may be taken have been gradually broadened, while presidential discretion has been narrowed.

Table 4.7 (see page 88) lists Section 301 cases by year and by outcome.[31] Taking only the petitions accepted, the number of cases per year remained stable during most of the 1980s. The year 1989 was something of an exception on account of the introduction of Super 301. The table also shows that United States Trade Representative (USTR) started to self-initiate cases in 1985, as a result of widespread dissatisfaction in Congress with the apparent inactivity of the administration in trade matters.[32]

The analysis of case outcomes in table 4.7 is an attempt to evaluate how effective Section 301 has been, bearing in mind the attention it has received as the cutting edge of aggressive, reciprocity-based, foreign-market opening initiatives by the United States. Section 301 is the most overtly political, and least circumscribed statute in terms of remedies and retaliatory possibilities. It is the counterpart to the more "technical" statutes of U.S. trade policy and by its very nature generates a negotiating demand on trading partners under a more or less implicit threat of retaliation. The negotiation is one-sided, since it amounts to a demand for the removal of some measure or the cessation of some policy, on grounds of unfairness or illegality. The process sometimes

Table 4.7
Section 301 Cases, 1975–90

Year	Number of cases filed	Number of petitions rejected	Initiated by USTR	Outcomes			
				No case or no identifiable results	Trade-liberalizing result	Retaliation	Uncertain trade effects
1975	—	—	—	2	2	—	2
1976	—	—	—	1	2	1	1
1977	—	—	—	1	1	1	—
1978	—	—	—	—	—	1	1
1979	—	—	—	2	3	—	—
1980	2	2	—	—	—	—	—
1981	—	—	—	8	—	1	1
1982	1	1	—	3	2	—	2
1983	1	1	—	4	2	—	1
1984	1	1	1	2	—	1	—
1985	5	5	4	—	3	1	1
1986	5	5	4	1	3	1	1
1987	2	2	1	1	1	2	1
1988	14[b]	7	1	—	—	—	—
1989	4[b]	n.a.	—	3	7	—	—
1990	3	n.a.	1	3	1	—	—
Total	98	24	10	29	26	8	11

Source: Based on data supplied by the Office of the United States Trade Representative. [a] Five of these cases involved specialty steel, and they ended up as Section 301 cases in which relief was granted. [b] This figure does not include petitions in respect of which no investigation was conducted. [c] These cases are too recent for the outcome to be determined.

involves multilateral dealings under GATT, where illegality is charged within the GATT's sphere of competence, and sometimes does not. Even where GATT is involved, the right of unilateral retaliation is retained under domestic law. By its unilateral nature, such retaliation would not win the approval of GATT.

For the purpose of discussion, four outcomes from Section 301 cases are distinguished. First, some cases are simply dropped or dealt with elsewhere, or no identifiable result occurs. Second, some cases yield a trade-liberalizing result, generally because they persuade a country that is the subject of a complaint to take liberalizing action. Third, in some cases the United States has retaliated because a trading partner has been unwilling to take the action demanded. Finally, a number of cases have resulted in action, but not the kind of action that allows a ready judgment of its likely trade effects. Items included in this category could end up as liberalizing, as trade inhibiting, or as having no effect at all.

There is a significant element of subjectivity in this exercise and plenty of room for argument at the margin in some cases.[33] Therefore, the analysis should be considered a general indication of what has happened under Section 301, and not a definitive and uncontroversial statement on each case. With this caveat, the two most interesting columns are those involving trade-liberalizing results and retaliation. Of the seventy-seven cases pursued between 1975 and 1990, twenty-seven of them (a little more than one third) had the kinds of results that Section 301 is supposed to produce.[34] Even if a liberalizing outcome could be claimed for a few more cases, the success rate is probably not as high as protagonists of this policy had hoped, particularly bearing in mind its costs in terms of trade friction.

The retaliation outcomes covered just over 10 percent of all the cases. This is an unequivocally negative outcome, since it simply reduces trading opportunities for all concerned. Academic observers of U.S. trade policy tend to regard policies based on the threat of retaliation to be of limited use in a country like the United States,[35] arguing that it is difficult to bluff in a democracy, particularly one with institutional characteristics like those of the United States. Therefore, unless there is a willingness to carry out retaliatory threats, a problem of credibility emerges. If there is a willingness to retaliate, the policy turns out to be costly, in terms of both the trade costs of the retaliation and the risk of counterretaliation.

The division in table 4.8 (see page 90) of the Section 301 cases among the countries affected provides further insight into the use of the retaliatory weapon. In three out of eight cases where retaliation occurred, the European Community was the target, twice it was Japan, and Canada, Brazil, and

Table 4.8
Section 301: Cases by Countries, 1975–90

| COUNTRIES | TOTAL | OUTCOMES | | | | |
		NO CASE OR NO IDENTIFI- ABLE RESULT	TRADE LIBERALIZING RESULT	RETALIATION	UNCERTAIN TRADE EFFECTS
EC	26	13	4	3	6
Japan	11	1	7	2	1
Korea	8	1	7	—	—
Canada	7	2	2	1	2
Taiwan	5	2	3	—	—
Argentina	5	2	—	1	2
Brazil	4	2	1	1	—
Others	11	8	3	—	—
Total	77	31	27	8	11

EC : European Community
Source: Based on data supplied by the Office of the United States Trade Representative.

Argentina accounted for the other three cases.[36] The cases involving the European Community have probably been the least successful. Two of them provoked counterretaliation and another almost did.[37] The Brazilian case was highly politicized, since it involved retaliation on Brazilian goods in response to an allegation of inadequate intellectual property protection in the Brazilian pharmaceuticals sector. Brazil complained to the GATT in a case that it would almost certainly have won, had it not withdrawn the case following the removal of the U.S. restrictions in 1990. The U.S. action would have been interpreted as unilateral and unjustified discrimination against Brazil.

One other important observation to be made about the information in table 4.8 is that a far higher success rate in securing trade liberalization has been scored with Japan and Korea than with any other countries. Japan and Korea account for half of all successful Section 301 outcomes, but for only 17 percent of all the cases investigated. This means that 68 percent of all cases brought against these two countries resulted in trade liberalization. By contrast, the European Community accounted for one third of all Section 301 cases brought and only 15 percent of the successful outcomes.[38] The United States appears, therefore, to have been much more successful in persuading Japan and Korea to do what they are asked than the European Community. How much longer the retaliation threat can be expected to work on Japan and Korea is a matter of speculation. The experience of using Super 301 against Japan suggests that there are limits to the responsiveness of the Japanese to demands and threats based on unilateral determinations of actionable behavior. In terms of guaranteeing more open and stable markets, aggressive unilateralism may well cease to have any positive effects at all beyond the short term. At the same time, the policy carries all the downside costs of embittered trade relations, which doubtless explains the restraint shown by the administration with respect to Section 301.

Unfair Trade: Super and Special 301

The Omnibus Trade and Competitiveness Act of 1988 introduced new and more strident Section 301 features. Super 301 requires an activist stance by the administration and no longer leaves the use of the provision to executive discretion. Specifically, the act requires that the USTR identify U.S. trade-liberalizing priorities in 1989 and 1990, for specific countries and practices. The USTR must then initiate investigations and seek the removal of the measures. This process can take from twelve to eighteen months.

Special 301 is the intellectual property provision. The USTR must identify countries that deny adequate intellectual property protection. Mention should also be made of special provisions of a similar nature to Super and

Special 301 involving telecommunications trade and government procurement. In the case of telecommunications trade, the USTR had to identify priority foreign countries with which negotiations would be carried out with a view to increasing U.S. market opportunities. For government procurement, a report was required in 1990 indicating the extent to which foreign countries discriminated against U.S. products or services in their procurement practices. This exercise did not produce any immediate results, but may lead either to dispute-settlement procedures under the GATT Code on Government Procurement, if the country concerned is a code signatory, or to bilateral consultations and possibly retaliation.

The administration has used these new Section 301 provisions with a good deal of circumspection, no doubt recognizing their high potential for damaging trade policy. In January 1989, the European Community and Korea were named as priority countries under the telecommunications provisions. Super and Special 301 determinations were made in May 1989. Under Super 301, five practices and three countries were identified. These were: quantitative import restrictions in Brazil, government procurement of satellites and supercomputers in Japan, technical standards on forestry products in Japan, and export performance requirements and protection of the insurance market in India. As regards Special 301, the USTR invented the concept of a Watch List, rather than naming any priority countries. Two categories of country were identified: those on the Watch List and those on the Priority Watch List. There were eight countries on the Priority Watch List[39] and seventeen on the Watch List.[40]

The second (and final for Super 301) round of decisions on Super and Special 301, required by the end of April 1990, showed even more restraint than the earlier ones. The only country designated under Super 301 was India, once again for alleged barriers to foreign investment and to foreign participation in the Indian insurance market. As regards the 1989 designations, the accusations against Japan were rolled into a more broad-based exercise called the Structural Impediments Initiative (SII).[41] The case against Brazil was dropped in May 1990 on the grounds that Brazil had made progress on the designated practices. Finally, in spite of a finding that India's investment and insurance practices were "unreasonable" under the 1989 Super 301 investigation, and in spite of redesignation for the same practices in 1990, the USTR decided in June 1990 not to take retaliatory action. The reason given for this decision was that retaliation would be inappropriate because investment and services were under negotiation in the Uruguay Round.

On Special 301, there were no further designations in 1990, and modifications were made in the Watch Lists during the year after the 1989 designations.

Mexico, which had been on the Priority Watch List, was no longer designated, while three other countries that had been on the Priority Watch List
were moved to the Watch List[42] and one country was dropped from the Watch
List.[43] In April 1991, India, China, and Thailand were named as priority countries under Special 301 (not placed on the Watch List). Australia and the
European Community were placed on the Priority Watch List. Twenty-three
countries remained on the Watch List. Following the April 1992 designations,
there were still twenty-three countries on the Watch List (not all the same
ones as in 1991)[44] and eight countries and the European community on the
Priority Watch List.[45] Since the introduction of Special 301, only Malaysia,
Mexico, and Portugal have been removed from all lists.

So restrained was the Bush administration in using Super and Special
301 that not a single case of retaliation resulted (in contrast to the regular
Section 301 procedures). But this does not remove the difficulties for the current administration that these provisions have created. They place the administration in a no-win situation. On one hand, in constant badgering and
criticism, Congress has charged successive administrations with not using the
provisions aggressively enough. On the other hand, designated foreign countries have been reluctant to cooperate, resenting the unilateral, intrusive, and
accusatory flavor of the designations. In effect, none of the countries designated under Super 301 were disposed to cooperate. Japan's designation was
rolled into the SII, a bilateral negotiation predicated upon the assumption
that problems should be solved through action by both Japan and the United
States. Brazil's designation could be dropped because a new government
brought trade-liberalizing reforms. India consistently refused to undertake
what it regarded as negotiations under duress. This suggests that this particular adventure in aggressive trade policy has not been a success. Its trade policy benefits have been minimal, and it has generated gratuitous political
tensions. Its high profile and its automaticity have militated against constructive dialogue on specific policy problems. It was no doubt a source of
some relief to the Bush administration that under the 1988 Omnibus Trade
and Competitiveness Act, Super 301 lapsed after the 1990 designations. On
the other hand, how long it will be before some similar arrangement is again
legislated by Congress is a matter of speculation. At least three bills were
introduced in the House and Senate toward the end of 1991 that proposed to
reintroduce Super 301.[46] Provisions in some of this proposed legislation would
further reduce the discretion of the administration to decline from taking
action under Super 301, and would permit Congress to trigger Super 301 cases.

Section 301, and in particular its recent extensions, have led to much
criticism of the United States by its trading partners, both in GATT and

elsewhere.[47] Why do foreign governments feel so strongly about this issue? First, Section 301 relies in many instances on unilateral interpretations of legitimate and illegitimate trade practices. It therefore sets multilateral processes aside. Second, action under Section 301, based on these unilateral interpretations, carries the stigma and at least implicit accusation of unfair behavior on the part of a targeted country. Third, the statute gives the appearance of being based on the assumption that the United States is less protectionist, more correct, and more respectful of international trade discipline than the targeted countries. Fourth, Section 301 is an important vehicle for locating U.S. trade problems in foreign behavior. Fifth, the recent modifications in Section 301 force the executive branch to name countries as unfair traders, even in the absence of any dispute or complaint. Sixth, the design of Section 301 means that the only real limit on executive action is self-restraint. This makes for instability and uncertainty. Seventh, Section 301 can be used as a threat to extract a voluntary restraint commitment from an exporter. Finally, the suspicion remains that one objective of Section 301 is to define, and to some extent pre-empt, the outcome of multilateral trade negotiations. Domestic legislation has been designed and used to favor particular results in multilateral trade negotiations. To sum up, in Hudec's words:

> Foreign reactions have been sharpened by irritation over the self-righteous tone of the new law. The detailed procedures are structured as a series of public investigations and decisions which makes them appear to be "trade crimes" trials. Foreign governments have bristled at having their policies "tried" in this manner and have gone out of their way to ridicule the quasi-judicial appearance of these procedures. Section 301 proceedings, they note, are a totally one-sided affair in which the United States plays both prosecutor and judge, in which the defendants are tried in absentia, and in which Congress has ordained certain guilty verdicts in advance, particularly with regard to Japan.[48]

To the extent that these foreign attitudes and misgivings prevail, Section 301, particularly in its more aggressive and activist manifestations, can only cause a deterioration in international trade relations and achieve limited success in its declared intent to open markets. If political resistance to this approach builds up in a country, Section 301 actions might lead to a slowdown of trade liberalization or even to closed markets. This could happen without any retaliatory action by the United States. Two interesting questions remain about Section 301, which have not yet been explicitly addressed. First, is Section 301 illegal in a GATT sense? Second, how protectionist is it?

To take the legal question first, Section 301 will only infringe the GATT in particular circumstances. Where a case involves a GATT issue, Section 301 requires that GATT action be pursued, which leads to GATT consultations and, in unresolved cases, to a dispute-settlement procedure. There is nothing illegal about the process that far, and a problem would only arise if retaliatory measures were taken without GATT authorization. In cases involving non-GATT issues, which currently include such questions as intellectual property rights and investment regimes, a problem of GATT consistency arises only when retaliatory action is taken in an area of GATT competence. In short, Section 301 actions fall afoul of GATT law only when they lead to unauthorized retaliation.[49]

Hudec has developed an ingenious argument about the legality question, which goes beyond the formal issue of when Section 301 actions infringe the GATT. He contends that when a system of rules breaks down, as arguably the GATT system has, the doctrine of self-help or justified disobedience may provide a sound defense for a Section 301-type policy that is GATT-illegal. Hudec's argument is particularly interesting in that he sets rigid standards that would have to be met in order for the disobedience to be justified. The most important of these is that the disobedient country must apply the same standards to its own behavior as those it demands from other countries. But Hudec argues that the 1988 amendments to Section 301 "are based on an outrageous premise—namely, that the commands of Section 301 do not apply to the United States. . . . [This] one-sided premise has . . . corrupted the substantive content of the new Section 301, leading Congress to include many substantive standards that are wholly unreasonable on any terms."[50]

As for the question whether Section 301 is protectionist, the answer is not clear-cut. Protectionism can hardly be characterized as its primary intent. There are plenty of superior instruments for that purpose. However, it can have protectionist consequences in three important ways. First, a Section 301 action may lead to retaliation by the affected party, as has been the case with the European Community. Second, it may provoke negative protectionist reactions in other countries. Third, and most important, it may foster market-sharing arrangements based on import undertakings by trading partners. Thus, there are certainly circumstances in which Section 301 may lead to protectionist outcomes. Section 301 action contributed, for example, to the establishment of a market-sharing arrangement in semiconductors (chapter 5).

An argument sometimes heard, especially in the liberal trading community in the United States, is that Section 301 contributes to maintaining an open trading system by diverting domestic protectionist sentiment away from closing the American market and toward opening foreign markets. Export opportunities then become more important, the reasoning goes, than looking for ways of inhibiting imports. Abstracting for a moment from likely foreign reactions to such a strategy, the argument might seem to make sense at first glance, but it does not for two important reasons. First, it reinforces the myth that the only trade problems facing the United States are those provoked by foreign misbehavior. In this way, Section 301 smooths the path for protection seekers that go to the explicitly market-closing trade remedies predicated upon foreign unfairness, such as the antidumping and countervailing-duty statutes.

The second reason Section 301 is unconvincing as an antiprotectionist device is based on an argument developed by J. Michael Finger.[51] It is that the diversion of so much attention to foreign market opening, through the rhetoric of fair trade, has broken the historic link between import-inhibiting and export-expanding interests. The tension between these two interest groups shaped the U.S. position in multilateral trade negotiations over many years. Exporters would try to persuade the government to accede to foreign demands for improved access to the U.S. market in the knowledge that these "concessions" would lead to improved opportunities for U.S. exports in foreign markets. But now, prying open foreign markets has become an activity independent of U.S. import policy, thus largely releasing protected domestic industries from the pressures exerted by export interests and the administration that would argue for reductions in U.S. trade barriers as a quid pro quo for similar action by foreign governments. Fair trade rhetoric and crowbar politics have been assigned the task of improving foreign market access.

CHAPTER 5

SECTORAL TRADE POLICY

To gain insights into the causes and consequences of trading arrangements dominated by political negotiation and bureaucratic direction, this chapter examines trade policy trends in some detail in four sectors: steel, textiles and clothing, automobiles, and semiconductors. These sectors illustrate some of the effects of managed trade, which are also discernible in other sectors where comparable arrangements exist.[1]

Many sectoral deals start life as the result of petitions and complaints from disaffected domestic producers, relying on one or another of the unfair trade statutes discussed in the previous chapter. Or they might grow out of some exaggerated legislative proposal that promises the foreign industry concerned a fate considerably worse than a negotiated restraint agreement. A sectoral deal generally starts against a background of trade friction and ends with a negotiated agreement that takes the parties outside the recognized norms of the trading system. An adversarial situation is settled, temporarily, by setting aside the rules. Despite the economic costs and inherent instability of these kinds of arrangements, the fact that they are based on negotiation and cooperation makes them a particular threat to the multilateral trading system.

Underlying the tendency to adopt sectoral expedients such as those discussed here are the broader tensions that have characterized recent trade relations. These have been especially apparent among the three main players, the United States, Japan, and the European Community (EC). Japan has been the center of many disputes with the United States and EC that are about more than just trade interests in specific sectors. A basic question for many has been whether market-oriented trade policies can be maintained with Japan without giving that country an unfair and ultimately damaging advantage. This is in large part the origin of the clamor for industrial policy, and of increasingly strident demands for fairness. Some U.S. and EC remonstrations look like assaults on the Japanese way of life, or simply demands for assimilation. The popular expression "Japan bashing" describes this kind of all-encompassing attack.[2]

Almost every aspect of the debate about the true nature of Japan and its participation in international trade is contentious. How far is Japan an "unfair" trading country rather than simply a more dynamic economy with higher savings and investment rates than those of its trading partners? How appropriate is Japan's level and composition of trade in relation to what its geography and resource endowments suggest they should be? If difficulties of access to Japan's market are less and less about trade barriers, is the problem other policy obstacles, cultural differences, or organizational structures? Or is the problem one of uncompetitiveness, poor management, and even inertia among U.S. and European companies? Would the trade frictions peter out if changes in macroeconomic policies eradicated bilateral trade imbalances? The literature on these issues is burgeoning, but writings are often as emotional as they are factual, and agreement is elusive. Meanwhile, a succession of trade disputes make the trading system look more and more ragged. Sectoral deals, in all cases involving export restraints or import commitments from Japan, seem to serve only as stop-gap arrangements, attesting to the inherent instability of permanent negotiations about trade shares.

The chances are remote that stability can grow out of trade disputes that are defined unilaterally in terms of dishonorable behavior and whose solution is sought through demands and threats. Even if specific issues appear to be settled, and a tough stance makes good copy at home, the accumulated effects of confrontational politics are overwhelmingly negative as far as the Japanese response is concerned. As Tsurumi puts it:

> In Japan, the image of the United States as a fat, lazy, incessant nag that blames Japan for its own problems has steadily been gaining ground. Many Japanese are fed up with Washington's endless demands. In response to Washington's most recent trade-related threats, therefore, Japanese bureaucrats have begun to openly discuss Japan's "second-strike capabilities"—in particular the use of its financial power to teach the United States a lesson and, if necessary, to bring the U.S. economy to its knees. . . . With every new

American demand, the United States is seen as an ever more unreasonable bully whose leadership and trust can no longer be relied upon. Thus Japan's traditional deference to U.S. leadership is increasingly being questioned, especially by a new generation that neither remembers World War II nor feels any debt to the United States for its generous postwar policies.[3]

Any improvement in the trading environment between Japan and the United States has to come from cooperative and balanced negotiations. Genuine disputes and questions about the legitimacy of trade practices should be settled through multilateral due process, on the basis of prior agreement on the rules of the trading system. An escalation of unilateral demands, even where these result in negotiated restraints or commitments, will not improve trading opportunities or enhance the prospects for mutually beneficial cooperation.

The United States has tended to address its difficulties with Japan very largely outside of the General Agreement on Tariffs and Trade framework, but has used GATT dispute-settlement procedures when they reinforce the U.S. position.[4] Politically, Japan, like most other contracting parties, does not like to ignore GATT rulings. Apart from the Section 301 process, discussed in chapter 4, and the sectoral disputes discussed below,[5] the United States has attempted to promote separate initiatives or processes for dealing with trade friction. The two most important of these are the 1985 Market-Oriented Sector-Selective (MOSS) talks, and the 1989 Structural Impediments Initiative (SII). These exercises have been promoted by the administration as a response to the kinds of criticisms quoted above. They seem intended to divert potential conflict, and formal litigation, into a specific negotiating process that is expected to produce tangible results.

For the MOSS talks, specific Japanese market-access issues were selected.[6] The sectors involved were telecommunications, electronics, medical equipment and pharmaceuticals, forestry products, and transportation machinery and auto parts. The declared objectives of the talks were to identify and seek the removal of specific tariff and nontariff barriers to market access in Japan. Views differ on how successful the MOSS process was, although it did result in some tariff reductions and other Japanese concessions. In effect, if success is to be measured by the creation of market opportunities, simply looking at export figures is not helpful because of the range of exogenous factors that affect trade flows. Even though MOSS was less confrontational than some bilateral episodes in the recent past (such as the semiconductor dispute — see below), it was still firmly based on the premise that Japan had an obligation to liberalize unilaterally, which to a degree implied an unfair-trader stigma. Nevertheless, the Japanese probably found MOSS preferable to litigation and threats of retaliation.

The SII was launched in July 1989 shortly after Japan had been named one of three unfair trading countries under Super 301. As noted, the SII was seen as a way of dealing with that designation in a less confrontational manner. Unlike MOSS, the SII was designed to solve problems in both countries, but it was much more wide-ranging and unfocused. It was intended to identify and solve structural impediments to trade. The United States identified its areas of concern as being saving and investment, land-use policy, pricing mechanisms, domestic distribution systems, antitrust policy, and "keiretsu"[7] relationships. Where the U.S. concern with savings and investment might be in part characterized as the charge that the Japanese do not consume enough, the Japanese in their turn listed low American saving as one of their concerns. Other issues identified by the Japanese included improvements in corporate competitiveness, export promotion, work force training, and education. The SII was completed and a final report issued in June 1990. Commitments were made by both sides on the issues raised, although it must be said that these commitments were loosely worded and mostly of the "best endeavors" variety. Final agreement on the SII was considerably facilitated by President George Bush's announcement that he accepted that taxes may need to be raised in order to address the budget deficit. Previously, the administration had opposed any tax increases. Action on the budget deficit was one of the most important items on the Japanese shopping list.

In subsequent bilateral reviews of the SII in 1990, 1991, and 1992, Japan and the United States have criticized one another for a lack of progress with respect to SII commitments. Japan has remarked on what it sees as a lack of serious action on the U.S. budget deficit and on the encouragement of private savings and corporate investment. The United States has claimed that Japan's efforts have been inadequate to deal with monopolistic corporate behavior and the distribution system, and to lessen the exclusivity imposed by keiretsu relationships.

In March 1992, Senate Finance International Trade Committee Chairman Max Baucus (D.-Mont.) stated that the SII had been a failure.[8] He argued that quantitative targets should be set, as this was the only way to secure Japanese compliance. He also wanted a renewed Super 301 to replace the SII. These statements are typical of a belief in Congress that confrontation and unilateral demands produce better results than negotiation. Shifting from the SII back to Super 301 would eliminate that part of the process that permits Japan to express a view on what needs attention in the United States. It would fit well with that strand of American policy thinking that seeks to place as much blame as possible for perceived domestic difficulties on the behavior of foreigners. On the other hand, considering the broad and unfocused character of the SII, it will probably be a source of friction only if either party expects far-reaching action to result from it.

In trade relations between the United States and the European Community, contrasts with the Japanese relationship are stark. There is little philosophical content in debates between the United States and the Community, although on balance the EC is more likely than the United States to prefer interventionist or regulatory solutions to trade problems. Also, unlike the Japanese case, the United States does not make demands for unilateral action that go to the roots of European culture, politics, and social and economic organization. In common with the Japanese relationship, U.S.-EC trade problems may be solved through sectoral arrangements of the kind discussed in the rest of this chapter.

Trade friction between the United States and the European Community in the last few years has been dominated by two sectors, namely steel and agriculture.[9] Robert Hudec, analyzing GATT disputes between the United States and the EC, has shown how a variety of agricultural and agricultural subsidy issues dominated disputes between the two in the 1980s.[10] Hudec argues that, although the EC's common agricultural policy (CAP) was an irritant, the United States also had a political appreciation of the fact that the CAP was essential to the identity of the EC. As the 1980s wore on, however, it became increasingly difficult for the United States to live with an unreformed CAP. As will be seen later in this study, different views over the content and pace of agricultural reform have been central to the difficulties encountered in multilateral trade negotiations.

SECTORAL ARRANGEMENTS

Steel

The steel industry has secured one of the most complete systems of managed trade in the manufacturing sector, not least because supply and demand conditions, and relative competitive positions, have changed dramatically over the last thirty years. If not a secular tendency toward excess production capacity, severe market gluts have accumulated in years of slack demand. Production facilities have expanded rapidly in Japan and a number of newly industrializing countries (NICs), placing severe pressure upon European and U.S. producers. Much more of total production is exported now compared to a few decades ago. In 1950, only 10 percent of world steel production was exported; in 1983, 26 percent.[11] In 1950, imports accounted for only 1 percent of U.S. steel consumption; 20 percent in 1983.[12]

In the United States a predominant issue has been why so much of its domestic steel market has been lost to foreign suppliers.[13] It is recognized that the early successes in selling to the U.S market were abetted by labor disputes in the domestic industry that caused supply shortages. There is less agreement on how far the competitiveness of U.S. steel production was undermined by a failure to adapt to new technologies requiring substantial new investments and to what extent changes in relative labor and raw material costs were a causal factor. In one of the most extensive recent studies of the steel industry, Howell and others[14] argue that the technological lag was not significant but that relatively higher U.S. production costs were important.

The other, more contentious issue is how far differing levels of government support in various countries were responsible for the decline of the U.S. steel industry. The U.S. industry, and many commentators, believe that domestic steel production has been badly exposed to foreign subsidization, and that competition has been as much against the treasuries of other governments as foreign producers. As Howell and others put it, "[T]he massive subsidy injections and other forms of direct state financial aid which are pervasive throughout the world steel industry have no U.S. counterpart."[15] A contesting view is presented by Anderson and Rugman,[16] who argue not only that the U.S. steel industry has received non-negligible subsidies, but that these are underestimated because state and municipal subsidies are excluded from the available calculations. They also note that little work has been done on this issue. Subsidy levels in the United States have probably been lower than those in other steel-producing countries, although the magnitudes and weights to be assigned to different explanations of the decline of the U.S. industry, are likely to remain disputed issues. On the other hand, the industry has scored major successes in its drive to secure protection from foreign competition. According to Jaime de Melo and David Tarr, the cost in terms of forgone national income from imposing quotas on steel exports to the United States amount to $0.5–2.4 billion (depending on elasticity assumptions).[17]

As early as 1966, U.S. steel producers sought import quotas on steel. During the same period, the industry filed many antidumping petitions, only a small fraction of them successful. Fearful of the imposition of trade controls, the European and Japanese industries agreed to restrict their exports to the U.S. market. These arrangements ran from 1969 to 1971. They were renewed in 1972 for a further three years, but had little effect in 1973 and 1974 on account of increased steel demand. Again in 1975, however, slack demand resulted in excess production and a search for export markets. Following a

1976 import-relief petition filed under Section 201 of the Trade Act of 1974, the United States tried and failed to negotiate export-restraint agreements with Sweden and the EC on five categories of specialty steel, and so imposed import quotas. Japan concluded a restraint agreement with the United States on these products. Apart from specialty steel, however, the U.S. market remained largely open until the adoption of the trigger price mechanism (TPM) in 1978. Meanwhile, the EC had negotiated a series of "voluntary" export restraint agreements (VERs) with its foreign suppliers, which were justified as an alternative to antidumping duties.

By 1978, increased penetration of the U.S. market, predominantly by Japan and the EC, led to renewed pressure for protection. Once again, numerous antidumping petitions were filed in order to apply pressure on the government. Instead of negotiating fresh export restraint agreements, which were offered by suppliers, the Carter administration introduced the TPM. This established a set of trigger prices, based on the production costs of the most efficient producer (Japan at the time), such that any imports entering the United States below those prices would automatically provoke a self-initiated, accelerated antidumping investigation. This was, in effect, a minimum price import regime. The steel industry considered that the TPM worked satisfactorily for about one year; then methods were developed to circumvent it.

Dissatisfaction with the working of the TPM led to the filing of several antidumping petitions against European producers in 1980. The TPM was suspended during the antidumping investigations but restored again later in the year in a strengthened form, including a new import antisurge mechanism. A financial aid package was also put together for the domestic steel industry. Producers remained dissatisfied with the TPM, and competitive pressure was mounting as a result of the strengthening dollar and reduced demand for steel. In 1982, the steel industry filed over 200 antidumping and countervailing-duty (CVD) petitions, which effectively killed the TPM and led to a number of positive dumping and subsidy findings. Some thirty-eight European steel producers were found by the Commerce Department to be relying on subsidies. Toward the end of 1982, the EC negotiated a VER, whose effect was to reduce exports of 10 bulk steel products by 9 percent and remove the threat of additional U.S. import duties. Agreement was not reached on steel tubes and pipes. Japan had been informally restraining its steel exports to the United States for several years.

The next episode came in 1983, when a Section 201 investigation on specialty steel led to a finding of injury and a recommendation by the International Trade Commission (USITC) for import relief. The presidential relief decision led to the imposition of tariffs and quotas on certain products, with the understanding that export restraint agreements may be negotiated. This Section 201 investigation had been ordered by the president following the filing of Section 301 petitions (unfair trading practices) in 1981 against Austria, France, Italy, Sweden, and the United Kingdom on specialty steel products. Since this was finally a Section 201 action, the United States was required to offer compensation for its restrictions.[18] A failure to reach agreement on compensation with the EC led in 1984 to retaliation by the EC on alarm systems, sporting goods, and petrochemicals.

In 1984, the final episode leading to comprehensive VERs for the steel industry was played out. Although the 1982 restraint agreement with the EC on carbon steel (and the less formal understanding with Japan) had reduced imports from those sources, new suppliers such as Korea, Brazil, and Mexico had achieved significant import penetration. To deal with this situation, the steel industry orchestrated a legislative proposal for a statutory quota of 15 percent on steel imports, filed many antidumping and countervailing-duty petitions, and also filed a Section 201 petition for import relief. The USITC found serious injury under the Section 201 petition and recommended a series of tariff quotas and quotas for a period of five years.

This left President Reagan to decide whether or not to impose import restrictions. He had to weigh up the prospect of compensation or retaliation from foreign suppliers if he granted relief, as well as the costs of protection, against the likely industry and congressional reaction if he did not. The U.S. Trade Representative William Brock explained that "[T]he President has clearly determined that protectionism is not in the national interest. It costs jobs, raises prices and undermines our ability to compete here and abroad."[19] Yet as if VERs were not protectionist and did not cost jobs, raise prices, and undermine competitiveness, the president then announced a national policy for the steel industry, encompassing a wide range of steel products and countries. The USTR was instructed to:

> Negotiate "surge control" arrangements or understandings . . . with countries whose exports to the United States have increased significantly in recent years due to an unfair surge in imports—unfair because of dumping, subsidization, or diversion from other importing countries who have restricted access to their markets.[20]

This was a remarkable statement. Apart from the strange distinction made between protection and VERs, the entire grounds of the debate were shifted away from import relief considerations to the assertion that the United States was reacting to unfair foreign trade practices. The administration had bought wholesale into the logic that the industry had to promote in order to justify its regular resort to the unfair trade statutes. Moreover, the VERs were negotiated across the whole range of steel products, with many countries, in circumstances where it was apparently no longer necessary to establish that the domestic industry had been injured or that foreign suppliers were resorting to some impermissible trade practice.

The national policy for the steel industry was intended to reduce imports to 18.5 percent of domestic consumption, or 20.2 percent if semifinished steel was included. Congress quickly passed the necessary legislation to enforce the VERs, making the arrangements conditional on modernization by the domestic industry, and providing retraining assistance for displaced workers. After difficult beginnings, the Reagan steel program, which was to run until September 1989, began to produce the desired effects for domestic producers. The import penetration ratio fell from 26.4 percent in 1984 to 21.3 percent in 1987. Restricted suppliers were not meeting their quotas, and the only reason the established target had not been met was increased exports by nonrestrained countries, in particular, Canada.

The steel issue was comparatively subdued until early 1989, when a debate started about whether or not the steel VER program was to be renewed. President Bush had equivocated on the issue in his election campaign, talking both of the need for genuine competition in the steel industry and of renewing the VER program in the interim. The 1989 debate was different from earlier episodes in the steel story for two main reasons. First, a coalition of steel users, organized more seriously than ever before, lobbied for support in Congress, with some success. Some of the steel-using sectors active in this process were manufacturers of construction equipment, agricultural equipment, metal products, and household appliances, as well as forgers, metal-stampers, and shipbuilders. The antiprotection lobby[21] was also given a boost by reports from the USITC and the General Accounting Office that were critical of the VER program. The USITC report argued that the program had raised costs to users, which resulted in significant export market losses. It was also argued that while the steel industry had lost $12 billion from 1982 to 1986, it had made profits of $1 billion and $2 billion in 1987 and 1988, respectively, and therefore did not need any more protection.

Despite all this activity, the protection lobby remained strong, and the industry resorted to its traditional tactic of threatening hundreds of antidumping and countervailing-duty petitions. As a final compromise, President Bush renewed the VER program in October 1989 for only thirty months, instead of the five years demanded. The program incorporated built-in expansion factors and more flexible short-supply arrangements. More important, a Steel Trade Liberalization Program was also announced, with the objective of eliminating trade-distorting practices in the sector in all countries. The program called for an international consensus on government disciplines with respect to state aid and other trade-distorting interventions.

At the initiative of the United States, multilateral negotiations for the establishment of a Multilateral Steel Agreement (MSA) took place in Geneva from 1990 onward, in parallel to but separate from the Uruguay Round negotiations. Thirty-six countries participated in these negotiations, designed to eliminate quantitative trade restrictions and tariffs, regulate the use of antidumping and countervailing-duty remedies, control subsidization, and introduce special dispute settlement procedures. It was never clear, given its exclusive sectoral form, whether the MSA would promote free trade (its declared intent) or degenerate into a market-sharing arrangement (similar to that regulating textiles and clothing).

The United States wished to conclude the MSA negotiations before the expiry of its VER program, on March 31, 1992. But negotiations broke down that day, as agreement remained elusive on several key elements of the proposed MSA. The position then adopted by the administration was that the VERs were not going to be renegotiated and that the U.S. industry had the necessary unfair trade remedies at its disposal. Taking the administration at its word, twelve domestic companies filed forty-eight antidumping petitions and thirty-six countervailing-duty petitions against twenty-one countries (all major foreign suppliers) on a variety of flat-rolled steel products that accounted for about 6 percent of the domestic market.

The reactions of trading partners to these moves were strong. The EC Commission rejected subsidy allegations, arguing that any crisis in the U.S. steel industry reflected the "inability of the major integrated producers to compete successfully with the more streamlined and efficient American "mini-mills."[22] A spokesman for the Japanese steel industry also denied subsidization charges, arguing that "American steelmakers should look inward to discover the real cause of their problems. . . . Japanese and other overseas steelmakers are not the cause of U.S. overcapacity, the destructive price competition for market share among integrated mills and mini-mills, or the recession."[23] Both the EC and Japan argued that the antidumping and countervailing-duty actions were tantamount to trade harassment. They also pointed out that most foreign suppliers, including the EC, Japan, and Korea had not been filling their quotas under the VER arrangements.

The definition of dumping used under the U.S. statute and regulations makes dumping findings highly likely in the cases where dumping is alleged (chapter 4). This means that the final decision on actions to be taken will rely on the injury finding. But through this process blame for the ills of the industry has been placed squarely and exclusively at the door of misbehaving foreigners.

Textiles and Clothing

The textiles and clothing sector has the distinction of being the only manufacturing industry to have acquired a special status in international trade arrangements, as a result of a negotiated departure from GATT rules. The industry acquired this status gradually over a period of years, while trade restrictions were relentlessly extended to cover more and more products and countries.

The strength of protectionist sentiment in the textiles and clothing industry derive from several sources. The technical characteristics of the industry mean that it can develop rapidly in new locations, so barriers to entry are often practically nonexistent and, above normal profits, difficult to generate.[24] Many branches of the industry are labor intensive, making relative wage costs a crucial element of competitiveness. It is an old and traditional industry, employing many workers, one that figures prominently in the early stages of industrialization.

The story of how the textiles and clothing industry came to be a special case began in the 1950s, although some trade restraint agreements had been reached between the United States and Japan as early as the 1930s.[25] As Japanese postwar recovery began to have repercussions in international markets in the 1950s, textiles and clothing industries in the industrial countries were among the first to feel the effects. When Japan acceded to the GATT in 1955, a number of existing members initially invoked the nonapplication provisions of the GATT in order to be able to continue to apply GATT-illegal restrictions to Japanese imports, including textiles and clothing.[26] As the main sponsor of Japanese membership in GATT, the United States could hardly refuse to apply the provisions of the agreement to the trade between the two countries. In an early example of what has become a traditional method of ensuring opacity and a lack of accountability in the twilight zone of GATT legality, the United States persuaded Japan in 1956 to restrict its exports on a "voluntary" basis.

Under continuing pressure from the domestic industry, President John F. Kennedy called for a multilateral trade-restricting arrangement in 1961, which took shape as the Short-Term Arrangement Regarding International Trade in Textiles. The Short-Term Arrangement (STA) embodied a network of restrictions involving 16 countries and over 60 product categories. The STA was succeeded by the Long-Term Arrangement (LTA) in 1962. The LTA had been foreseen in the STA, and its successful negotiation was a precondition that President Kennedy had to meet to secure negotiating authority from Congress for what became the Kennedy Round. The LTA lasted, with two extensions, until 1974.

Once again, in the early 1970s, the administration had to bargain for multilateral negotiating authority. This time it was President Richard M. Nixon for the Tokyo Round, and the textile and clothing industry wanted a more effective mechanism of protection. The result was the Multi-Fiber Arrangement (MFA) of 1974. This arrangement lasted until 1977, to be replaced by MFA II in 1978, by MFA III in 1982, and MFA IV in 1986. MFA IV expired in 1991. If the Uruguay Round had been completed on schedule at the end of 1990, a ten-year phase-out arrangement would probably have superseded MFA IV. As it was, MFA IV was extended for a further 17 months, until the end of December 1992.

The increasing restrictiveness of these successive arrangements is easy to trace.[27] While the STA involved sixteen countries and about sixty products, MFA IV encompasses forty-one signatories (counting the EC as one) and thousands of product categories. The STA only covered cotton products; the LTA extended coverage to cotton blends, MFA I to all textiles and clothing of wool, cotton, and synthetic fibers, and MFA IV to vegetable fibers and silk blends. A notable feature of the MFA is that the countries whose exports are restricted are all developing countries and the countries that are protected are all industrial countries. This has given trade relations in the textile sector a distinctly north-south flavor. More seriously, it has led to significant trade diversion at the expense of the restricted countries.[28]

The concepts developed under the MFA and its predecessors bear little relation to those usually associated with trade rules, and they have provided ample scope for protection seekers, with the active support of their governments, to inhibit imports. For example, the notion of "market disruption" is the conceptual equivalent of injury in the GATT context, but there is no question under the MFA of any injury determination. Restrictions are negotiated periodically on a bilateral basis and take the form of VERs. There are no mechanisms for establishing causality between market disruption and import flows. The Textiles Surveillance Body, created by the MFA, rules on the propriety of MFA restrictions, within the MFA guidelines.

The idea implicit in the MFA that "low cost" suppliers should have lesser guarantees against trade restraints is contrary to the principles of the trading system. The MFA is intrinsically discriminatory, ensuring that the benefits of specialization through trade cannot be enjoyed on a generalized basis. The concept of "minimum viable production" was introduced into the MFA as a way of restricting imports below the levels permitted by the standard restriction formula of the MFA. The same purpose is achieved with the notion of "reasonable departures." Thus, the MFA is not only a thoroughly protectionist mechanism, it has also become less and less able to define stable minimum levels of access or increasing access.

As far as mainstream trading rules are concerned, the MFA is in several respects a far cry from what the GATT would require. As noted, the GATT demands a standard of proof of material injury and causality for safeguard or import relief actions, whereas the MFA is expressed in terms that permit restrictions to be based on nothing more than differences in relative prices. The imposition of quantitative trade controls is not legal under GATT, despite continuing debate over the exact status of VERs under GATT. Most fundamentally of all, the essence of the MFA is the capacity to select targets for trade control on a discriminatory basis, while the GATT's most basic tenet is the most-favored-nation (MFN) rule. A technical analysis of the differences between the MFA and the GATT would yield further instances of incompatibility, but the above illustrations suffice to show how far the MFA departs from the basic principles of the trading system.

What of the costs of the MFA? In the restricting country, the costs fall on consumers and the economy at large. Protection raises prices of imported goods and import substitutes[29] and misallocates productive resources to less efficient uses. In the case of the MFA, there is an added twist, because the benefits of higher prices, or the rents associated with trade restrictions, may not go to the importing government or to domestic quota holders, but rather to the foreign suppliers who administer the restrictions in the shape of VERs. A number of quantitative estimates have been made of the costs of protection in the textiles and clothing industries. One of the most thorough estimates for the United States is that of William Cline,[30] who concludes:

> Tariff and quota protection raise import prices by an estimated 53 percent for apparel and 28 percent for textiles. Total consumer costs of protection amount to $7.6 billion annually in apparel and $2.8 billion in textiles. Total protection preserves 214,200 direct jobs in apparel and 20,700 jobs in textiles. The average American household thus pays $238 every year to retain some 235,000 jobs in the textile and apparel sectors rather than elsewhere in the economy. The consumer cost per job saved is approximately $82,000 in apparel and $135,000 in textiles. . . . The net welfare costs to all Americans are smaller; after deducting transfers to producers and government, the net annual costs amount to $7.3 billion in apparel

and $811 million in textiles. However, the employment benefits are far smaller than this cost. Evaluated on the basis of average duration of unemployment and average wage, the annualized costs of transitional unemployment resulting from elimination of protection amount to only about 3 percent to 4 percent of the net welfare costs of protection.

In a more recent study using a computable general equilibrium model, Irene Trela and John Whalley[31] calculated that the removal by industrial countries of all tariff and nontariff restrictions on textiles and clothing would result in a net world welfare gain of $15 billion. In this model, about one-half of the total estimated gain accrued to developing countries. Jaime de Melo and David Tarr estimate that the United States could enjoy a welfare gain of $7–15 billion (depending on elasticity assumptions) by removing all textile and clothing quotas.[32]

In its Article 1, the MFA specifies its objectives as being:

> . . . to achieve the expansion of trade, the reduction of barriers to such trade and the progressive liberalization of world trade in textiles products, while at the same time ensuring the orderly and equitable development of this trade and avoidance of disruptive effects in individual markets and on individual lines of production in both importing and exporting countries.[33]

Experience with the MFA would suggest a lot of emphasis on the second part of this sentence, and scarcely any at all on trade expansion, barrier reduction, and progressive liberalization.

Martin Wolf and others conclude in their 1984 study of the costs of protection in the textiles and clothing industry that: "The MFA is a monument to diplomatic compromise, political appeasement and bureaucratic obfuscation. A defense can hardly be made in economic terms."[34] The particular workings of the MFA and the exceptional success of domestic industrial lobbies have produced a systematic and effective system of protection. Its durability has doubtless been reinforced by the fact that the protection is directed at developing countries which have so far been ineffective in any form of retaliation[35] or in adopting any measures leading to the removal of the discrimination. It is one of the perverse effects of VER arrangements like those of the MFA that vested interests are built up among exporters in the restricted industry which favor the maintenance of the restraints. This is because of the rents that go with access to export quotas.

Negotiated trading arrangements such as the MFA allow governments overtly to use market access conditions for political ends, sometimes in a bizarre fashion. The use made by the United States of its textile quotas following the Gulf War is a case in point. To compensate Turkey for the economic costs incurred as a result of its support for the coalition, including the loss of its oil pipeline revenue, the United States doubled Turkey's apparel quota. The United States then persuaded Hong Kong, as "a 'contribution' to the U.S. war effort,"[36] to reduce its textile exports to the United States by the equivalent of 16 million shirts (27 million square meter equivalents), estimated to be worth $125 million in forgone sales. Korea and Taiwan were also pressured to make similar contributions to the Gulf War. Increasing the price of clothing to the American public is a strange way indeed for the government to seek contributions to the war effort.

Like other sectors that have succeeded in establishing managed trade arrangements to promote protectionist ends, the textile and clothing industry has harnessed legislative procedures for its own ends. The industry has orchestrated the introduction of highly protectionist proposed legislation. In 1985, Congressman Ed Jenkins (D.-Ga.) introduced a textile bill that would have sharply reduced imports from major suppliers and restricted future growth in all imports, including from industrial countries, to no more than 1 percent a year. According to Destler and Odell,[37] the bill picked up unexpected and significant support on account of the prevailing mood in Congress at that time, making it necessary for the president to exercise a veto. Instead of following the normal procedure of letting the matter drop or seeking to override the presidential veto immediately, the supporters of the bill managed to schedule the vote on the override for eight months later, which would be just after the negotiations in Geneva on MFA IV. This was a highly effective tactic, which almost certainly resulted in a harder U.S. position in the MFA negotiations. In the event, however, the textile industry was dissatisfied with the results of the MFA IV negotiation, and the bill gathered further support, leaving only a very narrow margin of eight House votes upholding the veto. A similar effort was made in 1987 and 1988, when the Jenkins Bill was reintroduced, and again President Reagan exercised his veto right.

There is one important contrast between steel and textiles. In the case of steel industry protection, much emphasis has been placed on the argument that measures against imports are necessary because of the unfair trade practices of foreign suppliers, despite the fact that no attempt is made seriously to establish the case. In textiles and clothing, on the other hand, the fair trade rhetoric has hardly been employed at all. That the MFA is simply protectionist does not seem to create any difficulty for legislators or the administration.

Perhaps this phenomenon can be explained by the nature of both the arrangement and its victims. The MFA is in some sense official, including at the international level; if a sin is collectively practiced it loses much of its stigma. The idea has been imprinted on the collective psyche that this is a unique, quite special case. The victims, domestic consumers and developing-country exporters, are either not sufficiently touched by, or aware of the costs they bear (the consumers), or are too weak (non-quota holding exporters) to do anything about it. Another part of the explanation may be that as long as both textiles and clothing are protected, no intermediate or user industry is going to protest the cost effects of the MFA. Importers and retailers are not sufficiently powerful by themselves. In any event, they can be partly neutralized by accusations of a lack of patriotism if they oppose too vigorously measures whose avowed cause is the protection of American jobs.

If policy in the textile and clothing industry changes, it will have to happen on an internationally coordinated basis. It is difficult to see countries acting unilaterally to any significant degree, whether they are inside or outside current MFA arrangements.[38] Moreover, unless the consumer movement in industrial countries mobilizes, domestic pressure is unlikely to build effectively against protection in these industries, considering the strength of the textile lobby. This leaves the developing-country exporters as the only probable source of pressure for change. Despite what is made of vested interests within developing countries in favor of maintaining MFA restrictions in their present form, most developing-country governments are committed to its eradication. The beginnings of this pressure are manifest, and developing countries are likely to have growing success in holding other trading interests hostage to progress in the textile field. A coordinated approach of this nature will be increasingly hard to resist.

The textiles and clothing sector arrangements foreseen in the draft North American Free Trade Agreement (NAFTA)[39] demonstrate the strength of the U.S. domestic lobby. Far from presaging the demise of the MFA, the NAFTA brings Mexico under the North American protectionist umbrella. In exchange for improved access for Mexican apparel production, Mexico will be required to source virtually all textile inputs, down to fiber and yarn, within the free trade area. This highly restrictive arrangement is achieved through the NAFTA rules of origin.[40]

Automobiles

In the auto industry, protectionist pressures have proved impossible to resist in the United States and Europe, leading yet another manufacturing sector toward market sharing. Whereas, in 1973, only 1 percent of automobile imports in the industrial world[41] were subject to discriminatory restrictions, by the early 1980s, almost 50 percent were.[42] From the mid-1970s, conditions in the auto industry began to change rapidly. The 1973 oil crisis was in part responsible, since it led to a reduction in demand for cars, and a structural shift in the industry toward smaller, more fuel-efficient vehicles. This in turn implied the need for additional investments and technological innovation. These developments coincided with the emergence of Japan as a major auto exporter, placing additional pressure on European and U.S. manufacturers. The situation deteriorated further in the late 1970s and early 1980s as a result of the recession.

In the United States, the United Auto Workers (UAW) filed a Section 201 petition in 1981 requesting import relief. The USITC investigation established that the industry was suffering injury but did not recommend import relief because imports were not considered the major cause of the injury. By this time, the industry was losing money, and some 200,000 auto workers and more in supplier industries had been laid off.[43] It was therefore likely that action would be taken. Moreover, President Reagan had recognized the need to do something about auto imports during his election campaign, rather as President Bush did eight years later in regard to steel.

In Congress the intention to press for action was clear from the very beginning of President Reagan's term. Senator John C. Danforth (R.-Mo.) introduced a bill that would impose statutory import quotas on Japanese cars for three years. According to Destler,[44] it was not intended that the bill should become law but was rather aimed at exerting pressure on the Japanese and the administration. In view of the broad trade stance of the Reagan administration, it was reluctance to be seen to be taking protectionist action so soon after assuming office. The obvious solution was a VER, and in view of the alternative, the Japanese were willing to negotiate a restraint agreement.[45] The administration did not want to be seen to be doing that either, even if it was less transparent, and preferred to maintain the fiction that any trade restraint would be entirely at the discretion of Japan.

In the event, the Japanese government announced a unilateral commitment in May 1981, to restrict auto exports to the United States over a period of two to three years to 1.68 million units a year, with a built-in growth factor for any market expansion. The arrangement would be reviewed in the third year.

A 1989 Report of the Advisory Committee for Trade Policy and Negotiations (ACTPN) on the U.S.-Japan trade problem makes interesting reading on the auto restraint issue:

> To this day, Administration officials insist that the VER was a non-agreement resulting from a non-negotiation. There is little reason

to doubt them; it was MITI [Japan's Ministry of International Trade and Industry] and not the Administration that was strongly in favor of restrictions. Administration officials apparently did no more than comment on the Japanese proposals as they evolved.[46]

The argument is disingenuous. It is like saying that a man asked to be shot in the foot, without mentioning that he had the choice of being shot in the foot or in the head. But the ACTPN position is helpful for one of the arguments made in the Advisory Committee's report: that the lesson from the auto episode was that it was dangerous to give the Japanese the initiative in trade issues. This view seems to be founded on the assertion that by raising car prices, the VER had increased the profits of the Japanese industry, and that "because the agreement was truly a voluntary action by the Japanese Government, the administration had no control over its extension or demise."[47] Despite the subsequent claim that the administration wished to see the restraint done away with, there has been little evidence of this intention.[48]

The truth about what was asked for, what was offered, and by whom has become a little clearer, if President Reagan's autobiography is to be believed.[49] According to Reagan, in March 1981 the cabinet had a lively debate about whether to impose mandatory import quotas on Japanese autos, during which several members of the cabinet and staff, including David Stockman (budget director), had expressed firm opposition. The rest of the story is worth quoting in full:

> As I listened to the debate, I wondered if there might be a way in which we could maintain the integrity of our position in favor of free trade while at the same time doing something to help Detroit and ease the plight of thousands of laid-off assembly-line workers.
>
> The Japanese weren't playing fair in the trade game. But I knew what quotas might lead to; I didn't want to start an all-out trade war, so I asked if anyone had any suggestions for striking a balance between the two positions. George Bush spoke up:
>
> "We're *all* for free enterprise, but would any of us find fault if Japan announced without any request from us that they were going to *voluntarily* reduce their exports of autos to America?"
>
> I knew the Japanese read our newspapers and must know about the sentiment building up in Congress for quotas on their cars; I also

knew there must be some apprehension in Tokyo that, once Congress imposed quotas on automobiles, there was a good possibility it might try to limit imports of other Japanese products.

I liked George's idea and told the cabinet I'd heard enough and would make a decision, but didn't tell them what it was. After the meeting, I met privately with Secretary of State Al Haig and told him to call our ambassador in Tokyo, Mike Mansfield, and have him pass the word informally to Japanese Foreign Minister Masayoshi Ito, who was scheduled to make a visit to Washington in a few days, that pressure was building in Congress for passage of a bill establishing mandatory quotas. I told him to suggest that an announcement of a *voluntary* cutback by Japan might head it off.

. . . Foreign Minister Ito of Japan was brought into the Oval Office for a brief meeting. . . . I told him that our Republican administration firmly opposed import quotas but that strong sentiment was building in Congress among Democrats to impose them.

"I don't know whether I'll be able to stop them," I said, "But I think if you *voluntarily* set a limit on your automobile exports to this country, it would probably head off the bills pending in Congress and there wouldn't be any mandatory quotas."[50]

Why autos were not made into a fair trade issue is an interesting question. If the same circumstances emerged now, or had emerged six or seven years later than they did, would fair trade and reciprocity arguments have been kept out of the debate? It is somewhat doubtful, since there seems to be less and less need to prove an infringement of any established requirement, rule, or practice before crying foul. In any event, because there was no allegation of a misdemeanor on Japan's part, the administration had to make it look as if trade restrictions had nothing to do with protectionism in the industry.

The VER was increased to 1.85 million units in 1984, and then to 2.3 million in 1985. There it remained until March 1992, and was then slashed to 1.65 units, the lowest level since VERs were introduced in 1981. The reduction may have partly reflected increased production at Japanese facilities in the United States, but was no doubt also influenced by the trade tensions that manifested themselves in early 1992 (see below). In 1985, President Reagan did say that he would not seek a renewal of the agreement, an oblique signal from a government that supposedly had not requested it in the first place. The

U.S. industry has consistently pressed for a reduction in the size of the quota, and no congressional initiatives have been made for its removal. The quota has remained unfilled since 1987, as Japanese exporters have settled into a pattern of self-disciplined restriction while also manufacturing within in the U.S. market.

Besides restricting Japanese exports by one means or another, the UAW also sought to induce Japanese investment in the United States as a way of maintaining employment levels. The chosen instrument for this purpose was to seek congressional sponsorship for domestic content legislation. In 1982, Congressman Richard Ottinger (D.-N.Y.) obliged by introducing a domestic content bill by which the larger the sales in the U.S. market, the more domestic content foreign cars would have to embody, up to a maximum of 90 percent. The administration was strenuously opposed to the idea. Although USTR Brock had said in 1981 in a remark giving tacit approval to restrictions on car imports that "there are times when you have to take some steps backwards to go forward,"[51] he described the domestic content legislation proposal as "the worst piece of economic legislation since the 1930s."[52] The draft legislation never reached the Senate floor, even though the House had approved a modified version.

After demands for domestic content legislation were frustrated, the UAW began to lobby for the replacement of the VER with a more explicit market-sharing arrangement to include limits on Japanese investment in the U.S. auto sector.[53] This was a reversal of the earlier insistence on more Japanese investment. In effect, such an arrangement would restrict imports of component parts of Japanese vehicles as well as the finished product.

The decade-long battle between the United States and Japan in the auto sector took on a new dimension in January 1992 with a visit by President Bush to Japan. What was supposed to be a state visit looked more like a sales visit, as the president's entourage was dominated by industrialists, and the occasion was used to press for market opening measures. The pressure focused largely on autos and auto parts, but the agenda also included computers, paper products, flat glass, semiconductors, procurement, financial markets, and legal services. The U.S. position was simply that Japan should buy more goods and services from the United States.

As a backdrop to the visit, Congressman Richard Gephardt (D.-Mo.) and five of his colleagues introduced a bill[54] that restricted U.S. auto imports from Japan by up to 1.25 million units over a five-year period unless Japan reduced its trade surplus with the United States by 20 percent a year. The bill also envisaged a minimum 60 percent local content requirement for Japanese cars made in the United States to qualify as local manufactures. The Gephardt initiative was reminiscent of his 1986 amendment to proposed trade legislation that eventually became the Omnibus Trade and Competitiveness Act of 1988, where emphasis was placed on balancing the value of trade bilaterally (chapter 6).

The Japanese agreed to purchase auto parts worth $19 billion annually by the end of fiscal 1994 and increase purchases of cars to 20,000 units — less than 0.5 percent of the total Japanese market. As had occurred earlier in the case of semiconductor purchasing commitments forced upon Japan (see below), an argument erupted as to whether the Japanese had made a firm quantitative commitment or merely a best endeavors undertaking. Although the distinction might be important in terms of whether such targets were enforceable, or whether failure to meet them was in some way punishable, undertakings like these infringe the most basic tenets of an open and competitive trading system. Also unstable, they become a recurring source of tension, which easily spills over into the broader relationships between countries.

Moreover, the inconsistency of calling for more competitive and less cozy markets arrangements on one hand, and making demands (for purchasing commitments) that force firms to collude and industries to cooperate with government on the other, seems to be lost on the promoters of market-sharing solutions. It makes as little sense as subscribing to an industrial policy and railing against unfair trade practices all in the same breath (chapter 1).

A further issue raised by politically generated demands of this nature is whether the goods concerned are of the requisite quality and design. It emerged from the controversy caused by President Bush's Japan trip that U.S. auto makers were hoping to sell American cars that had not even been adapted for driving on the left-hand side of the road. The story that large American cars are favored by gangsters and dentists in Japan may be apocryphal. If true, however, gangster preferences might more appropriately be counted as exports of the American film industry. The partiality of dentists remains a mystery.

As in textiles and clothing, the expression of trade restrictions in quantitative terms induced Japanese car manufacturers to upgrade the quality of their products to secure additional value per unit sold. Even allowing for this effect, however, significant price rises can be expected to result from VERs. Crandall, for example, calculated that the price of imported Japanese cars had increased by some $900 on average, while domestic cars had gone up by around $400, implying a consumer cost per job protected of $160,000 a year.[55] De Melo and Tarr have estimated that the removal of restrictions against Japanese autos would imply a national income gain for the United States of around $10 billion.[56] Since auto protection was engineered through "voluntary" export restraints, consumer or other interest groups wishing to protest this situation would have some difficulty in knowing whom to hold accountable. That same lack of accountability is likely to contribute to the longevity of the measure.

Semiconductors

Trade relations in the semiconductor industry have been contentious and confused. They have been heated because in the United States the fortunes of the semiconductor industry have become symbolic of national economic and security interests, and national pride. They have been confused because they have generated contradictory and conflicting market outcomes and disputed interpretations of supposedly secret deals. They have been important systemically because they explicitly raise questions about the relation between market sharing and discrimination against third parties. They have also ushered in a first foray by the United States into industrial policy proper on an industrywide basis.[57]

The semiconductor industry is unlike the steel, textile, and automobile industries because it is a new industry on the technological frontier, not an old one, fighting a rearguard action against underlying uncompetitiveness. The survival and competitiveness of the semiconductor industry is also widely regarded as vital to the economic and political fortunes of the United States as a nation in the decades to come. However, the semiconductor industry is similar to the others mentioned in that a commanding position was undermined in a short period of time by foreign competitors.[58] After leading the industry worldwide with inventions and innovations until the mid-1970s, the U.S. industry's market position and technological capacity were threatened or overtaken by Japanese industry.[59]

Manufacturers in the United States developed integrated circuits, dynamic random access memories (DRAMs), and the first generations of improved DRAMs. By the late 1970s, however, Japan was producing DRAMs at low cost and taking larger and larger shares of the market for these products. According to Prestowitz, the United States share of the world market for all memory products fell from 75 percent in 1979 to just over 25 percent in 1986, while the Japanese share moved up from 25 percent to 65 percent in the same period.[60] Between them, the United States and Japan accounted for over 90 percent of the world market. Reacting to the beginnings of these trends, the U.S. industry began in the early 1980s to exert pressure on the administration for action to counter Japanese incursion, arguing that the Japanese had succeeded in challenging U.S. dominance in its own market, and elsewhere, by a combination of dumping and domestic protection.

The administration's first attempts to restrain alleged dumping in the U.S. market by Japanese firms were largely informal. The Commerce Department suggested to Japanese negotiators that price monitoring, which could provoke antidumping action, might be undertaken. According to Prestowitz's account of events, this informal warning worked for a short time and prices stabilized. Then the Justice Department indicated its intention to investigate possible antitrust violations on the strength of price-fixing allegations against Japanese firms. This was the first episode in what was a central difficulty in the U.S. stance on the semiconductor issue, namely, that price undertakings aimed at avoiding antidumping actions led in practical terms to cartelization, price rises, and trade restrictions. This difficulty went beyond merely creating a contradictory situation in the United States; it also led to third-country protests and GATT litigation.

The U.S. industry wanted three things from the Japanese. The first was a cessation of alleged dumping in the U.S. market; the second, a cessation of such dumping in other markets; and the third, an increased share of the Japanese market for U.S. producers. After several months of discussion, the first agreement with the Japanese was reached, toward the end of 1982. Japan agreed to "seek to ensure" equivalent opportunities in the domestic market to those enjoyed by Japanese firms in the U.S. market. A short three months later, pressure for something more concrete resumed, as the industry saw no improvement in the situation. The second agreement, concluded a year after the first, involved an informal undertaking by the Japanese to encourage domestic firms to buy more U.S. chips and develop long-term relationships with U.S. suppliers.

The second agreement was regarded as more satisfactory than its predecessor, but market conditions changed markedly in 1984. Demand for semiconductors was dropping, the Japanese took the lead in introducing the newest generation of 256K RAMs, and markets were oversupplied at low and apparently uneconomical prices. The emphasis of the U.S. industry's campaign for more favorable operating conditions shifted in 1985 from access to the Japanese market to include antidumping petitions against Japanese sales in the United States. Being 1985, when the value of the dollar had peaked and the administration had embarked upon its new activist trade stance, the efforts of the industry were complemented by those of the government. A veritable barrage of trade-remedy actions was unleashed on the Japanese.

The Semiconductor Industry Association (SIA) filed a Section 301 petition in June 1985, alleging the existence of major barriers to the sale of foreign semiconductors in Japan. The petition was accepted and an investigation initiated. In the same month, Micron Technology filed an antidumping petition on 64K DRAMS. In their preliminary investigations, the Commerce Department found dumping and the USITC found injury. In December the Commerce Department announced preliminary dumping margins ranging from 9 percent to 94 percent. Three other firms then filed an antidumping petition at the beginning of October on erasable programmable read-only memories (EPROMs), which led in March 1986 to a preliminary dumping margin assessment of between 30 percent and 188 percent. Micron Technology then filed an antitrust suit, also in October 1985, charging predatory pricing by six Japanese firms. In December, the Commerce Department self-initiated an antidumping investigation on DRAMS of 256K and higher, which led to preliminary dumping margin determinations ranging from some 20 percent to 109 percent. Finally, in March 1986 the USITC initiated a Section 337 investigation as a result of a petition from Texas Instruments alleging the violation of patents on semiconductors by Japanese and Korean manufacturers.

In sum, by March 1986, Japan was faced with one Section 301 case, three antidumping cases, one antitrust suit, and one intellectual property infringement case. Although this situation may not have been entirely orchestrated, the intent was clearly to force the Japanese to negotiate and make concessions to the United States, rather than allow the legal procedures to run their course.[61]

One important reason why the U.S. industry wanted to avoid imposing antidumping duties was that it knew the price increases involved would make the United States an "island of high prices," which would reduce demand for the U.S. product and impair the performance of domestic industries using domestically produced semiconductors. Under an agreement with Japan, on the other hand, prices could be raised worldwide, since between them the United States and Japan accounted for 90 percent or more of the market. For their part, the Japanese did not want to be shut out of the U.S. market, which would have been the outcome of the antidumping actions in some product lines. Also, if the Section 301 case had run its course, it could have spilled over into other sectors and meant more trade friction.

After arduous negotiations, a five-year agreement was finally signed by the United States and Japan at the end of July 1986. Under the Arrangement concerning Trade in Semiconductor Products, Japan would monitor the costs and prices of semiconductor exports to all markets and would do all in its power to prevent dumping. In addition, Japan would encourage its domestic producers and users to purchase more American semiconductors. To this end, an organization would be established to help foreign producers to increase their sales in Japan, and long-term supply relationships would be promoted. Finally, foreign companies were to be assured of fair access to patents in Japan.

A side letter accompanying the formal agreement referred to the objective of increasing the American share of the Japanese market to 20 percent by 1991. The supposed secrecy of this part of the arrangement is not difficult to understand. The United States hardly wished to be seen to be negotiating a fixed market share for itself; the negative European reaction would have been energetic. The degree of sensitivity to the consistency of these demands with the U.S. image of itself as a fair trader, and to trading-partner reaction, has diminished significantly in recent times, as illustrated by the 1992 auto and auto parts episode. For the Japanese, secrecy would lessen the firmness of any commitment, if for no other reason than that substantial enforcement problems could be expected from an agreement whose content was in dispute. In the event, the side letter was the source of acrimony and tension three years later, when it was no longer secret. MITI officials denied that there was any commitment on Japan's part to secure a 20 percent share of the Japanese market for U.S. producers. At the same time, USTR Carla Hills was reported as saying that in her view Japan had "committed itself to afford the U.S. industry a 20 percent market share by 1991.[62]

As a result of the semiconductor arrangement, the president suspended the Section 301 investigation, but made it clear that any infringement was actionable under Section 301. As far as the antidumping actions were concerned, the Department of Commerce announced fair market values for different categories of chips that were significantly above recent market prices. Any sales at less than fair value would trigger antidumping actions. This, in effect, was simply a minimum import price regime, the product of a negotiation, and not of an "objective" application of a statute designed to remedy injury to a domestic producer.

This arrangement soon ran into difficulties in GATT. The EC brought a complaint in late 1986 and requested the establishment of a dispute-settlement panel to rule on the legality of the agreement. It was the Japanese who were in the dock, since they were the ones taking action to enforce the arrangement. The EC made three specific complaints about the arrangement. First, the monitoring of sales to third parties by the Japanese authorities contravened the GATT provisions making import or export controls illegal (Article XI), and also infringed the antidumping provisions (Article VI). Second, the arrangement contained provisions about access to the Japanese market that would lead to discrimination against third parties (contrary to Article I). Third, the lack of clarity surrounding the arrangement infringed the GATT provisions on transparency (Article X). Canada added its weight to the EC complaint, arguing that the export-monitoring itself was discriminatory, and also contravened the GATT provision that governments should not prevent enterprises within their jurisdictions from acting in accordance with commercial considerations (Article XVII).

Naturally, the other major trading partners of the United States did not want world prices of a product inflated to accommodate a U.S. industry in trouble. Neither did they like the idea that the United States might have used its influence and power to secure a favorable position for itself in the Japanese market.

In the event, the GATT panel concluded that the monitoring arrangements went beyond mere surveillance and constituted a coherent system for restricting exports of semiconductors below a specified price. They were therefore GATT-inconsistent as far as countries other than the United States were concerned. The panel did not, however, find evidence of discrimination in favor of the United States as regards Japan's market access measures. Depending on the real contents of the side letter, its consideration by the panel might have reached a different conclusion. Japan has acted on the monitoring procedures in order to bring them into line with the GATT.

The market-access provisions of the semiconductor arrangement are significant from a systemic angle, as Bhagwati has shown.[63] Essentially, the argument is that in addition to VERs, new trade-policy instruments are emerging such as the "voluntary import expansion" (VIE) commitment, which further expand the scope for the bilateral exertion of reciprocity-driven, quantity-oriented, protectionism. In its most discriminatory form, it is export protection precisely analogous to import protection. It is the latest, most intrusive form of market sharing to have been developed, and in many ways is a logical outcome of the Section 301, and especially the Super 301, process.

Jagdish Bhagwati notes four other instances where VIE solutions to trade disputes have been sought, or produced.[64] Two of them concern Japan. In one case, pressure to open the beef market was apparently applied in terms of a quota expansion instead of quota removal. The argument was that quota removal would have given all foreign suppliers nondiscriminatory and competitive access to the Japanese market, whereas a modified quota would continue to guarantee a certain U.S. market share. In the second Japanese case, in response to a Section 301 case concerning leather, the offer by Japan to replace quotas with tariffs was not welcome, for the same reason as in the beef case. The other two cases involved Korea. One concerned the discriminatory opening of the insurance market. The other was the charge that to respond to U.S. complaints about the trade deficit between the two countries, Korea intended to switch almost all its agricultural and certain manufactured imports to U.S. suppliers. It is questionable how far these outcomes actually occurred, or were actively sought as a matter of policy. In any event, the semiconductor story shows how it can happen; and the 1992 auto episode, how it can be repeated.

The battle between the United States and Japan did not calm down after the conclusion of the semiconductor arrangement. Only nine months after the arrangement came into force, President Reagan retaliated against Japan for alleged noncompliance. The U.S. complaints related both to third-country dumping and domestic market access. The retaliation involved imposing tariffs of 100 percent on Japanese products valued at $300 million. Of this amount, $135 million was in respect to the third-country dumping charge[65] and $165 million was for market access. This was by far the worst case ever of retaliation against Japan under the unfair trade procedures of Section 301.[66] In response to the action, Japan cut production further. In recognition of this action, two months later, in June 1987, the president withdrew retaliation worth $51 million in respect to the third-country dumping allegation. Japan continued to control export prices and quantities to third markets, and in November all the retaliation pertaining to third-country dumping was removed. On account of continuing U.S. dissatisfaction with the level of market penetration attained in Japan, however, the additional tariffs on trade of $165 million remained in force, until signature of a new five-year agreement on June 4, 1991. The new agreement repeats the commitment to raise the U.S. share of the market to 20 percent, this time by the end of 1992.

On this round, there was little coyness about the objective of increasing the foreign share of Japan's domestic market.[67] Japanese firms are to be encouraged to incorporate U.S.-made chips into their products as part of the drive to increase foreign penetration of the Japanese market. The new agreement also incorporates an expedited antidumping procedure, which short-circuits normal investigating procedures if a case is triggered. The precise meaning of the 20 percent market-share target, and the question of the strength of the commitment, will probably still give rise to disagreements unless it is met to the satisfaction of U.S. exporters. By mid-1992, several members of Congress and the administration had already complained by mid-1992 that Japan was not taking the market share commitment seriously enough, and that the 20 percent target share would not be reached by year-end. The Japanese government meanwhile was reported to have been trying to persuade Japanese industry to buy more U.S. computer chips.[68] The semiconductor issue will be a running sore in U.S.-Japan trade relations for some time to come, as U.S. producers, backed by government, seek to wrest a larger share of the Japanese market from domestic producers by political means. The five-year extension of the semiconductor agreement supports the view that, once market-sharing arrangements of this nature are allowed, they will become hardy perennials.

Another consequence of the semiconductor arrangement was its effects on supply and demand in the U.S. market. As early as the end of 1986, the American Electronics Association was complaining to the administration about the arrangement's effects on the price of semiconductors. By 1988, there was a shortage of semiconductors and chip users were demanding an easing of the arrangement to encourage larger shipments of semiconductors from Japan to the U.S. market. In response, the Commerce Department revised the definition of fair value to be used in dumping cases. In other words, the Commerce Department made it less likely that dumping actions would be brought on low-priced sales, in the hope of encouraging further trade. That the definition of fair price could be altered solely as a function of supply and demand in the domestic market says much about the arbitrariness of the definitions used in antidumping procedures.

This aspect of the semiconductor story is similar to that of steel. If protection is given to one industry that produces an input for another, the second industry is inevitably placed at a disadvantage. The fact that the consumer who pays the costs of protection is an organized producer, and thus the protected item is not a final good, focuses attention on the message that protection is not free. Because user industries can organize and protest effectively, where consumers and retailers have more difficulty, there is greater public awareness of what is being done at the behest of protection seekers.

Finally, an important spin-off from the semiconductor issue was the establishment in 1988 of a research consortium known as Sematech (Semiconductor Manufacturing Technology). All the major U.S. semiconductor manufacturers are affiliated to Sematech, which has an annual budget of $250 million. Half of this amount is provided by the government. Sematech aims to restore the U.S. industry to its former leadership position by the mid-1990s. Its focus is on research and development (R&D) rather than on product manufacture. Although such an initiative might have run afoul of the antitrust laws, the National Cooperation Research Act of 1984 seems to provide an antitrust exemption for R&D joint ventures.

Economies of scale in R&D, and the high costs involved, make a pooling of resources attractive, and such arrangements do not necessarily have to lead to a cartelized industry. The involvement of government, however, means that the industry is receiving a subsidy, and in effect, an industrial policy has been established. Apart from the issues relating to industrial policy discussed in chapter 1, there is a trade policy issue. In the semiconductor industry, the United States is indulging in precisely the kind of activity for which it designed its unfair trade statutes to use against foreigners. While the adage that "if you can't beat them, join them" might apply, it is difficult to see how such a stance can be squared with the pursuit of reciprocity via the unfair trade remedies. More generally, this raises the question of how far, in its own behavior, the United States meets the standards it sets for foreigners.

LESSONS FROM SECTORAL TRADE POLICY

Some of the main conclusions emerging from these four sectoral cases are summarized here. First, the industries most prone to administrative intervention involve markets that are subject to important changes in supply and demand or competitive conditions. As a consequence, less efficient or less protected industries have to contend with import surges and reduced export-market opportunities.

Second, any suggestion that market-sharing arrangements are a temporary palliative, designed to allow a breathing space for adjustment, or are an effective way of persuading trading partners to eliminate alleged unfair trading practices should be treated with utmost caution. Once in place, these arrangements are extremely difficult to abolish. They nearly always provide long-term protection to domestic industry and may lead to wage pressure and reduced adjustment efforts in the beneficiary industries. Powerful vested interest groups cooperate very effectively to ensure the longevity of market-sharing arrangements.

Third, the protection associated with market-sharing arrangements in particular sectors seems to follow an almost inexorable law of expansion in at least three senses. First, the product coverage of the arrangements expands as affected producers take advantage of substitution possibilities among similar or related products, thus shifting pressure to unprotected sectors. Then, the number of countries subject to restraint expands as market space vacated by controlled foreign sources is taken up by unrestrained foreign suppliers, or as transshipment arrangements through third countries are perfected. Finally, protection through market sharing in one country leads to similar arrangements in other countries, either because they lose market share in the protected foreign market, or because exports from third countries are diverted to them. These tendencies can be documented in the textile, clothing, and steel sectors, among others.

Fourth, recent developments in the steel industry, and to a lesser extent in semiconductors, illustrate how antiprotection interests may moderate protectionist outcomes. An important point is whether the protected sector produces final goods or inputs into the production of other goods. For inputs, protection either has to be extended to the user industry or pressure will build up in opposition to the favorable arrangements secured by producers of inputs. This process, as described above in the case of steel, provides a useful public illustration of the truism, not always adequately appreciated, that not every industry, or even most industries, can be protected. Protection can only be given to some industries at the expense of another part of the economy.[69] It is not something that simply disadvantages foreigners.

A fifth observation, which is more relevant in the United States than elsewhere, also concerns the spread effects to the economy at large of arrangements that are supposedly special and sector specific. In chapter 3, it was shown how different trade remedies had been modified over time, becoming increasingly likely to produce trade-restricting outcomes. Although this has not been documented in any detail in this study, much of the inspiration for modifications to trade legislation originates in industries that are seeking special protection. This tendency applies generally, but more especially to antidumping and countervailing-duty legislation. The recent idea, for example, that private antidumping actions should be allowed, and new provisions on repeated dumping and short life-cycle products, came from the semiconductor industry. Destler and Odell[70] have argued that the likelihood of resistance from user industries or consumers to this sort of legislative activity is lower than when protectionist demands are overt. Nevertheless, when the special case industries are successful in changing generic provisions in their favor, the effects can spread to all industries.

Sixth, the statutes and legislative processes are sometimes harnessed by protectionist interests to secure market-sharing arrangements. Decisions to negotiate export restraints in the sectors discussed have frequently been preceded by trade-remedy petitions or legislative proposals that have made a negotiated market-sharing arrangement seem a more attractive alternative. The threat of something worse than market-sharing can work both on the administration and the exporting country or firms. This does not mean that the unfair trade remedies are never used to address unfair trade. Rather, the problem arises when the statutes or legislative processes are abused as a means of harassing fairly traded competitive imports. Heightened political involvement at the sectoral level, combined with a cumulative protectionist bias infused into the unfair trade statutes, diminishes the likelihood that any notion of fairness, legitimate or otherwise, will be given serious consideration, or measured against alternative explanations of the afflictions besetting an industry that might be of domestic provenance. Crying foul and mustering political support may soon be all it takes to dull import competition or seize foreign market share.

Seventh, using the statutes as threats may influence the content of the statutes themselves. If unfair trade laws are invoked mainly to persuade trading partners to negotiate self-restraint arrangements, this objective can influence the design of the laws. In other words, the laws may be developed as much as mechanisms for issuing threats as actual trade remedies. To the degree that this occurs, the statutes are likely to lose their effectiveness as credible trade remedies, becoming ever more strident in content. Then they can no longer work in anything other than an excessively protectionist manner when they are actually applied.

Eighth, the experience of the steel and semiconductor industries seems to suggest that when a sectoral issue achieves a sufficiently high political profile, some of the restraining requirements of the statutes are ignored, as if they were irrelevant niceties. This occurs less with Section 301 because of the virtual absence of legal restraints on action that the president may take. But in both steel and semiconductors, due process was set aside with respect to antidumping (semiconductors) and countervailing-duty (steel) procedures, although action was nevertheless taken or provoked on the basis of the justifications offered by the relevant provisions. This abuse of the statutes in more politicized circumstances than usual undermines the credibility of the overall U.S. trade policy stance. A similar slippage occurs when devices such as the trigger-price mechanism or predetermined less-than-fair values are used to institute de facto minimum import prices.

Finally, managed trade can be an additional and sometimes extraordinary source of trade instability and political tension—quite apart from the deadweight economic costs of reduced trading opportunities. The stories told in this chapter are persuasive evidence of the inherent instability of attempts to determine trade flows by administrative fiat. Permanent negotiations among national polities simply do not create reasonable trading conditions over any appreciable length of time. This should be hardly surprising, since every decision to intervene in a protectionist manner implies action that will redistribute, and in the aggregate usually reduce, national income. Agreements between countries also distribute gains and losses between the parties involved. The more sectors become managed in the fashion described here, the harder it is to see how trade can be relied upon as a source of growth and increased national welfare.

CHAPTER 6

RESPONSIBILITY AVOIDANCE IN THE TRADE POLICY PROCESS

Recognizing its vulnerability to protectionist demands, Congress developed methods after 1934 to insulate itself from these one-sided pressures for import restraints.[1] Besides delegating negotiating authority, efforts were made to refine legalistic remedies against unfairly traded imports and unfair foreign trade practices. These remedies gave every appearance of objectivity and automaticity, seemingly responding only to the facts of a case and expunging any consideration of politics from trade policy decisions at the detailed industry level. Legislators could refer constituent demands for action against imports or foreign trade practices to officials responsible for administering established procedures. The president was, in any case, less vulnerable to special interest groups than were individual legislators and in a better position to take a broad view when discretionary decisions were called for. At the same time, the design of trade statutes, and the procedures associated with them, gave Congress the opportunity to exercise adequate control over the behavior of the executive.

Besides delegated negotiating authority and sanitized trade policy instruments, the system needed an escape valve. This was built into the system such that pressing and politicized sectoral problems could be dealt with as special cases through direct legislative action. This route was reserved for such industries as textiles, agriculture, petroleum, and steel. As long as these industries remained few, and a modicum of agreement existed nationally that they were indeed deserving cases, these special arrangements did not risk becoming the Achilles heel of the entire edifice.

From the beginning, the delegation of trade policy functions to the executive was undertaken with reserve by Congress. The legislative branch of government could not abrogate its constitutional responsibilities entirely, even if it had wanted to. There had to be some responsiveness to constituency demands, reflected partly in the special case industries that were dealt with legislatively or given special deals, and partly in limits imposed on the freedom of maneuver of the executive. It was all a matter of balance.

HOW RESPONSIBILITY IS AVOIDED

The above characterization of postwar U.S. trade policy has been masterfully presented by Destler.[2] But do these arrangements still function so well? The policy framework and decisionmaking apparatus have been worked on over the years in ways that have repoliticized trade policy, increased the likelihood of protectionist decisions in favor of particular industries, and reduced the accountability of the executive and legislative branches of government for trade policy outcomes. A major part of this story is action by Congress to reassert control over trade policy, but often in ways that blur the locus of responsibility for policy decisions.

The disposition of gains and losses from trade measures imparts a strong bias in favor of protectionist outcomes.[3] Although gainers from more open trade could more than compensate the losers (assuming efficiency gains from specialization through trade), the concentration of losses among a few producers and the diffusion of gains among many consumers favors a trade-restricting outcome. Despite some evidence that consumer interests organize to confront protectionist pressure, as in steel (chapter 5),[4] organized labor and industry wield a formidable force in the political struggle over trade policy decisions. Therefore, a weakening of mechanisms built into the decisionmaking process to deflect protectionist pressure will move the system naturally toward an antitrade bias.

The mechanisms originally developed for avoiding constituency demands for protection were probably never explicitly presented as part of a coherent strategy under which the Congress gave up some of its authority. Changes were made incrementally, and the process was never described as a transfer of power or abrogation of congressional responsibility. Changes in the relationship between Congress and the executive are easier to present as a secular trend with the benefit of hindsight. Since no neat package rearranged trade policy functions, it is not possible to say exactly when contrary tendencies overtook the beneficial features of arrangements involving the delegation of trade policy responsibilities. Nor is it possible to name a date when Congress started clawing back trade policy authority, or denying it to the president.

"Responsibility avoidance" in trade policymaking had been facilitated by curtailment of presidential authority through various adjustments to the statutes, the promotion of fair trade rhetoric, and reliance on export restraint arrangements. These same modalities have also served to smooth the path for protection seekers.[5]

The Curtailment of Presidential Authority

Congress has modified the statutes over the years to reduce the president's discretionary authority over trade policy in three principal areas: through increased controls on delegated negotiating authority, restrictions imposed via the statutes themselves, and changes in institutional arrangements and functions.

Congress has maintained control over the executive by granting limited, time-bound tariff negotiating authority. Occasionally, too, the authority has been circumscribed by additional provisions. A particularly restrictive measure was taken, for example, when the president's negotiating authority was renewed in 1948. A "peril point" concept was introduced, whereby the Tariff Commission (later the United States International Trade Commission, USITC) could limit the extent of tariff reductions by determining the point at which a reduction would cause material injury to a domestic industry. The systematic application of the peril point could have arrested trade liberalization altogether. The provision was repealed in 1949, reestablished in 1951, and finally eliminated in 1962. The obvious intent behind the provision was to inhibit tariff reductions to which the president might otherwise agree.

The president faced additional legislative controls in 1974, in the context of the grant of authority to negotiate nontariff measures in the Tokyo Round. The grant of nontariff measure negotiating authority had become a sensitive issue after the Kennedy Round (1964–67), when an Anti-Dumping Code and a Chemicals Agreement which concerned the American Selling Price[6] mechanism had been negotiated internationally but could not take effect because Congress refused to implement them.[7] President Richard M. Nixon requested negotiating authority for nontariff measures that would permit the implementation of negotiated results if Congress did not disapprove within ninety days. This, combined with a request for unlimited tariff-negotiating authority, was rejected. What eventually emerged was the fast-track approval.

The Omnibus Trade and Competitiveness Act of 1988 further limited presidential authority in this matter by providing that the fast-track procedure may be nullified if the executive branch fails to consult adequately with Congress.

While the delegation of trade policy authority by Congress to the executive may be expected to lend more coherence to policymaking in the trade field and lead to less protectionist outcomes, a less positive side should be mentioned. The delegation of authority is both incomplete and short term. Thus, when international trade negotiations are in prospect, as they have been once every decade or so for the last thirty years, the president has to approach Congress for authority to negotiate. It is one thing when authority defines the terms of the negotiations and delineates what is negotiable, but it is quite another when the authority is bargained against sectoral protectionist interests.

Horse-trading has become the pattern. Trade bills whose ostensible purpose is to create opportunities for further trade liberalization have come to serve also as vehicles for additional protection. Textile lobbies have been particularly effective in this regard. President John F. Kennedy had to agree to the Short-Term Arrangement on textiles in 1961 to garner support for the Kennedy Round. This arrangement restricted cotton textile exports to the United States from seventeen countries. The Long-Term Arrangement was put in place the following year. President Nixon faced a comparable situation in the early 1970s in respect of the Tokyo Round, and the Multi-Fiber Arrangement was born in 1974. The announcement of a program of voluntary restrictions on steel by President Ronald Reagan in 1984 was crucial in marshaling support for the Trade Act of 1984. There were no multilateral trade negotiations in prospect in 1984, but the administration wanted negotiating authority for regional arrangements and to renew the Generalized System of Preferences. In the 1988 legislation providing authority for U.S. participation in the Uruguay Round, the administration not only had to swallow Super 301 but also certain sectoral reciprocity provisions. Examples abound of how these different occasions have been used to increase the restrictive effects of trade-remedy laws. To the extent that this kind of legislative activity occurs, U.S. participation in the multilateral trading system is held hostage to some of the more powerful domestic industrial interests in the United States.

Incremental changes in the statutes dealing with remedies against unfair trade have frequently lessened presidential discretion, reflecting a belief in Congress that the executive branch has shown a tendency to be too liberal in trade policy. Thus, changes in trade laws have generally facilitated action that will restrict trade flows. A notable example of this tendency is the reform of the escape clause, or safeguard provisions. Until 1958, the president was required to explain his reasons to Congress if he rejected a petition for protection following an injury finding and recommendation from the Tariff Commission. Since the 1958 Trade Agreements Extension Act, however, Congress has had the power to override a presidential rejection of an affirmative injury finding and recommendation for relief by the USITC.[8] Congress has persisted in trying to make it easier for petitioners to receive relief, even though the statute (Section 201 of the Trade Act of 1974) has fallen into disuse. Congress would no doubt have wished for greater success in curtailing the use of presidential authority to deny relief.

Section 301 of the Trade Act of 1974 has received similar treatment. In 1979, for example, flexibility in processing petitions was reduced by the introduction of statutory time limits. In 1984, pressure was imposed on the president to self-initiate Section 301 cases. This pressure was turned into a legal necessity with the introduction of Super and Special 301 in 1988. The president's right to decide upon what action to take in Section 301 cases was reduced in 1988 when retaliation against "unjustifiable" trade practices became obligatory.

Through Section 301, Congress has armed the executive with a potent policy weapon. Self-restraint on the potential for massive action against U.S. trading partners is the bottom line. The law allows the president to do virtually what he likes to force policy changes in other countries, and in the name of retaliation, restrict their exports to the United States. Each Section 301 amendment has made it possible for the president to be a little tougher over a wider range of issues. At the same time, however, Congress has been taking discretionary power away from the president. This denial of discretion may force the president to apply the enhanced Section 301 in circumstances where his better judgment dictates otherwise. However, the administration has managed to use Super and Special 301 with a great deal of restraint (chapter 4).

Important changes have been made in the antidumping and countervailing-duty statutes over the years. Procedures, as well as the definitions of dumping, subsidization, and injury have been continuously modified to facilitate the presentation of petitions and to increase the likelihood of action in favor of plaintiffs. Much of what has been done to the antidumping and countervailing-duty statutes has been intricate. These are highly technical instruments involving complicated procedures. Their very complexity gives them respectability and makes them seem objective, impartial, and unlikely candidates for subversion. Not readily apparent to the casual observer is the fact that they have been so worked over as to yield a high probability of a finding of dumping or subsidization.

As regards institutional arrangements aimed at diminishing presidential authority, the creation of the position of Special Trade Representative in the

Trade Expansion Act of 1962 is one example. In 1974, the STR became the United States Trade Representative, with strengthened authority. Other 1974 innovations were the rule that congressional representatives must be included on U.S. delegations to trade negotiations, and the establishment of private sector advisory committees on international trade matters. The latter arrangement was strengthened in the Omnibus Trade and Competitiveness Act of 1988. In the context of the Trade Agreements Act of 1979, the president was required to reorganize departmental functions to promote a more sympathetic attitude toward domestic producer interests. As a result, responsibility for managing aspects of antidumping and countervailing-duty statutes as well as certain national security provisions was transferred from the Treasury Department to the Department of Commerce.

The Quest for Fair Trade and Reciprocity

Much has been made of the growing emphasis in the United States on fair trade and reciprocity. The antidumping and countervailing-duty statutes, apart from being more than a match for any genuinely unfair trading practices, also double up as a safeguard mechanism of the kind Section 201 was designed to be. With a moribund Section 201 and highly probable findings of dumping or subsidy under the relevant investigatory procedures, it is basically the injury test in antidumping and countervailing cases that acts as the decision point about whether or not to limit imports. Apart from counteracting dumping and subsidies, therefore, the relevant statutes have made protection available to industries under the guise of actions designed to counter unfair foreign trade practices. Even before any duty is levied in an antidumping or countervailing-duty action, the harassment effect must be considered, where the mere act of initiating a case may reduce imports or raise their prices.

The picture with respect to Section 301 is more complex. In its various manifestations, Section 301 has been characterized as a crowbar, a less than subtle reference to the avowed purpose of the statute. It is designed and presented as a market-opening device and works upon the assumption that concerted action is required to rectify unfair trading behavior by other countries. The instrument has registered mixed success in meeting its primary objective (chapter 4). It has proved less effective with the European Community (EC) than with Asian countries. Because of its unilateral and essentially aggressive foundations, which require a credible threat of retaliation and pliant trading partners to be successful, frequent use of Section 301 is not a long-term option for the conduct of U.S. trade policy. In the meanwhile, Section 301 has soured international trade relations for no great gain and undermined confidence in the viability of the multilateral trading system. Moreover, it is doubtful that

U.S. trade policy meets the standards that Section 301 sets for other countries. It has also fed self-righteous indignation in some domestic circles, supporting the view that the only problem facing the U.S. economy in the trade field is the unfair trade policy behavior by foreigners.

Apart from raising the likelihood of protectionist actions and at times inhibiting trade liberalization that might otherwise have occurred, the modern emphasis on reciprocity and "unfairness" in trade policy has unfavorable systemic consequences. Reciprocity demands today have more to do with equivalence of outcomes in an ex post sense than with ex ante market opportunities (chapter 1). This trend toward an effects-based definition of reciprocal treatment is inevitably addressed in a bilateral, as opposed to a multilateral setting. It leads to discrimination and quantity-oriented market-sharing arrangements. Judgments about whether reciprocity has been served are not necessarily limited to single sectors. They might be made across sectors and across issues. The kinds of sectoral arrangements discussed in chapter 5 are all driven to some degree by reciprocity considerations.

Reliance on Export-Restraint Arrangements

A growing tendency to resort to various kinds of negotiated export-restraint arrangements was traced in chapter 4. Much can be said about the destructive effect of these arrangements from a systemic point of view, about their insidious reliance on negotiation under threat, about their important historic role as the gateway to full-fledged sectoral market-sharing arrangements, and about their suppression of profitable trading opportunities. In this context, however, the key point is that export-restraint agreements obviate the need for government in the protecting country to take any trade policy action or any responsibility for the consequences of restricted trade. It was shown in chapter 5, in the context of the automobile sector, how implicit the threat of import restrictions and the consequent negotiation can be, so that the exporting country is portrayed as acting entirely independently, almost spontaneously.

Some of the sectors where export-restraint agreements predominate have ended up that way as a result of campaigns based on the unfair trade statutes. Massive filings of antidumping or antisubsidy actions, for example, have preceded steel restraint arrangements. Similar activity took place with respect to semiconductors before a negotiated agreement emerged. The specter of unfair trade does not have to be raised in order for export-restraint agreements to be struck. It did not prove necessary for motor vehicles for textiles. Thus, export-restraint arrangements can stand on their own as useful mechanisms for promoting protectionist outcomes for which the government of the protecting country is ostensibly not responsible.

Most of the arguments about responsibility avoidance put forward in this chapter concern the behavior of Congress. But the growing use of voluntary export restraints (VERs) does raise interesting questions about the role of the executive branch in promoting protectionist outcomes without seeming to be responsible for their formulation or implementation. VERs produce what Martin Wolf[9] and others have characterized as "no hands" protection, since it is the victim of protection (the exporting country) that administers the restriction. Nivola argues that the administration can be as sensitive to domestic pressure groups as Congress and must also respond to them.[10] This may be particularly true for election campaigns, as demonstrated by President Reagan in the case of automobiles and President Bush in the case of steel. To the extent that the administration feels compelled to satisfy demands for trade restrictions, it is tempting to do so in a way that minimizes the likelihood of being stigmatized as protectionist. Moreover, the automobile episode in 1981 shows how VERs can appeal to the administration as a way of heading off overt demands for protection from Congress. Thus, in negotiating VERs, the administration may be responding to pressure from the affected industry, from Congress, or from both.

This is one policy area where Congress has not taken authority away from the executive branch. Initiatives by the administration that end up in VERs would, on the contrary, be welcomed by many congressmen. However, the promotion of VERs by the administration leads to contradictory behavior. With one hand, the administration seeks to strengthen the multilateral trading system as a bulwark against protectionist pressures from Congress, but it undermines the system with the other by negotiating GATT-illegal VERs.

Rhetoric versus Responsibility in Congress

Another factor that influences the content of trade legislation is the manner in which the legislative process is conducted in Congress. Some lawmakers welcome the luxury of adopting positions for which they do not have to assume responsibility. Some members of the legislature sponsor exaggerated or extreme trade bills in Congress in the knowledge that the proposals will be killed by their colleagues, by the administration, or through procedural attrition.[11] The constitutional division of powers, together with delegated trade policy authority, act as a filter. To a degree, the successful promotion of manifestly protectionist legislation or policy outcomes would be risky, since being branded a protectionist does not seem to pay politically.[12] On the other hand, if unstoppable momentum gathers behind a proposal to restrict trade, its promoters can lessen the risk of a protectionist stigma by emphasizing unfair foreign trade practices rather than simply appealing for policy favors.

The practice of making exaggerated legislative proposals can be identified in the formulation stages of each of the trade acts (chapter 3), although the degree of excess seems to have intensified over time. For illustrative purposes, it will suffice to mention some of the proposals that were floated in the legislative process culminating in the Omnibus Trade and Competitiveness Act of 1988. In the months and years leading up to the passage of the act, literally hundreds of trade bills were presented in Congress, many of which would have made Smoot-Hawley seem friendly to foreign governments. And unlike Smoot-Hawley, they were mostly accusatory in tone and built upon reciprocity demands and unfair trade remedies.

Some of the more trade-restricting features of earlier versions of the 1988 act[13] would have: established quotas on imports of lamb and steel; created a private right of action in U.S. courts for customs fraud, in addition to current administrative remedies; excluded repeat offenders of U.S. customs laws from the U.S. market; removed presidential discretion regarding relief in Section 201 cases; mandated retaliation in Section 301 cases, including cases of mandatory "self-initiation"; redefined the term "subsidy" to expand the application of countervailing-duty law; provided a private right of action in U.S. courts for dumping in addition to the antidumping law; and amended antidumping and countervailing-duty laws in an array of other ways that would have increased the number of petitions filed, raised the likelihood of injury findings, and increased the probability and magnitude of protection being granted.

Among the more infamous proposals was the 1986 Gephardt Amendment. This required retaliation against countries found to have "excessive and unwarranted" trade surpluses with the United States. The term "excessive" was mechanically defined by a formula. "Unwarranted" meant that the USTR found that the country maintained a pattern of unfair trade practices harmful to the trade interests of the United States and contributing to its trade surplus. Six months were given for reaching an agreement that would lead to a 10 percent annual reduction in the bilateral surplus. Failing agreement, retaliation was mandated. The considerable impracticality of the proposal, its vagueness on procedures, its solid foundations in economic illiteracy,[14] and the fact that such a provision could be used against the United States in some of its trade relationships did not prevent the proposal from gathering support. Key features of Super 301 emerged from this initiative.

In terms of the above characterization of the politics of trade policy formulation, the functional explanation for these tendencies is straightforward. If Congress delegates its trade policy responsibilities, or if lawmakers know that their proposals will be tamed or killed along the way, a bit of wild talk does no harm and can be useful. Members of Congress can be seen as sensitive to the difficulties of their lobbying constituents and outraged at alleged foreign malpractice in the trade field. It is an excellent opportunity for playing to the gallery. The executive branch may also benefit from these arrangements. Not only can the president and cabinet officials be seen as effective in defining and defending a higher national interest as they help to knock away the uglier features of draft trade legislation, but the process also gives them ammunition in negotiations with foreign governments. Negotiators can point to an angry Congress and maintain harder positions, emphasizing a role as intermediary between foreign and domestic interests. But this politically useful game inevitably feeds through into trade policy decisions.

Credibility is difficult to maintain in the medium and long term if every congressional trade legislation proposal goes nowhere. There must be some positive success rate. Systematic overstatement will impart a protectionist, and in the case of unfair trade remedies, also a confrontational bias in trade policy outcomes. Proposals originating in Congress are likely to appear in legislation, though in diluted form. The promulgation of Super 301 as a reflection of the Gephardt Amendment is one such example.

Second, it is impossible to control fully and orchestrate the legislative process. Judging from Destler's description of how the Trade and Tariff Act of 1984 was legislated,[15] much is left to chance in the rush and pressure of the process. Rhetorical escalation carries risks. The game relies on the skill and hard work of a few talented individuals and could spin out of control. In a world where almost no protectionist proposal is regarded as outrageous, the objectives and expectations of lobbyists and sectoral protectionist interests are bound to extend much beyond what they would have been in an disciplined climate, where legislative proposals more nearly reflected legislative ambitions. Thus, the escalation spirals upward.

Third, beneath the bluster and exaggeration, lie real concerns. There is no precise, identifiable dividing line between bluff and serious proposals. Even if the theater were taken out the legislative exercise, members of Congress would not expect their every proposal to come law. A democratic process is at work. Blurring the distinction between substance and form sows confusion and makes rational outcomes more elusive.

Finally, the cost of systematic overstatement in the legislative process must also be weighed in terms of its effects on foreign governments. It is tempting for foreigners to regard the process as indicative of a lack of self-restraint, proper procedural control, and political leadership. Moreover, protectionist posturing and confrontational accusations of unilaterally defined unfair trading practices might provoke retaliation, almost certainly complicate negotiations, and put the multilateral trading system at risk.

THE COSTS OF RESPONSIBILITY AVOIDANCE

Domestic Consequences

Apart from any arguments that might be made about the political and constitutional implications of the situation described above, the costs in terms of increased levels of protection are one of the most relevant domestic considerations. This applies as much to any actual increase in the level of protection as it does to the potential created for future protectionist outcomes. An attempt was made in chapter 4 to gauge how much more protectionist U.S. trade policy became in the 1980s. The difficulty of quantifying such estimates with any accuracy was emphasized, but it was nevertheless argued that a protectionist trend was discernible. Aggregate data suggested more restrictive tendencies, and perhaps also that the United States had been catching up with its traditionally more protectionist trading partners. This conclusion was reinforced by a qualitative examination of the way in which the trade statutes had been modified in successive trade acts and also the frequency with which they had been employed.

The precise extent to which the politics of responsibility avoidance gives rise to trade-restricting outcomes is a matter of conjecture. But it would be difficult to argue convincingly that there is not an important connection. Finally, although the costs of protection have not been closely examined in this study, other work at the sectoral level in the United States and other countries points to substantial welfare costs from arrangements such as those for textiles, steel, and automobiles. A less direct cost of these arrangements is their powerful demonstration effect for other, less privileged sectors.

Implications for the Multilateral Trading System

A consideration of the effects of recent trade policy developments on the multilateral trading system and U.S. participation in the system anticipates much of the discussion in the next section of this study. Nevertheless, a few comments will be made at this stage. Giving out mixed signals is a fundamental problem for U.S. trade policy behavior. On one hand, policy trends, especially the development of Section 301 of the 1974 Trade Act, and a growing interest in regionalism, suggest that the United States has serious doubts about continuing to rely on multilateral approaches to its trade relations. The question is bound to be asked whether the U.S. commitment to multilateralism is slipping, after three decades as the centerpiece of U.S. trade policy. If it is slipping, does it signal indecision or a new vision of U.S. trade interests? On the other hand, U.S. policy pronouncements and active participation in the international trading system, particularly in the Uruguay Round, tend to contradict the idea that the United States has given up on multilateralism.

In what has become a popular and highly charged debate, a number of alternatives to multilateralism are being put forward. Most proposals of this kind seem to be founded on the assumption that, through continuous friendly negotiation, countries will able to decide how to divide up the economic pie and split the benefits of specialization through trade. It is highly unlikely that such arrangements will be sufficiently stable and amicable to secure the economic benefits offered by a multilateral approach to trade relations. Dividing up markets through political processes is a sure recipe for reducing trading opportunities. If countries do not want to forgo those benefits and retreat into more autarkic arrangements, there is no practical alternative to the pursuit of multilateral trading arrangements. This does not necessarily rule out regional integration initiatives, but it does exclude administered trade and discriminatory arrangements motivated by protectionist objectives.

If the United States has not decided to abandon its postwar reliance on multilateralism, its current trade policy orientation is greatly complicating its role in the trading system. As for the system itself, part of the apparent U.S. departure from multilateral due process may well be strategic, aimed at multilateralizing particular policy approaches through the threat of unilateral action. If that is so, the policy will at best be effective only in the short term and at the cost of undermining confidence in the ability of the multilateral trading system to deliver the benefits that are promised for it.

A more fundamental question is what hope the multilateral trading system has of survival without a U.S. commitment to its preservation. The answer is that it has very little hope. Whatever may be said about the relative decline of the United States and its diminished power on the world scene, order in international trade relations cannot be maintained if the United States has no sense of policy direction. And if the United States chooses a route different from multilateralism, the world will not be far behind.

III THE MULTILATERAL TRADING SYSTEM

CHAPTER 7

THE TRADING SYSTEM UNDER STRAIN

S ome of what is today perceived as growing weakness in the international
trading system is rooted in deficiencies in the initial design and operation
of the system. Thinking in terms of a Golden Age in the history of the
General Agreement on Tariffs and Trade (GATT) is a mistake. The rules
have always been ignored or circumvented in some areas. There has also been
something of a "conspiracy" of noncompliance that has largely ceased to function, partly because the United States is no longer willing to indulge trans-
gressions in the name of an overriding strategic interest. The Golden Age
view is problematic in that it may lead to the conclusion that what once
worked well has become entirely unworkable, calling for radical new
approaches. The story of the GATT has always been a mixture of success and
failure, of adaptation and compromise, and of a struggle to preserve certain
principles in the face of political exigencies. Just because the struggle has
intensified, it does not mean that the principles are no longer valid.

Among the early flaws in the system were the mercantilistic foundations
of the GATT, its failure to cover sectors such as agriculture and textiles, and
weak rules in such areas as subsidies (chapter 1). At the institutional level, the
provisional status of the GATT and the grandfather clause have been undermining influences. In addition, the success of the GATT in reducing tariffs
has not only exposed its relative powerlessness in dealing with nontariff barriers to trade but may have also encouraged the use of such other measures as
quantitative restrictions.

The trading system is under greater strain today than ever before. Views differ as to the sources of the problem, how serious it is, how well the GATT has held up, and what viable alternatives are available. Protectionism rose to a new postwar plateau in the 1980s, and the seeming incapacity of the system to reverse the trend may be ascribed to a range of factors. Three important explanations for the current difficulties, all dealt with in chapter 1, are recalled here.

First, growing economic interdependence, as captured by the notion of globalization, has raised additional sensitivities and put pressure on existing trading arrangements. In the early days of GATT, trade flows were a less important component of economic activity for many countries, and so they worried less about the competitive and adjustment pressures engendered by trade flows. Increased economic contact among countries has introduced new potential areas of conflict of interest and has also undermined the "conspiracy" of noncompliance referred to above.

In addition, new trade regulation issues have emerged. More and more countries want international commitments on trade in services and international factor flows. Trade in services, and the factor-related issues of intellectual property rights and certain kinds of investment policies, are important elements of recent international trade negotiations. Closer economic ties have demonstrated that the rules of international trade are unacceptably narrow and circumscribed if limited to border measures affecting trade in goods. The GATT trading system becomes increasingly marginalized as an international regulatory mechanism if it does not reach into policy areas traditionally regarded as internal and does not cover additional areas of economic activity. Thus, old failures and new pressures both weigh on the trading system as a result of increased interdependence, which at the same time intensifies protectionist pressure and creates demands for disciplines in new areas.

Second, changing power relationships have generated additional tensions. These have arisen both because of the difficulties for some countries in adjusting to economic dynamism in others and because of growing doubts that the present construction of the "rules of the game" is sufficiently balanced and equitable to mediate trade relations. The industrial policy debate, which in its more modern manifestations is about managed trade and market sharing, exposes these strains. The growing emphasis in U.S. trade policy upon reciprocity and fair trade is a part of the same phenomenon.

Some critics of the GATT would support systemic modifications to deal with perceived weaknesses in the traditional approach to trade regulation. These critics would argue that the GATT's market-based and nondiscriminatory orientation has allowed Japan and certain other countries to benefit inordinately from GATT-type arrangements without opening their domestic markets sufficiently to imports. In other words, the charge is that Japan has not offered reciprocity. This is an "unfairness" platform on an economywide scale and has been embraced in different ways in both the European Community (EC) and the United States. This kind of argument has been in part a response to new competitive realities, and to Japan's own vigorous growth. It has led to adjustment pressures and protection in the United States and Europe. There are strong grounds for believing that the kind of institutional and regulatory reform that would be designed to take the unfairness out of trade relations and guarantee reciprocity, essentially by managing transactions bureaucratically, would simply deflect adjustment pressure and generate more protectionist outcomes.

Third, macroeconomic disequilibria have incited new protectionist demands and growing skepticism about the capacity of existing trading arrangements to protect adequately the interests of domestic producers (chapter 1). In the United States, the twin deficits and the strong dollar contributed greatly to protectionist pressures, particularly in the first half of the 1980s. More serious still, arguments about the deindustrialization of America, and about threats to the national interest from increased imports, have mystified sectoral protectionist demands and led to frequent calls for trade controls. Yet, recognition is widespread that trade restrictions would have little or no effect on the trade deficit.

PRINCIPLES OF THE GATT SYSTEM

Some Theoretical Considerations

The GATT is a multipurpose instrument, aimed at promoting trade liberalization and guaranteeing stable conditions of market access through a set of rules and a dispute-settlement system. Trade liberalization is seen as a continuing objective, the idea being to move trading arrangements consistently in the direction of freer trade. The GATT does not claim to secure free trade. The original concept of the GATT is too pragmatic for that. If trade policy is moving away from freer trade, however, the GATT system would be failing in one of its basic objectives.[1]

Relating every aspect of the GATT system to clear propositions in economic theory is no straightforward matter. The GATT has to respond to a variety of real-world pressures, and several aspects of the rules seem suboptimal from an economist's perspective. That would also be true of the GATT's mercantilist bent, except in rather restricted circumstances.[2] Nevertheless, if one were to try to identify the theoretical underpinning of the GATT, it would certainly be articulated around the theory of comparative advantage, relying on the existence of welfare gains from specialization through unrestricted trade. In short, the case would be for free trade, with the possibility of minor departures in carefully specified circumstances. The GATT, for example, accommodates the infant-industry case for protection, based on the idea that, because of market failure, "learning-by-doing" costs in new activities cannot be fully recouped by the firms that incur them.[3] In this case, the absence of government support of one kind or another leads to a socially suboptimal outcome.

Examples of GATT rules departing from the free trade paradigm are easy to cite but more difficult to justify theoretically than the infant-industry argument. The very idea of the tariff, for example, which the GATT permits, is contrary to free trade, and may only be justified on national welfare grounds occasionally, if a country is a large enough player in the market to be able to lower the price of a good through the imposition of a tariff.[4] Similarly, the imposition of trade restrictions to protect an ailing industry, as permitted under the GATT safeguards provisions, is not easy to justify in theory, except perhaps in terms of fairly sophisticated arguments about seeking a wider distribution of temporary adjustment costs, which would otherwise fall exclusively on producers displaced by imports. Another example is the use of quantitative trade restrictions, which are permitted by the GATT in a variety of exceptional circumstances, but which can usually be shown to be inferior to price-based measures. Many other instances could be cited where there would at least be grounds for debate on the theoretical justification for allowing policy interventions.[5]

Seeming inconsistencies of this nature have been broadly tolerated as politically indispensable and regarded as nonfatal to the system if kept within controlled limits. Nonetheless, a concerted theoretical attack has emerged on the free trade paradigm as a basis for policy. The central idea in this body of theory is that perfect markets are so rarely a reasonable representation of economic reality that policy prescriptions based on perfect competition assumptions are unable to identify opportunities for increasing economic welfare that exist precisely because of market imperfections. Because such opportunities are assumed to exist in a non-negligible number of cases, free trade is a poor guide to policy. The new theories are associated with a small number of economists, among whom the most frequently cited are Krugman, Helpman, Brander, Spencer, Dixit, and Grossman.[6]

The new theories are based on two main kinds of arguments. One is that markets do not often provide the vital elements of automatic adjustment that equalize returns to factors of production (capital and labor) among different uses, and in the process guarantee the best possible allocation of resources within the economy. This does not occur, the theory goes, because barriers to entry permit established firms to earn additional profits, or "rents." The presence of economies of scale in production is one factor that may inhibit entry and make it easier for incumbent firms to earn monopolistic profits. The perfect competition model assumes constant returns to scale, such that the relative size of firms has nothing to do with their competitiveness or efficiency. Once it has been established that rents exist, the issue is who appropriates them. Theory establishes cases where "strategic" policy interventions can secure additional rents for one country at the expense of another. There is, therefore, a case for intervening to favor certain industries.

The second line of argument upon which the new theories are based has been mentioned above in the context of the infant-industry case for protection. Although this justification for protection has been the subject of some contention, it is a very old one, going back to the original formulation of the theory of comparative advantage. In the new theories, the emphasis is somewhat different, falling less on the learning process among the work force than on the dynamics of technological innovation. The idea is that because the original investors in research and development cannot fully capture the returns on their outlays, high-technology activities will be underinvested. Similarly, if other governments support such activities, foreign firms will have an unfair advantage over their unsupported domestic rivals. That is a case for targeting, or in other words, for an industrial policy.

While at the abstract level of theory, these arguments undermine the case for a trade policy that prizes nonintervention in all or most circumstances, at the practical level, a number of serious problems arise with the interventionist prescriptions. A basic difficulty stems from the fact that strategic trade policy is not merely a matter of assigning welfare gains between countries from trading or from not trading. Interventions have a direct impact in the domestic economy. How are the right choices to be made? At a technical level, the specification of industry-selection criteria that are beyond political dispute is impossible,[7] thus leading to politically determined outcomes. This dilemma has given rise to the literature on the political economy of protection,[8] which analyzes inbuilt biases in the political system that tend to engender protectionist outcomes. Once the possibility of intervention to favor selected industries is conceded, the selection process will all too frequently be hijacked by well-organized lobbies in search of protection. The strategic trade policy justification for protection is insidious and difficult to deal with because it provides a theoretical case for protection based on a notion of the national interest, or national welfare. Individual firms benefit because it is argued to be in the national interest for them to do so.

Theoretical models recommending intervention to capture an economic rent or internalize a market failure are highly sensitive to small variations in the parameters or assumptions of the models.[9] This raises additional doubts about their reliability as guides to policy. Finally, theories that find in favor of strategic policy interventions cannot foresee the possibility that foreign governments will retaliate at what they might be reasonably expected to see as predatory, beggar-thy-neighbor policies. Retaliation could wipe out strategic gains and carry additional costs by souring the overall trading environment.

Although these considerations argue against building a trade policy around the prescriptions of the new trade policy, they do not invalidate the theoretical challenge to the free trade paradigm. Improved knowledge and analytical techniques may in time give the new theories more practical relevance. As Krugman puts it, the new theories produce a new justification for noninterventionist trade policy:

> This is not the old argument that free trade is optimal because markets are efficient. Instead, it is a sadder but wiser argument for free trade as a rule of thumb in a world whose politics are as imperfect as its markets.[10]

The Rules of the System

The GATT system has five primary mechanisms for promoting freer trade, security of market access, and trade policy transparency. These are institutional arrangements to promote multilateral trade negotiations, binding attained levels of trade liberalization, guaranteeing nondiscrimination, ensuring the rule that tariffs should be the only instrument of protection, and promoting accountability in multilateral trade policy.

Through incremental trade liberalization, improved market access is attained in trade negotiations. Tariffs are then bound in schedules of concessions that form an integral part of the GATT. These tariff bindings can subsequently be renegotiated, but any increase in a bound tariff must be compensated by a new or reduced tariff binding on some other product. Tariff negotiations have generally been held bilaterally between countries with predominant supplying interests, then multilateralized on a nondiscriminatory basis in the context of a negotiating round. More recently, a formula approach has supplemented bilateral procedures, whereby a range of tariffs are subject to predetermined cuts by several countries. These periodic tariff-cutting exercises have led to significant duty reductions by the major trading countries over the last forty years.

Two rules give the GATT system its central policy orientation: nondiscrimination, or the most-favored-nation (MFN) principle,[11] and the exclusivity of tariffs or taxes as the only permissible form of protection. Most GATT norms are designed to support these two rules, to provide controlled exceptions to them, or to protect attained levels of trade liberalization. This structure will be briefly explained here.[12] Nondiscrimination, supported by the exclusion of quantitative restrictions, is the single most important characteristic of the system.

The Most-Favored-Nation Principle

The MFN, established in Article I of the GATT, provides that all foreign suppliers will be treated equally and without discrimination in respect of all duties and charges and all rules and formalities connected with imports and exports. There are four broad categories of departure from the nondiscrimination rule. They deal with unfair trade practices, special exceptions, regional trading arrangements, and discriminatory arrangements or special rules in favor of developing countries. These are precisely some of the areas where the GATT system has been unable to maintain its authority over trade policy behavior.

GATT Article VI permits countries to apply antidumping or countervailing-duty measures if injurious dumping or subsidization occurs. The rules seek to control the use of such measures, ensuring that unfair trade practices are proven, that the antidumping or countervailing duties strictly respond to actual or threatened injury, and that there is clear causality between the injury and an unfair trade practice. These supposedly reactive mechanisms, designed to deal with unfair trade practices, seem increasingly to have served protectionist designs in a discriminatory, nontransparent fashion.[13]

Articles XX and XXI of the GATT foresee circumstances in which nondiscriminatory action may be taken to impede trade. Article XXI deals with national security considerations; Article XX covers such matters as public health, safety and morals, the protection of patents and of national treasures, the conservation of natural resources, and the management of scarce commodities. This list is not exhaustive, and few disputes have arisen in this area, principally because most of the exceptions are considered natural and necessary.[14]

Preferential regional arrangements are a third exception to the MFN principle. Article XXIV of the GATT allows the establishment of free trade areas and customs unions. The provisions are designed to ensure that any such arrangements will encourage the creation of new trading opportunities among the parties involved, as opposed to diverting trade away from third parties. Four basic rules are supposed to ensure this result. First, substantially all trade must be covered by the arrangements, so that they do not simply promote a few trade-diverting sectoral deals. Second, trade barriers must be eliminated, not merely reduced on a preferential basis. Third, external trade barriers toward third parties must be no higher on average after the establishment of a free trade area or customs union than they were before. Finally, recognizing that these kinds of arrangements will be phased in over time, Article XXIV requires a clear plan to be established and declared for the transition. This has been one of the weak points in the GATT, and ever since the European Community's creation in the late 1950s, Article XXIV has been a source of contention. As more and more countries take an interest in regional trading arrangements, this weakness becomes more problematic for multilateralism.

Preferential trading arrangements among developing countries are covered in separate provisions. In the early 1970s, a group of developing countries had established a protocol under which they exchanged tariff preferences among themselves.[15] This arrangement did not envisage the creation of a customs union or free trade area, and no other provisions in the GATT system offered legal cover. A waiver under GATT Article XXV was therefore granted for ten years, in November 1971. However, in the "Enabling Clause,"[16] one of the instruments that emerged from the Tokyo Round, general legal cover was provided for these kinds of regional arrangements. None of the Article XXIV requirements applied, although the Enabling Clause states that such arrangements should aim to facilitate trade, should not create obstacles to the trade of third countries, and should not impede MFN-based trade liberalization. Regional arrangements among developing countries subject to the lesser disciplines of the Enabling Clause can only cover tariffs. The preferential removal of nontariff barriers still requires Article XXIV coverage or a waiver. Finally, the Enabling Clause does not provide legal cover for arrangements between industrial and developing countries such as the Caribbean Basin Initiative of the United States. That kind of arrangement has been a source of disagreement for many years, ever since the European Community sought to justify its preferential trading arrangements with former colonies and dependencies.[17] As with arrangements among developing countries involving nontariff measures, Article XXIV coverage or a waiver is required.

The fourth exception to the MFN principle has already been touched upon. It concerns special arrangements for developing countries, recognizing their particular financial, trade, and development needs. Under the Enabling Clause, specific legal cover is provided for the Generalized System of Preferences (GSP),[18] for special and differential treatment under the Tokyo Round Codes,[19] for regional arrangements among developing countries, and for special treatment in favor of the least developed countries.[20] There are two other important features of the Enabling Clause, apart from its specific provisions allowing departures from the MFN principle. These are the juxtaposed statements on reciprocity and graduation. On one hand, the Enabling Clause states that industrial countries do not expect to receive reciprocal commitments from developing countries that are inconsistent with the latter's individual development, financial, and trade needs. On the other hand, the Enabling Clause also states that developing countries expect to participate more fully in the framework of GATT rights and obligations as their development and trade situation improves. These essentially nonquantifiable, political provisions have given rise to endless debate and disagreement in the GATT. An important objective of the United States in the Uruguay Round was to raise the level of developing-country obligations in GATT.

The Elimination of Quantitative Restrictions

Concerning the second major principle of the GATT system, Article XI provides for the general elimination of quantitative restrictions. To a certain degree, this may be seen as a principle that supports the MFN rule and promotes transparent trade policy. In the absence of discriminatory tariffs, it is difficult, though not impossible, to discriminate among trading partners without resorting to quantitative restrictions. Departures from MFN are almost always supported by quantitative rationing. As for transparency, the trade-restricting effects of quantitative measures are much more difficult to identify than those of price-based measures. In addition, economic efficiency and distributive issues are involved in the choice between quantitative restrictions and tariffs. With tariffs, revenue goes to governments, but under a quantitative regime it goes to importers or quota holders as economic rent. Where there are rents to be had, potential quota holders can be expected to participate in rent-seeking activities, which can be an important source of economic inefficiency. Other economic costs are associated with the likelihood that the distribution of quota rights will not correspond to an economic optimum of the kind that a system of rationing based on price would be expected to produce, and may itself cause unwanted distortions.[21]

The principle that eliminates quantitative restrictions is subject to a range of exceptions. However, all the foreseen exceptions are supposed, by definition, to be limited in duration. Quantitative restrictions are not intended as a permanent feature of the GATT system.[22] The first exceptions to the elimination rules, for agriculture, are provided in Article XI. These exceptions are carefully circumscribed, dealing essentially with critical commodity shortages and supply management. In effect, these exceptions have not helped in dealing with widespread disregard for GATT disciplines in agricultural trade.

In four other main instances, exceptions are permitted for the use of quantitative trade restrictions. First, quantitative trade restrictions may be applied under Article XXI for national security reasons, and under Article XX for such reasons as protecting health, public morals, national treasures, and gold and silver supplies, conserving exhaustible natural resources, participating in international commodity agreements, and supply management in specified circumstances.

Second, Articles XII and XVIII:B permit the use of quantitative trade restrictions when foreign exchange is in short supply. The more stringent Article XII is supposed to be used by industrial countries, and Article XVIII:B by developing countries. The distinction is not altogether rigid. Under a 1979 Declaration from the Tokyo Round,[23] the industrial countries came close to accepting that they would not invoke the balance-of-payments exception in the future. In practice, the provision has remained virtually moribund since that time.[24] Developing countries continue to use Article XVIII:B, and a major U.S. initiative in the Uruguay Round, supported by other industrial countries, has been to tighten disciplines in this area.

Third, Article XVIII:C permits countries to apply quantitative restrictions to foster the development or extension of an industry. This is the GATT "infant-industry" provision, available only to developing countries.[25] It has been used sparsely, principally because the balance-of-payments exception of Article XVIII:B has served as a surrogate. Quantitative restrictions taken in order to ration foreign exchange when reserves are low are difficult to distinguish from quantitative restrictions to protect specific domestic industries. The infant-industry provision can require compensation to be paid in the form of alternative trade liberalization measures if the restrictions fall on items subject to tariff bindings. In general, the balance-of-payments exception has been easier to use than the infant-industry exception.

Finally, the GATT safeguard provision, Article XIX, provides grounds for applying measures against imports, including quantitative restrictions. Safeguards are permitted when unexpectedly rapid import growth causes or threatens serious injury to a domestic industry as the consequence of obligations assumed under the GATT. Import-restricting measures must be compensated and must be temporary in nature. Although there is no clear statement on the matter, it is generally accepted that Article XIX should be applied on a nondiscriminatory basis. Of all the exceptions to mainstream GATT disciplines, this has been the least effectively controlled. Countries have increasingly preferred to use discriminatory measures of protection, often in the form of voluntary export restraints (VERs), rather than submit to Article XIX disciplines. The GATT safeguards provision has thus fallen largely into disuse, and the lack of proper multilateral discipline in this area is generally cited as a major failure of the GATT system.

The Protection of Trade-Liberalization Commitments

Trade-liberalization commitments under GATT constitute a combination of tariff bindings and disciplines on the use of other restrictive measures or policies. The rules limiting the use of quantitative restrictions are central to the protection of the value of tariff bindings, as are the procedures for renegotiating bindings. National treatment, contained in Article III, is another important provision. The national treatment rule in the GATT is intended to ensure that no additional margin of protection against imports is provided through the application of internal measures in a way that discriminates in favor of domestic products. The national treatment requirement covers internal charges and taxes, mixing regulations, and all other laws, regulations, or requirements affecting the sale, offer for sale, purchase, transportation, distribution, or use of products. The two important exceptions to this rule are government procurement and government subsidies.

The national treatment rule is essential to the maintenance of definable market-access commitments and transparency, but it does take GATT commitments beyond the frontier. The GATT has never been restricted solely to disciplines on border measures because the possibility of policy substitution has made that impossible. However, as trade negotiations have impinged increasingly on matters other than the flow of goods from one country to another, so too have the kind of commitments necessary to maintain market access undertakings come increasingly to resemble national treatment rather than just MFN. While MFN has to do with nondiscrimination among foreign products, national treatment is about nondiscrimination between foreign and domestic products.

A final matter to be mentioned here is that of subsidies, covered by Article XVI of the GATT, as supplemented by the 1979 Tokyo Round Code on Subsidies and Countervailing Duties. In a sense, the subsidy rules are intended to protect access commitments with respect to the domestic market, but they are also about controlling intrusions into foreign markets via government assistance through subsidy payments. The rules outlaw export subsidies on manufactured products[26] but on primary products, state only that they should be avoided. Where subsidies are bestowed on primary products, they should not lead to a country's acquiring more than a fair share of trade in the subsidized product. This rule, based on a judgment of the effects of a policy, has proved impossible to enforce and is a major issue in agricultural trade. As far as production subsidies are concerned, disciplines are widely regarded as being weak. All that is required is that they should not be used in a way that adversely affects the industry of another country, or nullifies or impairs in any way benefits that would otherwise accrue under the GATT.

THE DEMISE OF THE NONDISCRIMINATION RULE

The increasing ineffectiveness of the MFN principle underlies much of the GATT trading system's difficulties in the last two decades. In political terms, the MFN principle gives the international trading system its cohesiveness. It helps to take the politics out of trade by guaranteeing countries equal rights of market access, irrespective of their size and bargaining power. It creates stability by reducing the likelihood that countries will be "picked off," either because they are dynamic or for other, noneconomic reasons. Nondiscriminatory trading arrangements gain legitimacy by minimizing arbitrary behavior and by promoting politically neutral outcomes in competition for markets. They also make it harder to reverse trade liberalization, since this cannot be done in a geographically selective manner. By contrast, a discriminatory system produces market outcomes that depend on administrative decisions, and whatever factors go into the determination of such decisions.

The MFN rule is important as an efficiency principle. In purely economic terms, nondiscriminatory market access ensures that producers and consumers can buy from the most desirable foreign source.[27] Less obviously, the absence of an MFN rule considerably complicates bilateral trading arrangements. In a non-MFN world, the advantages granted bilaterally to a trading partner derive in part from the fact that the same advantages are not available to other countries. When a country establishes a network of bilateral arrangements, therefore, it faces endless difficulties in balancing a series of mutually inconsistent discriminatory arrangements. Each time a trade barrier is reduced in a bilateral agreement, advantages associated with preferential access under a preexisting arrangement with another country are undermined. This problem is likely to reduce trade flows and opportunities for profitable specialization. It is also likely to generate political friction that would not exist under an MFN regime. The more the GATT's MFN rule is encroached upon, the more apparent these difficulties become. Indeed, this is one reason why the MFN principle became an increasingly common feature of international trade agreements as trade relations intensified among countries.[28]

The MFN principle is breaking down for two broad reasons. First, it is easier to engineer protectionist trade policy on a discriminatory basis. Non-MFN arrangements allow countries to be picked off. Political costs, and the potential economic costs of retaliation, are less if countries can be singled out for particular attention. Departures from the MFN principle have been a prominent feature of recent protectionist trade policy.

The second reason for the erosion of the MFN principle is more complex. It has to do with the weakening of a consensus about what the "rules of the game" should be. This has shown itself most clearly in friction among the major trading countries, especially with Japan. Both the United States and the West European countries have constantly criticized Japan's approach to economic and trade policy. The debate about how to reduce trade tensions with Japan is highly charged and raises many unresolved issues (chapter 5). In trade policy terms, the denial of MFN treatment to Japan in a growing number of sectors is a clear indication of the problem.

The MFN principle is under threat in four main areas: "first order" protectionism, conditional MFN, regionalism, and special treatment for developing countries.[29] Each quite distinct, these four nevertheless overlap in important ways.

"First Order" Protectionism

The MFN principle has fallen into disuse because, without it, protectionist policy is easier to manage at lower political and economic cost. The particular way in which discriminatory trade restricting measures have been designed and applied adds to the attraction of the non-MFN approach. Specifically, the use of voluntary export restraints and similar export-restricting devices deflects responsibility for protectionist outcomes away from domestic decisionmakers and petitioners. Exactly the same process is involved in the subversion of the antidumping and countervailing-duty statutes, where they become discriminatory protectionist devices instead of unfair trade remedies.

While the subversion of the antidumping and countervailing-duty statutes is straightforward, involving accumulated unilateral action to bend laws and regulations in the direction of serving protectionist interests,[30] the use of VERs is more intriguing. How is it that countries are persuaded to connive in the diminution of their trade prospects? The literature on this issue is growing.[31]

Part of the problem is that the GATT system does not give countries the necessary support to resist pressures for discriminatory trade restrictions. To a degree, the weakness of the GATT in this area simply reflects the unwillingness of governments to be bound by multilateral disciplines that they do not like. Because the GATT has no effective enforcement mechanisms beyond moral suasion and the possibility of allowing retaliation, it has always needed a consensus based on enlightened self-interest to operate effectively. In addition, because the architects of the GATT did not foresee the development of VERs, interpretations of what GATT law is on this issue can be competing.[32] Nevertheless, the mainstream view would be that export restraints negotiated by governments are almost certainly contrary to the letter and definitely contrary to the spirit of the GATT. A problem, however, is that the party technically guilty of breaching the GATT is the exporting country, not the importing country that provoked the restriction in the first place.[33] The price of connivance, then, is silence in the GATT. That is why the GATT has never formally arbitrated a complaint on this issue or made a ruling. It is also why VERs are such an insidious incursion upon the integrity of multilateralism.

A second part of the explanation for the robustness of VERs is that they are the outcome of a credible threat that the protecting country could do something worse than extract a restraint agreement to troublesome export interests. The obvious alternative to VERs is discriminatory import restrictions, but these have two important disadvantages from the exporting country's point of view. First, if unilateral action is taken, the trade restrictions are likely to bite more. In a negotiation on restriction levels, the outcome can be moderated. Second, and more important, the authority administering the restrictions is generally in a good position to extract the price benefit that reflects the scarcity premium generated by a quantitative restriction. In other words, restricting supply in the face of demand raises the price of a good, and this economic rent or scarcity premium generally accrues to the exporter under a VER, but to the importer under an arrangement administered through import quotas.

If this is true, why does the protecting government feel the need to bribe the exporting country with VER scarcity premia when this could be a benefit for the protecting country? It is the price that the victim extracts for connivance, ensuring that there will be no messy GATT litigation and enabling decisionmakers in the importing country to conceal their protectionist handiwork. Political relations are also more harmonious under a VER arrangement than they would be under an import quota regime.

Arguments have been developed in the United States in favor of converting VERs into import restrictions. C. Fred Bergsten and other economists from the Institute for International Economics in Washington have argued that VERs should be converted into auctioned import quotas that would be managed by the U.S. authorities.[34] Auctioned quotas would transfer windfall gains to the importing country's government and provide funds for adjustment assistance to enhance U.S. competitiveness. They would also take windfall profits away from foreign competitors, help to reduce the budget deficit, and promote more liberal trading arrangements.

Laura Megna Baugham has cast some doubts on these propositions, arguing that auctioned quotas would likely reduce competition by cartelizing industry, increase uncertainty for importers, involve significant administrative costs, and upset trading partners, including through GATT violations.[35] A number of these criticisms are anticipated by Bergsten and associates, but the key issues would seem to be whether auctioning quotas really would lead to more trade liberalization, and from a systemic perspective, whether they would help to eliminate discrimination among trading partners. The auction might increase pressure for trade liberalization over time, but an effective challenge to discrimination via this route is less likely.

The economic effects of VERs have been well documented.[36] In addition to the administrative, distributional, and efficiency consequences of nondiscriminatory quantitative trade restrictions, VERs carry further economic costs as a result of the selective restriction of exports from the most efficient traders.[37] In the exporting country, they tend to cartelize the affected industry, and generate vested interests in maintaining the arrangements by quota recipients who learn that managed trade allows them to operate without worrying about new competition.

A variant on the VER, which is also "voluntary" and quite possibly discriminatory, though not necessarily trade restricting, is what Bhagwati has referred to as voluntary import expansion (VIE) arrangements.[38] This was discussed in chapter 5 in the context of trade in semiconductors and autos. The VIE is an extension of protection from the domestic market to exports. The fact that it may lead to increased trade is hardly consoling for countries excluded from such a commitment, unless it is undertaken on a nondiscriminatory basis.[39] When the beneficiary exporting countries are inefficient suppliers of a product, the VIE achieves what export subsidies can, namely, a situation where increased trade is not virtuous, but welfare-reducing instead.

In short, VERs and similar "voluntary" arrangements that distort trade are the highest expression of "first-order" protection promoted through discrimination. Their economic costs may be considerable, and their damage to the multilateral trading system is ominous. If the proliferation of VERs is not soon checked, little will be left of the nondiscrimination principle. Unfortunately, the safeguards discussions in the Uruguay Round give little cause for optimism that a collective commitment to nondiscriminatory safeguards will be forthcoming in the near future. Even if it were, the problems raised by the protectionist abuse of antidumping and countervailing-duty provisions would also have to be addressed.

The kind of antiprotection activity analyzed by Destler and Odell[40] might develop further and mitigate protectionist trade policy outcomes. Antiprotection activity may indeed be expected to increase if protectionism spreads beyond some notion of a tolerable level. Also, as economic activities become increasingly integrated across frontiers, more and more interests are likely to be jeopardized by protectionist decisions. Moreover, discriminatory protection generally relies on quantitative restrictions and managed trade. Such arrangements require more or less permanent negotiations and are inherently unstable. They might, therefore, been seen as self-limiting. But signs of abatement have yet to appear. Discriminatory trading arrangements are spreading.

Bhagwati suggests that VER-type arrangements have had the virtue of making protection "porous," since not all imports have been controlled. For this reason, VERs might be seen as a way for the administration to reduce protection below what it would have otherwise been.[41] VERs might, therefore, be an efficient instrument for governments to head off uglier outcomes. An alternative view is that by allowing governments to avoid responsibility for protectionist actions, VERs may have increased protection. The best antidote to protection is not to soften its impact through subterfuge, but rather to make it and its effects plain for all to see. This difference of view is not easy to settle conclusively. Some relevant evidence would be to consider what has actually happened to trade flows where VERs have been applied. But then again, showing that trade flows have increased despite VERs does not provide a benchmark for assessing what the real protectionist effects of VERs have been. In any event, the same fundamental question arises. What happens to trade relations and trading opportunities as the system tends toward a managed, quantitatively oriented regime? The picture looks bleak, unless positive measures are taken to reverse current trends toward discriminatory trading arrangements.

Conditional MFN

Arrangements such as VERs were described above as "first-order" protectionism because of their unequivocally protectionist design. The situation with respect to conditional MFN is less clear. The GATT seeks to defend unconditional MFN, but the conditional variety is becoming more commonplace in trade policy. For the present purposes, conditional MFN arrangements are defined as the selective application of trade rules and disciplines, in contrast to the preferential market access arrangements set up geographically. As will be seen in the later discussion of regionalism, the distinction is somewhat artificial, particularly as regional arrangements come to encompass much more than just border measures defining the conditions of market access. The distinction does, however, allow the isolation of a number of different aspects of the growth of discrimination in trade policy.

Conditional MFN was a significant issue in GATT during the Tokyo Round (1973–79), when it became increasingly clear that the side agreements known as codes were not going to be adhered to by the entire membership of the GATT. The Tokyo Round codes covered technical barriers to trade, government procurement, subsidies and countervailing duties, customs valuation, import licensing procedures, and antidumping. Most of these agreements sought to clarify and extend policy disciplines in areas already covered by the GATT. The one exception was government procurement, which is specifically excluded from the GATT.[42] The provisions of that code clearly intend that its benefits should be extended to signatories only. For the rest of the codes, the presumption is clear, as far as GATT law is concerned, that even though not all members of GATT subscribe to the codes their benefits should be extended to all GATT members without discrimination.[43]

As Hufbauer and associates point out, in one sense the benefits of the codes cannot be extended universally, even without any discriminatory intent in their application.[44] The benefits that cannot be enjoyed without membership include the right to participate in decisions by the code committees, and to have access to consultation procedures and to dispute-settlement arrangements.

The real problem, however, is that the codes have introduced the potential for discrimination into the trading system. For the most part, conditional MFN has not been applied by code signatories against non-code signatories. The one notable exception to this is U.S. policy toward the Subsidies Code. Prior to signature of the Subsidies Code at the end of the Tokyo Round, the United States did not apply the injury test in countervailing-duty cases involving dutiable imports.[45] Because U.S. trade law did not require an injury test at the time the GATT came into force, the United States "grandfathered" this situation in GATT.[46] In exchange for agreeing to bring its domestic policy into line as part of the Tokyo Round package, the United States insisted that it would grant the injury test only to countries that accepted a commitment to phase out export subsidies on manufactured goods. This policy was made explicit and was written into U.S. law in the Trade Agreements Act of 1979. The issue has since been a contentious one for many developing countries because it is they who still retain the right under GATT and the Subsidies Code to use export subsidies on manufactured goods. This illustrates how a conditional MFN policy can be used to try to force other countries to accept commitments not otherwise required under the trading system.

Although there has not been any GATT litigation on this issue, it is unlikely that the United States could defend what amounts to an infringement of the MFN principle.[47]

The first postwar expression of a conditional MFN policy in U.S. domestic law appeared in the Trade Act of 1974. Under this legislation, the president was empowered to recommend the selective application of trade agreements if consistent with the terms of the agreement in question. In the Omnibus Trade and Competitiveness Act of 1988, this provision was strengthened, and the president must recommend that trade agreements be applied on a conditional MFN basis. Apart from the case of the Subsidies Code, conditional MFN is applied in relation to the Code on Technical Barriers to Trade and the Code on Government Procurement, but conditional MFN in the post-Tokyo Round period has been a serious issue only in relation to countervailing duties.

There are, however, two points to be made about this. First, although the discriminatory effects of conditional MFN were limited to only one policy area, a more general concern with the "code approach" is that it splinters the trading system and creates a multitiered system of contractual rights and obligations. This in turn means that opportunities for full participation in all aspects of rule making in the international trading system are restricted to a subset of GATT members. Second, conditional MFN arrangements are likely to become more commonplace as trade rules and disciplines spread to new areas. What are the implications of such a development for multilateralism?

Contradictory perspectives can be adopted with regard to conditional MFN. The one most prevalent in U.S. policy circles is that conditional MFN is indispensable to the preservation of the essence of multilateralism and to continuing trade liberalization. It is the only mechanism that will ensure that the system remains relevant and responsive to changed circumstances. This has become increasingly true, the argument goes, as international disciplines have extended beyond market-access commitments at the border to substantive policy rules.

The graphic descriptions of "free rider" and "foot dragger" are used to characterize the countries that threaten multilateralism and trade liberalization by their refusal to play a constructive part.[48] As Hufbauer and Schott explain, a free rider is a small country that can benefit from the trade liberalization of others under an unconditional MFN system without having to make any contribution of its own. This accusation is often leveled at developing countries. A foot dragger is a large country whose refusal to subscribe to an arrangement would make it inconceivable to extend the unconditional application of the benefits of such an arrangement to all parties. Hufbauer and

Schott believe that "[I]t is no exaggeration to say that free riders and foot drag-gers are debilitating the whole GATT system."[49] Conditional MFN is the only way to guard against the destructive use of veto power. These authors do, how-ever, also caution against the discriminatory abuse of conditional MFN.

An alternative view is likely to be held by smaller members of the trad-ing system. It is that the free rider characterization is just too simple and fails to capture the important reality that small countries are not as well placed as large ones to determine the substantive content of the rules of the system. Admitting the possibility of a conditional MFN approach removes the need to worry about accommodating the concerns and interests of the multitude of small trading countries that make up most of the GATT. These countries must either conform to the rules or accept exclusion. The more marked the differences between the small countries that are excluded and the larger coun-tries that make the deal, the more potentially damaging conditional MFN out-comes are likely to be. Rules might be designed precisely to inhibit upcoming, dynamic trading countries.

In practical terms, it is probably inevitable that conditional MFN will become more prominent, perhaps as much to guard against foot dragging as against free riding.[50] The problem of free riding has been somewhat exagger-ated. Conditional MFN has not been widely practiced under the Tokyo Round codes, and yet smaller countries have increasingly participated in these arrangements. This is because participation carries benefits as well as obliga-tions. The carrot has been more important than the stick.

If this argument is accepted, the case for conditional MFN is limited. If codes containing conditional MFN provisions are nevertheless inevitable, their containment and control could be ensured by four ground rules. First, all countries should be entitled to participate fully in the negotiation and design of codes. Second, as a quid pro quo for this participation, all countries would make a commitment eventually to subscribe to the codes. This would mean that the conditional application of MFN would not need to be designed as a form of threat, enticement, or punishment. It would be a practical, interim matter. Third, codes would be open-ended by definition, in the sense of dis-pensing with any additional entry negotiations. Countries joining codes would simply have to accept the obligations involved. Finally, the operation of the codes should be kept under full multilateral control. These ground rules should permit countries that are ready to broaden or deepen their multilateral com-mitments to do so, while protecting the interests of countries that cannot yet accept such commitments. Any attempt by the latter group of countries to exercise a veto power would make the arrangements unworkable and ensure that reduced groups of countries would make exclusive side agreements. The

Uruguay Round proposals for the establishment of a Multilateral Trade Organization (MTO) may be seen as a solution to the conditional MFN problem (chapter 10), since pratically all GATT agreements would be incorporated under a single institutional umbrella with universal membership. In some instances, however, such as trade in services, the intention of applying MFN conditionally seems to persist.

Regionalism

The United States reversed its policy on preferential regional trading blocs in the 1980s by signing free trade agreements with Israel and Canada and by developing the Caribbean Basin Initiative. The thrust of this policy has been reinforced through the North American Free Trade Agreement and the Enterprise for the Americas Initiative. Martin Wolf has argued that the policy switch by the United States toward regionalism is a "tacit admission of its relative economic and political decline."[51] Two related policy questions need to be addressed. First, are FTAs or customs unions necessarily conducive to a further opening of markets? Second, do these arrangements complement or destroy multilateralism? GATT Article XXIV tries to address precisely these two issues. It insists that an FTA or customs union must eliminate barriers on substantially all trade between the parties and that barriers must not be raised against third parties as the result of regional trading agreements. But Article XXIV is widely considered to have failed as an effective mechanism for controlling regionalism.

As regards the first question, it is recognized that FTAs cannot be relied upon to move the trading system toward liberalization. The trade-creation effects of an FTA will not necessarily exceed the trade-diversion effects. The argument that new growth opportunities created by preferential trade liberalization will be shared by third countries outside an FTA may be important, but again the question is essentially empirical. If a customs union is established rather than an FTA, there are likely to be pressures to raise external trade barriers to the level of the most protectionist country in the union. It can be argued that European agriculture would not be as protected as it is if the European Community were an FTA and not a customs union. This sort of situation raises doubts that regionalism can be seen as a sure stepping stone toward the development of greater nondiscriminatory trading opportunities.

Where multilateral trading arrangements have failed to open up trade in specific sectors (such as in agriculture, textile and clothing, steel, and autos), there is a risk that regionally based accommodations may solidify these protectionist arrangements. The draft NAFTA, for example, excludes textiles and apparel, automotive goods, and agriculture from general trade liberalization commitments. In these sectors, slower and less complete moves to integrate the market will be backed by a strong emphasis on the exclusion of third parties from any benefits that might accrue.

From a systemic perspective that seeks to defend multilateralism, FTAs might be considered acceptable if they create new trading opportunities, do not unduly distort trade, and do not create unassailable vested interests that would block the extension of liberalized trading arrangements on a nondiscriminatory basis. In other words, there would be less to worry about if regional agreements were regarded as interim measures, aimed at providing momentum for nondiscriminatory trade-liberalization efforts. But are FTAs and similar arrangements really seen as short-term stop-gaps? Support for regional trading arrangements does not always come from advocates of liberal trade. Other motivations and considerations intervene. For example, Canada proposed an FTA to the United States as a way of "ducking under" mounting U.S. protectionism under the unfair trade statutes. Canada was also motivated by a sense of frustration with cumbersome, seemingly unproductive multilateral attempts to deal with mounting trading problems. Mexico was prompted to propose its FTA with the United States primarily as a way to build investment opportunities around improved (and preferential) access to the U.S. market.

A widely quoted article by James Baker about the FTA between Canada and the United States, written when he was secretary to the treasury, states that "a strategic employment of bilateral agreements can actually sustain and support GATT."[52] The case is made that the GATT no longer works. Multilateralism is crumbling, and regional initiatives can shore it up, and give it a new lease on life. This scenario suggests that third countries are not to be shut out, but rather enticed by example to join in future trade-liberalization efforts. Thus, an FTA embodies the seeds of its own destruction.

Suppose instead that the problem is not merely one of temporary inertia or some countries' wanting to move faster than others, but is more fundamental and concerns the essence of the trading system itself. The issue then is not that the front-runners offer a demonstration effect, expecting that other countries will sign on when ready. Rather it is that the participants in regional initiatives are redefining the substance and direction of the trading system, closing off options for the latecomers. At a time when many aspects of the trading system are being reassessed and arrangements sought in new areas, this can be an important issue. In this connection, Secretary Baker argues that if there is no follow-up liberalization along the lines of the U.S.-Canada FTA at the multilateral level through the Uruguay Round, the United States "might be willing to explore a 'market liberalization club' approach, through minilateral arrangements or a series of bilateral agreements."[53] When this argument is added to the first one, an enticement becomes a threat, and a complement a substitute. It may end in the abandonment of multilateralism, not its rescue.

If the issue was merely one of improving market access by reducing trade barriers at the border, the debate about regionalism would be less important. The discussion would center on trade creation and trade diversion, and lines between acceptable and unacceptable arrangements could be made reasonably clear.[54] In recent years, however, attention has focused on modifying existing rules and on extending GATT disciplines to new areas. If countries redefine the system in the context of regional arrangements, what chances are there of later extending the same pattern of commitments to other countries, or of modifying the content of such commitments to bring other countries on board? Judging from the debates in the Uruguay Round, the task will be formidable if regional arrangements extend too far in these directions. Canada, the United States, and Mexico have concluded a draft NAFTA that covers (eventually if not initially) a whole range of issues subject to multilateral negotiation, including trade in services, investment, and intellectual property rights. Will these agreements meld easily into a multilateral setting at a later date? The problem may not yet be acute because many issues remain ill-defined or pending in the NAFTA. However, further movement in this direction would seriously threaten the possibility of generalizing increasingly complex, intrusive, and intertwined arrangements into a nondiscriminatory world. The question is no longer one of countries choosing different paces along the same road to the same destination. Now the direction of the road itself must be determined.[55]

For those proposing regional initiatives, as Preeg does to complement multilateral initiatives,[56] and as Hufbauer does to deepen and extend the reach of the system,[57] the above questions should not remain unanswered. The multilateral trading system cannot be insulated from parallel arrangements even when the intent is genuine to supplement multilateralism and ultimately promote nondiscrimination. It is not at all clear that countries can focus on regional agreements and maintain the same commitment to multilateralism.[58]

On the contrary, the way the NAFTA and Uruguay Round negotiations played out from 1991 onward showed how a regional initiative could steal the show. The long history of the European Community in GATT also shows how multilateral objectives and commitments can be subordinated to regional imperatives. The European Community has rarely taken any initiative to promote multilateralism in GATT, preferring a defensive posture with the minimal commitment to keeping the GATT visible as an instrument for coordinating and expressing EC external trade relations. This minimalist approach to GATT may be further accentuated in the immediate future as the

Community defines its identity in relation to potential members in the rest of Europe and tries to give substance to the Single European Act and the Maastricht Treaty commitments. In the longer term, a more fully integrated Europe may be able to adopt a constructive multilateral approach without accentuating internal divisions.

Regional trading arrangements, such as FTAs and customs unions, are not going to disappear. In the Americas and Europe they will receive increasing emphasis, if not immediately in Asia. In these circumstances, perhaps some ground rules could be worked out. These would seek to minimize the damage that regional arrangements might have on the integrity of a fully multilateral trading system based on nondiscrimination. They would allow that regionalism can be a stepping stone to multilateralism, where regional initiatives are a first response to the process of globalization. They would also recognize that any configuration of regional trading blocs in the foreseeable future is likely to cover 50 percent or less of world trade flows.

Regional initiatives could be guided by four principles, and the degree to which they were respected would be a litmus test of underlying intentions. Two of the rules forwarded here are suggested by Martin Wolf.[59] First, countries becoming involved in FTAs or the like should contemplate only one such arrangement. This rule would be important for the United States, which could drift into a network of trading arrangements. If that occurred, it would lead in a fairly short time to tension and conflict. A single evolving arrangement would be closer to the 1970s idea of GATT-plus,[60] which was a detailed proposal for GATT reform. The basic idea was that the GATT alone was not an adequate instrument to mediate trade relations because it could not respond fully to the interests of all its members, especially the differing needs and perspectives of the developing-country majority in the GATT and the industrial countries. An additional GATT-like arrangement therefore had to be created among industrial countries to improve the content of trade disciplines and their observance. The proposal was clearly intended to liberalize trade. This is also how some observers see the Tokyo Round codes.

As initiatives move ahead for regional integration through FTAs in the Americas, this issue will become increasingly crucial. The decision to negotiate a NAFTA comprising the United States, Canada, and Mexico was a move in the right direction. But the question is what will happen when more Latin American countries become involved in these negotiations with the United States. Will the United States negotiate free-standing FTAs with them or incorporate new countries into the NAFTA?[61] Ronald Wonnacott has described the former approach as a "hub-and-spoke" arrangement.[62] Such an approach is likely to lead to considerable complications for all parties concerned, but the decision on this issue will not be made by the United States alone. Already, a network of FTAs and customs unions is forming in Latin America. Agreements exist or are in prospect between Mexico and Chile; between Mexico, Colombia, and Venezuela; between Mexico and Costa Rica; between Venezuela and Chile; and between Brazil, Argentina, Uruguay, and Paraguay. Existing agreements are being strengthened such as the Andean Pact (Bolivia, Colombia, Ecuador, Peru, and Venezuela) and the Central American Common Market (Costa Rica, El Salvador, Guatemala, Honduras, and Nicaragua).

Second, regional arrangements should be open-ended, in the same sense as agreements involving particular rules that initially operate on a conditional MFN basis. Open-ended agreements would automatically define the conditions of adherence and would not involve any additional conditionality if a country wished to join a regional arrangement. Abiding by the established rules would suffice. This idea would be opposed by interests for which a regional arrangement is a mechanism for diverting trade or for securing particular privileges from a trading partner. Open-endedness would, however, ensure that regional arrangements were conceived as temporary expedients to advance genuinely open trading arrangements.

Third, the nondiscrimination principle should apply, save in exceptional circumstances, to all aspects of a regional arrangement dealing with substantive rule-making. The GATT-plus proposal went further than this, arguing that MFN should be a feature of specific market-opening commitments as well.[63] As international trade agreements touch upon an ever-greater range of activities and areas, the danger of irreversible fragmentation will increase with the number of exclusive variants in different areas. The exceptional circumstances where MFN treatment would not be extended to third parties would involve such practical matters as consultation and dispute-settlement provisions. Once again, a willingness to abide by this rule would suggest a multilateralist, trade-liberalizing intent behind regional initiatives.

Fourth, a commitment should be made to multilateral accountability. This means that regional arrangements should not only continue to require approval from GATT but their operation should also be subject to multilateral scrutiny.[64] This would help to ensure that regional arrangements do not go off on tangents that would make their integration into a wider framework more difficult. This is particularly important in a situation involving so much more than discipline over border measures. It would also be understood that the basic Article XXIV rules would be retained, and perhaps improved, to guard against regionalism of a protectionist bent and discriminatory sectoral deals. A particular problem that regional negotiations continually confront is how to deal with sectors that are not adequately disciplined at the multilateral level. The temptation to build on existing distortions is strong, but to do so creates additional vested interests against multilateral reform efforts.

These four principles, or something like them, could be used as a yardstick for the multilateral surveillance of regional arrangements. In particular, the protagonists of regional initiatives should have to show what they can achieve through an FTA or similar arrangement that could not be achieved multilaterally on an MFN basis. As Jeffrey Schott points out,[65] some issues involve many countries and cannot, therefore, be easily dealt with in the more restricted context of a regional arrangement. In such cases, the free riders and foot draggers may be too important to be excluded at any stage of the process. This, for example, is one reason the United States and Canada could not agree on establishing additional disciplines over production subsidies in their FTA. It is also the reason both this agreement and the draft NAFTA failed to improve antidumping and countervailing-duty disciplines.

Special Treatment for Developing Countries

One of the most contentious issues in GATT, particularly in the 1980s, has been the nature of developing-country participation in the trading system. For the industrial countries, and the United States in particular, a major objective in the Uruguay Round was to ensure that developing countries assume a higher level of GATT obligations. Exceptions permitted in the GATT rules for developing countries were outlined above.

The question of developing-country participation in the GATT system has been a source of disagreement since the beginning.[66] The charter for the International Trade Organization, which never came into force, contained a range of provisions relating to development (chapter 2). Developing countries were disappointed when these provisions did not see the light of day and did not start to join the GATT in appreciable numbers for several years. These countries expended a great deal of energy seeking exceptions to GATT disciplines on the grounds that the rules were overly restrictive. They argued that some respite would be required to develop and diversify their economies. Only later would they be in a position to subscribe fully to the disciplines of the trading system.

Another important plank in the developing-country campaign was the search for trade preferences. It took a sustained effort of well over ten years before preferences were recognized as a legitimate way of helping developing countries to expand their trade without causing unacceptable damage to the trading system. It was nearly twenty years before full legal cover was granted to preferences in the framework of the Generalized System of Preferences.

These preferences have been a mixed blessing, largely because industrial countries extend them unilaterally and selectively. They have not been a stable element in the trading system.

The respective views of industrial and developing countries of each other's behavior in the trading system are easy to caricature. A strong industrial country view of the matter would be that developing countries have invaded the trading system, numerically and in terms of demands that undermine its integrity. They have fought hard for modifications in the rules to exempt themselves from any disciplines, while at the same time expecting to benefit fully from industrial countries' obligations. To make matters worse, the developing countries have then complained loudly about industrial country protectionism.

A developing-country riposte, in similar vein, would be that the trading system is inherently inequitable, designed to serve the interests of the industrial countries. Industrial country protectionism has grown over the years. Protectionist outcomes have been frequent in areas of interest to the developing countries (textiles and clothing, agriculture, and steel). Moreover, departures from the MFN principle have often been aimed at dynamic developing countries. As their own protectionism has grown, the industrial countries have pressed developing countries ever harder for increased contributions and commitments to the trading system.

If this is an exaggerated presentation of the views industrial and developing countries hold of each other, it is the raw material of the debate between the two groups. Regrettably, many issues that are not simply "North-South" have come to be seen in such terms because politics and rhetoric have captured the discussion. Any attempt at a less partial evaluation of the issue would identify problems on both sides. For instance, developing countries have in some instances had largely unbridled access to trade restrictions. Industrial countries have become more protectionist in some areas, and developing countries have been on the receiving end of this trend.

How far have departures from the nondiscrimination rule in the name of developing countries' growth undermined the integrity of the MFN system? To the extent that special treatment for developing countries has involved exceptions from rules, it has worked like a reversed conditional MFN, the conditionality being attached to developing-country status. Because intended to be temporary or strictly circumstantial, however, it is less potentially damaging to the MFN system. It does not create discrimination in respect of third parties. If there are problems, they concern control, definition, and agreement about what is acceptable. This applies to the balance-of-payments and infant-industry exceptions as well as to the special arrangements contained in the Tokyo Round codes.

From a developing-country perspective, a disadvantage of separate and less stringent rules is that by concentrating on acquiring and exercising special rights under the system, developing countries have been less well placed to put pressure on the industrial countries to live up to their multilateral commitments. With only a little exaggeration, a picture can be drawn of industrial and developing countries conniving in, or tolerating, each other's departures from principle. On the other hand, in a system based on reciprocity, it has been difficult for developing countries to secure what they regard as adequate "payment" for any trade liberalization they may offer. Thus, a tendency has emerged for developing countries to liberalize unilaterally, to rely on their own interpretations of what their obligations are, and to participate correspondingly less in GATT processes.[67]

In the field of preferences, vested interests may be created that militate against nondiscriminatory trade liberalization. Preference margins can distort trade flows. Besides, in the case of the GSP, there is no continuity or stability in terms of market access. Political friction is generated as a result of the unilateral decisions by the industrial countries every year to redefine the product and country coverage of their GSP systems. Furthermore, sometimes GSP is used in an overtly political manner. The fact that industrial countries have never seen the GSP as a contractual commitment suggests that it will wither away more easily than some other preferential arrangements, even if that goes against the wishes of vested interest groups.

From about the mid-1980s onward, more and more developing countries have adopted far-reaching trade liberalization programs.[68] As the Uruguay Round dragged on beyond its December 1990 deadline, many of these countries became increasingly strident in their protests about how little the industrial countries were willing to do to fulfill their commitments under GATT and their declared objectives under the Uruguay Round. These criticisms reflected growing developing-country frustration, heightened by the fact that their trade liberalization programs have given them an increased stake in open and secure export markets. Developing countries stand to lose a great deal from continuing deterioration in the multilateral trading system, especially as they open up their domestic markets.

NEW CHALLENGES FOR THE TRADING SYSTEM

As the 1980s wore on, a series of largely uncoordinated but related issues absorbed an increasing amount of attention among the major trading countries. These became known as the "new issues," encompassing trade in services,

trade-related intellectual property rights, and trade-related investment measures. The attempt to bring the new issues into the GATT was defended as
necessary to keep the system relevant in the face of widespread changes in
international economic relations. The United States took the initiative in all
the new areas. In services, this reflected an increasing awareness not only that
service transactions were becoming more important internationally, but that
the United States probably enjoyed a comparative advantage in some services.

At the same time, increased levels of foreign investment had awakened
interest in the effects of foreign regulatory systems on investment conditions and
profitability. The international infrastructure for dealing with trade issues seemed
to offer the best context for seeking agreement on rules for protecting intellectual property and making investment laws and regulations more attractive to foreign capital. More generally, "globalization" trends in the world economy would,
sooner or later, have led to a search for international rules and regulations to
meet the new realities, regardless of whether the initiatives had come from the
United States and whether they had been made in the GATT context.

Unfortunately, the drive to update the trading system and make it
responsive to new realities in trade relations coincided with a crisis in the
existing system. This point was not lost on countries that were fearful of initiatives to extend the system into new areas. It was mainly the developing
countries that emphasized what they characterized as a contradiction. How in
good faith, they asked, could countries presume to design new arrangements
in uncharted waters, when they could not even live with what they had
already created? The point was valid, even if it masked the developing countries' unwillingness to become involved in discussions that would expose them
to further pressures for trade liberalization. The contrast between a lame and
compromised GATT, and a nearly obsessive pursuit of international commitments in new areas, serves to emphasize a point made earlier about the need
to address trade and trade-related issues in a multilateral context. These issues
are too multifaceted to be dealt with adequately in a geographically compart-
mentalized fashion. The sheer complexity of the issues and the many unresolved questions make a retreat into conditionality and regional arrangements
that much more dangerous for the long-term prospects of multilateralism.

What were the characteristics of the new issues that implied change for
the existing trading system? At its simplest, the pre-Uruguay Round trading
system was about goods and about the range of policies that determined the
conditions under which goods could be produced in one country and sold in
another. Services were relevant only to the extent that they were embodied
in, or linked to, goods. Investment rules and cross-border flows of factors of
production were scarcely mentioned.[69] This is what the services, investment,

and intellectual property issues have changed. Their introduction extended the purview of the trading system beyond goods markets to factor (and service) markets as well. In services, the link is somewhat indirect and concerns the fact that trade in many services requires a commercial presence of some kind, and therefore impinges on investment questions. Few services can be traded across borders in the same straightforward way as goods. The investment issue concerns the conditions under which capital may move from one country and locate in another. The intellectual property issue, at its most fundamental, is about how investments in human capital, as reflected in production techniques, designs, and so on, are to be protected from appropriation.

The challenge posed for the Uruguay Round was to develop disciplines in the new areas. A major prior difficulty was to convince all Uruguay Round participants that disciplines ought to be developed in these areas. A more serious issue has been how far GATT principles can be applied where international factor flows and a myriad of internal laws and regulations become relevant to the negotiations. Does it make sense to speak of MFN or nondiscrimination? Where does national treatment fit into the picture?

Perhaps the most important systemic innovation introduced explicitly by the new issues into the trading system is the substitution of national treatment for MFN. This happens because the new issues require negotiations about conditions facing producers instead of products. In other words, as producers (capital and labor) and not just products cross frontiers, producers want to benefit from the same conditions on the other side of the frontier as their domestic counterparts. This means equal treatment under the laws and regulations to which domestic producers must answer. This is what is understood by national treatment under GATT, applying to products rather than producers.

As the national treatment provision changes from playing a supportive role to MFN, and replaces it, there is no longer the same distinction between nondiscrimination among foreigners and nondiscrimination between foreigners and domestic producers. Once given access, a foreigner benefits from the equivalent of free trade upon receiving national treatment. The intrusiveness of this situation is what caused many countries so much concern about services negotiations in the Uruguay Round. It has provoked a search for alternative means of driving a wedge between domestic and foreign interests or denying full national treatment. Domestic subsidies and taxes could be applied to favor domestic producers over foreign producers located in the domestic market. In practice, direct regulation will likely be preferred as a means of denying full national treatment. Whether price-based instruments or regulations are used, the measures would have to apply equally to all foreign suppliers if discrimination in the MFN sense is to be avoided.

Because national treatment replaces MFN as the fundamental principle regulating access conditions when producers rather than products cross frontiers, international commitments in this area will introduce pressures for the standardization of domestic laws and regulations. This arises directly from a world in which reciprocity is a sine qua non of international agreements. The reciprocity imperative is a catalyst for conformity and standardization in a general sense. In the new areas, the pressure is more intense. The potential systemic threat deriving from this pressure is obvious. As the demand for reciprocity grows and is seen as achievable through standardizing laws and regulations, so too will the temptation intensify to break away from a multilateral approach to the issues. Negotiations that reach this far into areas traditionally regarded as strictly internal, and which threaten the undefinable but powerful concept of sovereignty, are bound to be difficult. Agreement will often appear elusive, or impossible. The temptation to establish "clubs" of like-minded countries may become hard to resist, especially where domestic interest groups clamor for concrete negotiating results. Yet just as the temptation to break away is greater, so too is the difficulty of retreating once the process has taken hold.

Avoiding wholesale conditionality and the development of a multiplicity of side arrangements, with all that would imply for the trading system, is perhaps the greatest negotiating challenge in the new areas. Linked to this, and similarly provoked by insistence upon "up-front" and precise reciprocity, is the risk that international agreements involving the new areas will dispense with the market, and replace it with permanent negotiations and managed trade. The potential for this to occur is greater in the services area, where market access is explicitly addressed, than in regard to the intellectual property and investment issues, where general rules can be developed. Experience with existing agreements involving trade in services, particularly in the transport sector, do not set a promising example. Reciprocity demands in recent years have come to focus increasingly on outcomes and less on opportunities. If this trend takes hold, it is hard to see how market sharing will be avoided, especially in services. Instead of contributing to the revitalization of an already embattled multilateral trading system, taking the new issues on board could sink it. The challenges posed by the new areas must be met head-on if this outcome is to be avoided.

CHAPTER 8

THE TRADING SYSTEM
AFTER THE TOKYO ROUND

An analysis of the multilateral trading system in the 1980s would be incomplete without an examination of events in the 1970s. International economic relations in that decade were dominated by the Tokyo Round of Multilateral Trade Negotiations, launched in September 1973 and completed in November 1979. The Tokyo Round was the seventh round of negotiations within the General Agreement on Tariffs and Trade (GATT).[1] Until the Kennedy Round, GATT negotiations had been exclusively about reducing and binding tariffs. Success or failure could be judged by the extent of tariff reductions, and these rounds steadily brought down the high tariffs of the immediate postwar period. By the end of the Torquay negotiation, average tariffs were 25 percent lower than in 1948. By the end of the Tokyo Round, the average tariff on manufactures in industrial countries would be less than 5 percent. Increasing developing-country participation in the negotiations also reflected the growing geographical coverage of the GATT. Twenty-three countries participated in the 1947 Geneva meeting; ninety-nine in the Tokyo Round.

The Tokyo Round was different from earlier rounds in that negotiations were not only about tariffs but also about a range of nontariff measures. An earlier attempt to deal with some nontariff issues, including antidumping during the Kennedy Round, had gone nowhere, owing largely to opposition from the U.S. Congress. With varying degrees of success, the Tokyo Round addressed tariffs, agriculture, and a range of trade policies, most of them covered by the GATT but thought to need clearer or stricter regulation. In addition, the negotiations covered several issues relating to the participation of developing countries in the trading system.

PREPARATIONS FOR THE TOKYO ROUND

At the end of the Kennedy Round in 1967, the U.S. Congress was in an uncooperative mood as far as international trade relations were concerned, and dissatisfied with the results of the negotiations.[2] This may have stemmed in part from the lack of progress in agriculture and nontariff measures, although nominal tariff reductions averaged about 35 percent. A more important source of congressional dissatisfaction was internal. Congress believed that the executive branch had exceeded its negotiating authority by subscribing to an antidumping agreement. In addition, the administration had negotiated away the American Selling Price (ASP) method of customs valuation, whereby the valuation basis for calculating import duties was taken to be the price in the home market of the same article produced domestically. ASP was applied to a limited range of imports, predominantly benzenoid chemicals and canned clams.

In agreeing to the 1967 antidumping code, the administration argued that it had not exceeded its negotiating authority because commitments under the code were consistent with existing domestic legislation in the United States.[3] Congress considered this line of argument an excuse for having bypassed the correct constitutional procedures for negotiations of this nature. As a mark of disapproval, Congress passed legislation providing that:

> Nothing contained in the International Antidumping Code . . . shall be construed to restrict the discretion of the U.S. Tariff Commission in performing its duties and functions under the Antidumping Act of 1921, and in performing their duties and functions under such Act the secretary of the Treasury and the Tariff Commission shall—
>
> (1) resolve any conflict between the . . . Code and . . . Act . . . in favor of the Act as applied by the agency administering the Act, and
>
> (2) take into account the provisions of the . . . Code only insofar as they are consistent with the . . . Act . . . as applied by the agency administering the Act.[4]

On ASP, the Senate had warned the executive branch, by a voice vote in June 1966, that it lacked the legislative authority to enter into an agreement with the European Community, involving an exchange of additional EC tariff reductions for abolition of the ASP. Despite ASP's minor effect on imports because of its restricted coverage and despite the attraction of additional significant reductions in European tariffs, Congress neglected to take the necessary legislative action to abolish ASP. These two incidents are recounted in some detail here because they give a flavor of congressional attitudes at the time toward the GATT and also because they had a strong influence on negotiating authority for the Tokyo Round.

In the closing days of the Kennedy Round, these issues were studied in several quarters, prompted by a prevailing sentiment that it was time to think about the future of trade policy and international trade relations in general. President Lyndon B. Johnson appointed a Public Advisory Committee on Trade Policy, representing private sector interests, and also instructed the administration to undertake a study of U.S. trade policy. While recognizing that U.S. trade policy remained liberal in orientation, it was argued that the nature of the trading system was changing, and that further trade liberalization could be achieved only through international negotiation.

In 1970 President Richard M. Nixon appointed a Commission on International Trade and Investment Policy (known as the Williams Commission) to continue examining issues facing the trading system. Winham gives a precise account of changing U.S. attitudes reflected in the commission's findings:

> The report [spoke] of a crisis of confidence growing within the United States over the operation of the international economic system. Foremost among the causes of this crisis was the increased pressure of imports in American markets, along with a perceived decreasing ability of the United States to capitalize on its comparative trade advantage because of foreign restrictions. The crisis had produced mounting pressures in the United States for import restrictions, growing demands for retaliation against restrictive measures abroad, and a prevailing sentiment that other nations were not doing their fair share in helping with the persistent deficit in the United States balance-of-payments.[5]

The diagnosis given in the Williams Commission report is interesting for two reasons. First, it recognizes the relative economic decline of the United States, at a time when the Vietnam War was ending and the European

Community and Japan were coming into their own as economic powers. Second, it ascribes the perceived economic malaise afflicting the United States first and foremost to the refusal of other countries to make a suitable contribution to the international economic system. This reasoning seems to be part of a tradition that has led to the kinds of policies and reciprocity demands discussed in part I. The issue is not so much whether this kind of criticism of other countries is valid; it undoubtedly is. The problem is that relying on politically appealing, one-dimensional analyses feeds indignation and self-righteousness. This makes it hard to identify the aspects of the situation whose provenance is domestic and harder still to find negotiated multilateral solutions to what are, after all, shared problems.

The solution proposed by the Williams Commission was to rely on multilateral processes, involving negotiations based on overall rather than sectoral reciprocity. The proposals did not envisage a wholesale renegotiation of the GATT, but rather the establishment of a series of codes to improve existing disciplines. This proposal was the origin of the negotiation of codes on nontariff measures in the Tokyo Round. The proposals for trade negotiations made by the Williams Commission received international endorsement in the Organization for Economic Cooperation and Development from a report of a group of eleven experts (the Rey group) appointed to examine problems in international trade. The Rey group was equally convinced of the fundamental changes afoot in the world economy and of the need to update the system to take account of the new situation. There was also agreement on the desirability of further significant trade liberalization, going beyond the traditional tariff-cutting exercises of past multilateral trade negotiations.

Congress and the Tokyo Round

By February 1972, the United States, the European Community, and Japan had all declared themselves in favor of a new round of multilateral trade negotiations. In the United States, the immediate issue to be faced by the administration was the kind of negotiating authority that should be sought, and how to go about securing it.

On the question of tariffs, the matter was relatively straightforward. The president could reasonably expect to be granted tariff-cutting authority along the traditional lines established under the Reciprocal Trade Agreements program in 1934. Such grants of authority had been made regularly down through the years. Much more preoccupying was what to do about negotiating authority for nontariff measures. The Tokyo Round was clearly going to focus on such measures, but a sharp lesson had been learned from the episodes involving the antidumping code and the ASP in the Kennedy Round. The executive branch was determined not to be placed again in the ignominious position of having Congress undo or refuse to implement the administration's international commitments. At the same time, the administration had to be able to negotiate with its trading partners with authority. A negotiation would not be credible if U.S. negotiating partners had to operate under the constant fear that agreements reached with the administration would be struck down or ignored by Congress.

The final arrangements to meet these difficulties were both innovative and imaginative, although it took some time to put them in place. President Nixon's opening proposals were contained in a trade bill submitted to Congress in April 1973. In addition to its negotiating-authority proposals, the bill had provisions relating to other matters, including the Generalized System of Preferences (GSP) for developing countries, the extension of MFN treatment to certain communist countries, reform of antidumping and countervailing-duty law, and the reformulation of statutes dealing with unfair and injuriously competitive imports.

The initial proposal on negotiating authority was for unlimited tariff-cutting authority and an arrangement whereby the executive branch would consult with Congress about any nontariff agreements it planned to make. Any such agreements would be presented in their final form for endorsement or rejection, with no possibility of amendment. Although the House of Representatives approved the formulation, the Senate did not. Part of the reason was constitutional, arising from concern over the legitimacy of the legislative veto. Also involved, however, were suspicions that the president was seeking to appropriate too much power from the constitutional preserve of Congress, that of foreign trade policymaking. This all took place during Watergate, when communications between the president and Congress were breaking down.

The final compromise was the fast-track authority. Under these arrangements, the president negotiates on nontariff matters and, ninety days before entering into any agreements, notifies Congress of his intentions. The president then consults with the relevant congressional committees, and the international agreements are finalized and presented to Congress for approval. Congress must then consider the legislation and vote up or down, with no possibility of amendment. This formula was seen as a way of maintaining congressional control over trade policy while at the same time enabling the executive branch to negotiate meaningfully at the international level. In the event, the system worked so well that Congress has continued to extend fast-track negotiating authority.

Two other mechanisms were introduced at this time to ensure that international commitments entered into by the United States would have adequate domestic support. First, arrangements were made for congressional representation on delegations to international negotiations. Certain congressional representatives were also entitled to full and regular progress briefings. Second, private sector committees were established to supply advice and information regarding priorities and strategies in the negotiation. An Advisory Committee for Trade and Policy Negotiations (ACTPN) was created, with the responsibility of giving an "advisory opinion" on the results of the negotiations. The ACTPN was supported by a network of twenty-seven Industry Sector Advisory Committees, organized by activities, which met regularly to receive information on issues and progress in the negotiations, and to express their own interests. Though somewhat cumbersome in administrative terms, these arrangements succeeeded in ensuring smooth internal adoption procedures at the end of the Tokyo Round.

The trade bill presented by President Nixon in April 1973 was not passed by Congress until December 1974, after President Gerald R. Ford had assumed office. This meant that for the early part of the Tokyo Round, the United States was negotiating without authority. Much of the delay could be explained by the poor state of relations between Congress and President Nixon at this time, but some members of Congress also opposed the proposals for extending MFN treatment to the Soviet Union. After a year's delay in the Senate, the bill passed, with the Jackson-Vanik amendment, tying MFN treatment for communist countries to their emigration policies.

CHALLENGES FOR THE TOKYO ROUND

As noted, the Williams Commission reflected the feeling that the trading system faced problems that threatened to make the system increasingly irrelevant. What, then, were these problems? First, tolerance for noncompliance with GATT disciplines was reaching an unacceptable level, one that called the integrity of the system into question. There had always been some noncompliance, connived at by countries either in the interests of some more pressing imperative or in a kind of unspoken alliance of mutual indulgence. Not only were countries straying from disciplines with greater regularity, but an implicit consensus around noncompliance was also breaking down along with the consensus about what the rules of the system should say. The weakening of this consensus was a direct result of shifts in relative global economic power and changes in the economic and policy environment. Insofar as these developments can be dated, the late 1960s, including the run-up to the Tokyo Round, seems to be a crucial period. This is manifestly demonstrated by the agenda for the Tokyo Round.

A second element weighing on trade relations was, precisely, the accumulated success of previous GATT tariff-cutting negotiations. As tariffs had come down, nontariff barriers assumed greater relative importance as instruments of trade policy, attracting more attention and playing a more important role in influencing trade flows. In addition, some substitution was taking place. As governments committed themselves to tariff reductions, they looked around for alternative instruments of trade control and easily found nontariff measures to do the job (chapter 4).

The focus on nontariff barriers led to work in the Tokyo Round on technical barriers to trade, customs valuation methods, subsidies, countervailing duties, and quantitative restrictions. Later, negotiations were also begun on government procurement and on antidumping, stimulated by a desire to standardize antidumping procedures with what had been agreed on countervailing duties. In addition, the group on quantitative restrictions worked on an import-licensing agreement.

For the negotiations on technical barriers, valuation, and import licensing, the objective was to prevent procedures associated with these activities from themselves becoming hidden barriers to trade.[6] Only the negotiations on procurement involved a policy not previously covered in any significant way by the GATT.

The negotiations on subsidies and countervailing duties had as one major objective the introduction of the injury test in the United States in countervailing-duty investigations. Although the injury test is required by the GATT, the United States had not applied it on account of its "grandfather" exception for preexisting legislation. In exchange, the United States sought improved disciplines on the use of subsidies, an area of minimal disciplines under the GATT.

Part of the evidence of creeping noncompliance with GATT disciplines rested heavily on the growth of discrimination in trade policy, especially in the area of safeguards. The principal GATT safeguard provision permits countries to take emergency measures to forestall serious injury or its threat to domestic industries. The measures may be tariffs or nontariff measures of temporary duration, and the countries taking measures are expected to compensate trading partners for lost trading opportunities or face retaliation. Much is amiss with the way safeguards are applied, and the provisions themselves are also considered inadequate. The unwillingness of countries to observe the safeguard rules is a major breach in GATT disciplines, and failure to deal with it was made a central issue in the Uruguay Round. At the heart of the safeguards issue is the use of voluntary export restraints (VERs).

Agriculture was another area of interest, probably the single most sensitive trading issue since well before the Tokyo Round. Successive attempts to deal with agricultural problems have failed, and it was the principal obstacle to the completion of the Uruguay Round. Agriculture escaped GATT disciplines virtually from the beginning. The rules make exceptions for agriculture, in respect of quantitative import restrictions and export subsidies, and countries have found different ways of circumventing what disciplines there are. The United States took a lead role in this process in the early 1950s when it declared its agricultural policy beyond the reach of GATT discipline and secured a GATT waiver to that effect in 1955. The European Community built its political unity and economic integration generally on the back of agricultural protectionism and maintains a seemingly unshakable attachment to the common agricultural policy (CAP). The key CAP mechanism, the variable import levy, is not subject to GATT discipline. Japan also protects its agriculture, making domestic prices of some products several times higher than world prices. A similar picture prevails in non-EC European countries. In other words, agriculture is a problem in most industrialized countries.

Prior to the Tokyo Round, and particularly in the Kennedy Round, the United States had started to agitate for increased disciplines in agriculture. This interest was specific to produce that the United States could export competitively, including wheat, feed grains, oilseeds, citrus, poultry, and tobacco. By contrast, U.S. protectionist interests remained strong in dairy, rice, sugar, cotton, meat, and wool. Despite this division within the sector, export interests were able to promote a negotiating position that favored increased discipline and some trade liberalization. In the Kennedy Round, the United States wanted to see a "tariffication," followed by a gradual negotiated reduction in these tariffs. The European Community, by contrast, introduced its concept of an aggregate measure of agricultural protection, known as the *montant de soutien*, for which it was seemingly prepared to negotiate in terms of some kind of ceiling, but not to reduce.

In essence, the EC position on agriculture was, and largely still is, that the CAP is sacrosanct, that stabilization is more important than liberalization, and that commodity arrangements and market sharing are the best way of dealing with any problems. Such ideas were and still are unattractive to the United States. The European Community wanted to keep the sector entirely separate from the rest of the Tokyo Round negotiation, and at the end of the day, refused to negotiate at all. That sectoral agreements were eventually reached for dairy and meat, where the United States and the Community share protectionist interests, testifies to the relative ease with which lowest common denominator interests can be accommodated in an international negotiation. Describing the meat and dairy arrangements as trade liberalizing would stretch the imagination. The International Dairy

Arrangement was built around minimum price commitments and the Arrangement Regarding Bovine Meat amounted to little more than a forum for the exchange of information.

Finally, the manner in which developing countries should participate in the trading system has been a source of difficulty and tension for many years. Some developing countries were active in the negotiations for an International Trade Organization in the late 1940s and had more interest in Havana Charter chapters on development and employment than in trade aspects. When the charter failed to materialize, participation in GATT was comparatively muted for several years. Not until the late 1950s and early 1960s did developing countries begin to assume a more active role in the GATT. Their fundamental preoccupation has been the belief that the system was designed only to serve industrial country interests. Developing countries have consistently claimed that GATT rules do not take account of the special needs created by their economic situation and urgent need for development. Developing countries have sought more flexible disciplines for their import regimes and unhampered preferential access for their exports to industrial country markets.

In a major review of the GATT in 1955, some provisions were modified to ensure more ready access to infant-industry and balance-of-payments protection for developing countries. During these years, developing countries invested a good deal of effort in trying to secure duty-free treatment for their exports to developed countries, but with only partial success. In the early 1960s, increased emphasis was placed on proposals for trade preferences. In 1964, three articles were added to the GATT, referred to as Part IV. This addition had symbolic significance in its explicit recognition that developing countries had special problems and needs. As for its content, however, developing countries were generally disappointed. The new provisions did not provide legal cover for a departure from nondiscriminatory treatment, which would have been necessary for preference systems. They merely specified some "best endeavors" commitments by industrial countries to give priority to the trade interests of developing countries and a commitment to seek to avoid imposing additional barriers to their trade. The other major Part IV innovation was a statement that developed countries did not expect reciprocity from developing countries. An interpretative note to the provision explained that:

> [T]he less-developed contracting parties should not be expected, in the course of trade negotiations, to make contributions which are inconsistent with their individual development, financial and trade needs, taking into consideration past trade developments.[7]

In the years right after the introduction of Part IV, during the Kennedy Round and later, the Generalized System of Preferences was developed, and developing-country tariff preferences were introduced by many industrial countries. The U.S. preference system was introduced after congressional authorization in the Trade Act of 1974. From a legal standpoint in the GATT, the GSP was covered by a ten-year waiver, commencing in 1971.

Developing-country strategy became more concerted and strident in the Tokyo Round than ever before. This reflected a number of factors. First, the relative position of developing countries had changed, as several of them had grown rapidly and begun to represent a new force in international trade. Second, the creation in 1964 of the United Nations Conference on Trade and Development (UNCTAD), had given developing countries a forum for coordinating and articulating common positions. Third, developing countries still felt that some features of the trading system were hostile to their interests. Finally, in the context of the Tokyo Round they opted for a strategy of consolidating and codifying their gains in the field of preferences and ensuring that the new agreements gave them special and differential treatment as a matter of course. They were partially successful in achieving these objectives, but how much they have benefited from the arrangements is questionable.

THE RESULTS OF THE TOKYO ROUND

The results of the Tokyo Round may be summarized under four headings: tariffs, nontariff measure agreements, the "framework" agreements, and unfinished business.

Tariffs

The nontariff results and the failure to reach agreement in certain key areas eclipsed the considerable tariff results of the Tokyo Round. After much debate, agreement was reached in 1977 to reduce tariffs across the board by a weighted formula proposed by the Swiss, reducing higher tariffs proportionately more than lower ones. Despite some product exemptions, the formula reduced tariff escalation. The formula was applied by major industrial countries, and the reductions were supplemented by tariff line negotiations, product by product, between countries. This bilateral negotiating, with subsequent multilateralization of exchanges, is the traditional GATT negotiating technique.

The weighted-average tariff reductions made on manufactured products by nine major industrial countries[8] in the Tokyo Round amounted to 34 percent of the pre-Tokyo Round rate, leaving an actual weighted average tariff of

4.7 percent.[9] The corresponding figures for the United States were 31 percent and 6.4 percent. Taking agriculture and industry together, about 27,000 tariff lines, 75 percent of all duty-bound tariff lines in industrial countries, were subject to reductions. Taken together, tariff reductions and bindings by all countries during the Tokyo Round covered trade worth $155 billion.

Nontariff Measures

Six agreements (codes) were established in the Tokyo Round on nontariff measures. These covered government procurement, technical barriers to trade, subsidies and countervailing duties, customs valuation, import licensing, and antidumping. Each one will be described briefly.

The Government Procurement Code, the only one of the six not rooted in the GATT, seeks to narrow government's scope for using preferential procurement to give domestic producers additional protection. The terms of the code apply only to purchasing entities in signatory countries listed in an annex to the agreement. Essentially, the code obligations are to extend national and nondiscriminatory treatment to fellow signatories in procurement matters.

The Code on Technical Barriers to Trade seeks to prevent the erection of unnecessary obstacles to trade, and to ensure nondiscrimination and national treatment with respect to standards, technical regulations, testing methods, and certification systems. It also encourages the adoption of international standards and spells out procedural obligations designed to ensure a maximum of transparency about standards and their application.

The code on subsidies and countervailing duties is formally known as the Agreement on Interpretation and Application of Articles VI, XVI, and XXIII. This Code seeks to clarify, but not significantly modify, preexisting rules on subsidies, to spell out procedures for using countervailing duties, and provide a dispute-settlement mechanism. One important change was the extension of the prohibition on export subsidies to metals and minerals. A code innovation was the introduction of the possibility of undertakings by exporters faced with countervailing-duty actions. In addition, its dispute-settlement procedures envisaged the possibility of bringing a complaint for nullification or impairment of trade benefits even where no legal violation has occurred. This concept also exists in the GATT but it was taken further in the subsidies code as a palliative for weak disciplines on production subsidies.

The customs valuation code is formally known as the Agreement on Implementation of Article VII. It seeks to establish a single, more precise system of customs valuation than the one described in Article VII of the GATT. Above all, customs valuation and the procedures associated with it should not act as a hidden barrier to trade. As far as actual valuation methods are concerned, the code sets out five methods of valuation, to be applied sequentially when a method higher in the hierarchy cannot be applied. Developing countries are permitted to phase in the code's provisions gradually, and are also permitted certain leeway with respect to the valuation methods.

The Agreement on Import Licensing Procedures establishes the principle that licensing procedures should be neutral in application and equitably administered. In effect, this code is straightforward and basically procedural in content.

The antidumping code, formally called the Agreement on Implementation of Article VI, is similar to the one on subsidies and countervailing duties, both conceptually and in some of its provisions. Like the countervailing-duty rules, the imposition of antidumping duties requires proof of injury to domestic producers and the duties must be just enough to remedy the injury. Thus, a clear, causal link must be established between injury and imports. A code innovation, similar to the countervailing-duty rules, is that price undertakings may be accepted from exporters as an alternative to antidumping duties.

Finally, in addition to the dairy and bovine meat agreements mentioned previously, a side agreement was reached on trade in civil aircraft. The Agreement on Trade in Civil Aircraft eliminates tariffs on all civil aircraft and their parts, directs that the provisions of the standards code and subsidies code apply to the sector, provides that the application of any nontariff measures be consistent with GATT practice, and prevents signatories from obliging domestic airlines to purchase domestically manufactured aircraft.

The "Framework" Agreements

Four "Framework" Agreements were the main result of the developing-country negotiating effort in the Tokyo Round. They sought a firm contractual basis for discriminatory treatment in their favor. Perhaps the most important of these is the Decision on Differential and More Favorable Treatment, Reciprocity and Fuller Participation of Developing Countries (also known as the Enabling Clause). The developing countries' opening position was that a standing legal basis should be created for exceptions from MFN to permit industrial countries to introduce preference systems in favor of the developing countries. Voluntary preferential arrangements were not envisaged, but rather an obligatory, nondiscriminatory system that would operate on the same footing as other GATT obligations, including those on dispute settlement, compensation, and retaliation.

In the end, the Enabling Clause provided a permanent legal basis for GSP but did not require individual countries to extend such treatment. The clause provides cover for special and differential treatment under the Tokyo Round codes but leaves details of such treatment to each code. Also, provision is made for tariff preference arrangements among developing countries, requiring no other legal cover and avoiding the more stringent requirements of the regular GATT procedures for customs unions and free trade areas. Finally, the Enabling Clause makes special provision for least developed countries.

Treatment of the reciprocity issue is one particularly interesting and important feature of the Enabling Clause. In the negotiations, the developing countries insisted on a reiteration of the principle of nonreciprocity, originally spelled out in Part IV. At the same time, the industrial countries argued that nonreciprocity could not be open-ended, since its fundamental justification was the development imperative, which would not last forever. Therefore, argued the industrial countries, in exchange for recognition of the nonreciprocity principle, the developing countries must make a commitment to participate more fully in the system as their development situation permits. The latter notion, known as the "graduation" concept, also appears in the Enabling Clause. As may be expected from such abstract formulations, the twin issues of nonreciprocity and graduation remain problematic and prominent in discussion between industrial and developing countries.

The other three Framework Agreements involve rules on the use of trade restrictions for balance-of-payments purposes (the Declaration on Trade Measures Taken for Balance-of-Payments Purposes), the infant-industry exception for developing countries (Safeguard Action for Development Purposes), and the Understanding Regarding Notification, Consultation, Dispute Settlement, and Surveillance. The text on import restrictions for balance-of-payments purposes recognizes the previously established practice in some countries of applying import deposits or surcharges on imports instead of quantitative restrictions. It also carries a presumption that industrial countries will eschew import restrictions to deal with the balance-of-payments. The changes in the infant-industry provisions make it easier for developing countries to protect new firms and industries. The text on dispute settlement attempts to improve procedural aspects of existing arrangements by expediting processes and making them as transparent as possible.

Unfinished Business

Individual views would vary on how successful the negotiations had been in the areas described above, but agreement would be nearly universal that the Tokyo Round failed in two key areas, safeguards and agriculture. In safeguards, agreement was almost reached on a code, but the code was rejected because it allowed for discriminatory application of safeguards. Developing countries, fearful of what discrimination would mean for their new and dynamic export industries, spearheaded rejection of the code. In retrospect, allowing discrimination in this key area of trade regulation would have fundamentally changed the trading system. Rejection of the code, however, left the safeguards issue at the top of the negotiating agenda, with no sign of a resolution in sight.

Despite the two sectoral agreements on agriculture and, in the view of some, doubtless because of the policy direction they implied, the Tokyo Round failed to deal effectively with this agriculture. Probably more than any other single factor, the consequences of repeated failure to come to terms with agriculture have helped to undermine the integrity and credibility of the trading system. It is remarkable how little the underlying issues have changed, and how the rhetoric and the issues of the Kennedy Round were re-run in the Tokyo Round, and in the Uruguay Round.

ADOPTING THE TOKYO ROUND RESULTS

By April 1979, most of the Tokyo Round results had been virtually finalized. Among the outstanding issues was safeguards, on which work continued in vain until the end of 1979. Discussions also continued on agriculture. There were additional outstanding matters to settle in the fields of customs valuation and antidumping, some bilateral tariff negotiations to complete, and some issues in tropical products. The dairy arrangement also had to be finalized. The rest of the Tokyo Round results were incorporated in a *Procès-Verbal* on April 12, 1979.

Between April and November 1979, domestic ratification processes took place. In the United States, the executive branch worried about whether Congress would endorse or try to undo its efforts. A mixture of factors ensured a smooth process. The executive branch had been at pains throughout to keep Congress informed and its members involved in the negotiations, where appropriate. The private sector had been courted as well. There would be no surprises. The only international commitment subsequently modified involved a minor change in the area of procurement to protect some small minority interests. From a domestic process perspective, the Tokyo Round was a resounding success, dramatically different from the embarrassments after the Kennedy Round.

In terms of the trading system, however, some difficult problems remained to be resolved when it came to adopting the results of the negotiations. This stemmed essentially from the juridical status of the codes, which were self-contained agreements subscribed to by only some of the GATT membership. The issue was what the legal rights of nonsignatories would be when they did not subscribe to the disciplines of the codes. At a more general level, the question was how to maintain the universality of the trading system. For countries outside the codes, mostly developing countries, the issues were how to protect their acquired GATT rights, how to ensure transparency, and how to avoid being excluded from deliberations and processes that might impinge on their trade interests.

After much debate, the solution settled upon was to incorporate the codes into the GATT system through a Decision, made on November 28, 1979, entitled Action by the Contracting Parties on the Multilateral Trade Negotiations. The decision read in part:

> The Contracting Parties reaffirm their intention to ensure the unity and consistency of the GATT system, and to this end they shall oversee the operation of the system as a whole and take action as appropriate.

> The Contracting Parties also note that existing rights and benefits under the GATT of Contracting Parties not being parties to these Agreements, including those derived from Article I, are not affected by these Agreements.

Finally, the text also says that the GATT contracting parties will receive regular reports from the committees and councils established under the agreements and that nonsignatories would have observer rights for proceedings under the codes. This compromise could not hide what was a major new departure within the trading system. One more level of rights and obligations had been added within the system and the challenge of maintaining a coherent whole became even greater than before.

THE LEGACY OF THE TOKYO ROUND

The Tokyo Round results were, like any other multifaceted and complex exercise of this nature, a mixture. The codes on standards, import licensing, and customs valuation have unequivocally improved the international trading system. The government procurement code was a major advance in the reach of international disciplines, but a large part of the international trading community does not participate in it. This results in part from an unwillingness among governments to surrender the patronage afforded by procurement, but also from the way code signatories have defined the price of subscribing to the code.

The codes on subsidies and countervailing duties and on antidumping have not been successful. These remedies against unfair trading practices have increasingly lent themselves to protectionist ends. The detailed and complex procedures established have left many issues unclear. At least in part because of the lack of precision in the international agreements, national statutes have developed beyond the purview of these agreements and increasingly resemble instruments of protection that may conveniently serve as surrogates for selective safeguards. The Tokyo Round innovation of permitting exporters and the importing country to agree on undertakings has almost certainly increased the incentives for domestic producers to invoke these procedures.

The unfinished business of agriculture and safeguards are obvious lacunae in the international trading system. The Tokyo Round could not wrap them up and whether the Uruguay Round will do better remains to be seen. These issues have been on the negotiating agenda for so long that they hold no mystery. The issue is simply whether the political will exists to do something about them.

By failing to deal with the safeguards issue, the Tokyo Round left unresolved the question of how far the erosion of the MFN principle would be allowed to go before new disciplines were agreed upon. Indeed, the Tokyo Round complicated matters by introducing another dimension to the issue, conditional MFN. Apart from conditional MFN, the questions of protection-driven discrimination, regionalism, and special and differential treatment for developing countries will remain contentious matters for a long time to come.

CHAPTER 9

THE INTER-ROUND YEARS: 1980–86

The world economic situation was difficult in the 1970s. Sluggish growth, commodity price fluctuations, a rising price level, negative real interest rates, investment inertia, and falling employment rates had all become cause for serious concern. Macroeconomic adjustment in the early 1980s caused a sharp recession, whose full effects were not felt until 1982. Economic circumstances could hardly have been less propitious for multilateral trade negotiations, especially when they involved immediate, visible, and concentrated political and social costs. The gains were less obvious and longer term. Already acute protectionist pressures had been growing. Secular pressures were also at work: the globalization of the world economy and a shift away from a unipolar world power structure toward a multipolar one.

Another factor weighed on the trading system: problems carried over from the Tokyo Round remained intractable. Agriculture and safeguards were prominent among them, but textiles, subsidies, remedies against unfair trade practices, and the role and responsibility of developing countries in the trading system came up repeatedly throughout the 1980s. Agriculture was being debated in much the same way it had been for several years without any political movement. At the heart of the issue was continued European resistance to the arguments of the United States and other countries about the need for action on domestic protection levels and export subsidies in agriculture. If Japan had felt obliged to take a position, it would not have been very different from that of the Europeans.

189

In safeguards, the European Community (EC), silently supported by other European countries, held to the historical sticking point, that refurbished safeguard rules prohibiting all selective import controls were unacceptable. Various ways of securing compromise on this point were suggested, and rejected. The developing countries would not budge on nondiscrimination, since they believed that doing so would fatally undermine the basic pillar of the General Agreement on Tariffs and Trade (GATT). Japan and the United States had not adopted a strong position.

As discussion ground on, industrial countries took more and more selective safeguard actions in sensitive industries. The dynamics of domestic decisionmaking processes made it impossible for governments to await a multilateral solution. Thus, the existing Article XIX obligation to refrain from taking discriminatory safeguard action was in practice set aside. As voluntary export restraints, orderly marketing arrangements, industry to industry deals, and similar bilateral trade restrictions proliferated, settling the issue in the GATT became more difficult. The demonstration effect of the growth of illegal discriminatory arrangements further convinced those opposing selectivity of the justness and importance of their cause. Countries initiating the arrangements would have more and more difficulty agreeing to a solution that would call into question what they had been doing.

A third crucial element in the situation of the early 1980s was that the trading system was being stalked by the so-called "new" issues. Through initiatives put in train by the United States, and in significant measure subsequently supported by other industrial countries, GATT members were being asked to engage in negotiations for international commitments in a range of areas that had not been covered by the GATT. Among these were trade in services, minimum international labor standards, intellectual property issues, aspects of trade in high-technology goods, and trade-related investment measures.[1] These moves were regarded with suspicion and trepidation by some countries, especially those in the developing world, which saw them as yet another vehicle for making the trading system more demanding on them and less responsive to their needs.

THE 1982 MINISTERIAL MEETING

Despite the Tokyo Round's positive results on balance and their implementation on schedule, the U.S. administration and other governments were increasingly persuaded that only fresh political initiatives could stem growing protectionism and disorder in the trading system.

Eighteen months after the Tokyo Round ended, the GATT Consultative Group of Eighteen (CG-18)[2] agreed in June 1981 that the overall situation in the trading system should be considered by a ministerial meeting during the annual meeting of the GATT contracting parties in Geneva in November 1982. The declared purpose of the meeting was "to examine the functioning of the multi-lateral trading system, and to reinforce the common efforts of the contracting parties to support and improve the system for the benefit of all nations."[3]

GATT focused on preparing for this ministerial meeting throughout 1982. The Preparatory Committee for the meeting compiled an inventory of issues that had been suggested for consideration by ministers over the previous year. The list was long,[4] twenty-five to thirty separate items. In GATT terms, this was an extraordinary development, perhaps most of all because of the suddenness with which it happened. Until the Tokyo Round, little consideration had been given to anything but tariffs. Most nontariff measures coming out of the Tokyo Round were elaborations on existing GATT provisions, except for the government procurement code. Suddenly, the GATT agenda was wide open. Partly unfinished business from the Tokyo Round, partly new issues, this lengthy list grew as countries added their own particular interests.

Once open season on the agenda had been declared, less time was available to address individual issues. It also presented new negotiating and coalitional possibilities. Uncertainty and concern were perhaps the most important messages conveyed by the diffuse agenda. No satisfactory way was found to pare down the list. Despite an intense work schedule and multiple efforts at drafting a ministerial declaration, the Preparatory Committee never came near agreement. This meant that around seventy ministers from eighty-eight countries were presented with a panoply of negotiating issues. The ministerial part of the meeting was scheduled to begin on Wednesday, November 24, and finish at mid-day the following Saturday. Ministers were still meeting in the small hours of Monday morning, November 29.

Even after the final text had been agreed, the consensus was called into question. Australia issued a strong condemnation of the entire meeting. Part of the statement, delivered on behalf of the trade minister, read:

> [T]he Minister . . . made it clear that what was needed from this meeting was a conclusion which contained a real political commitment which would help all of us to withstand the protectionist pressures which all of us now face.
>
> [T]he document before us . . . falls well short of this objective. It is a papering over of a number of the real issues. In most, if not all, of

the important issues, the words are vague, ambiguous and shrink from firm commitments.

As a result, Australia is not able to associate itself with this document and reluctantly cannot accept that, in itself, it represents a successful and adequate outcome to this meeting.[5]

The European Community also issued an interpretative dissenting statement (see below). The 1982 ministerial meeting was fractious and frustrating. Negotiating in public, ministers ended up fighting in public. Discord was very visible on fundamental issues facing the trading system, most notably in agriculture and safeguards, and a number of the new issues placed on the agenda by the United States. Though countries stopped short of an impasse that would have been interpreted as a collapse of the GATT, confidence in the multilateral trading system was shaken. To avoid stalemate, countries had to compromise. The United States, as one of the most active participants, and in a leadership role, found itself compromising on several fronts.

The Results of the Ministerial Meeting

The 1982 Ministerial Declaration[6] contains a political part and an operational part. The political part of the document starts with a frank diagnosis of the problems facing the trading system:

[T]he multilateral trading system . . . is seriously endangered. In the current crisis of the world economy, to which the lack of convergence in national economic policies has contributed, protectionist pressures on governments have multiplied, disregard of GATT disciplines has increased and certain shortcomings in the functioning of the GATT system have been accentuated.

This may be the most direct, shared statement ever made of what is wrong with the GATT trading system.

The "standstill and rollback" commitment was the second important feature of the political part of the declaration. The contracting parties undertook, individually and jointly:

[T]o make determined efforts to ensure that trade policies and measures are consistent with GATT principles and rules and to resist protectionist pressures in the formulation and implementation of national trade policy and in proposing legislation; and also to

refrain from taking or maintaining any measures inconsistent with
GATT and to make determined efforts to avoid measures which
would limit or distort international trade.

Before 1982, standstill commitments had consisted of an undertaking not to
increase trade restrictions during a negotiation only to be able to negotiate
them down again. The 1982 statement, however, is conceptually quite different. The standstill part is a promise not to behave in a GATT-illegal fashion.
The rollback part, to "refrain from . . . maintaining any measures inconsistent
with GATT," is a tacit admission of past wrong-doing.

Apart from the insight that this kind of commitment offers into the state
of international trading relations, it is remarkable that governments did not
mind limiting themselves to making "determined efforts" to abide by their
international treaty obligations. These concepts of standstill and rollback
became more entrenched and central to the GATT process in the Uruguay
Round. Standstill and rollback commitments do not fit well with the GATT's
juridical framework. Arguably, they weaken it. Although considerable political importance is attached to the commitments, the conclusion is difficult to
avoid that they are as likely to raise fundamental doubts about the meaning of
international undertakings as they are to influence trade policy decisions.

The disagreement that emerged over the wording of the standstill and
rollback commitment illustrates the folly of attempting to use political expedients to solve problems of legal obedience. The issue at stake was whether the
words "to make determined efforts" at the beginning of the paragraph quoted
above referred only to the commitment down to the semicolon, or whether
they also applied to the commitment "to refrain from taking or maintaining
any measures inconsistent with GATT." In other words, was the standstill and
rollback commitment of the "best endeavors" variety? If it was not, the commitment might be construed not merely as a variation on the motto of the Boy
Scouts, but as a firm undertaking to take no GATT-illegal measures and to
remove those taken in the past.

The text can be interpreted either way. Language of this kind does not
reflect the limited literary skills of its drafters; it is heavily negotiated.
Sometimes such formulations offer constructive ambiguity. This one, however,
is more a case of destructive obfuscation. That the point was contentious is
borne out in the unilateral statement issued by the European Community after
the ministerial meeting:

> As regards the undertaking . . . to refrain from taking or maintain-
> ing any measure inconsistent with GATT, the Communities

consider this undertaking to mean that its best efforts will be deployed to avoid taking or maintaining such measures.[7]

An undertaking was also made in the political part of the declaration to "abstain from taking restrictive trade measures, for reasons of a non-economic character, not consistent with the General Agreement." This language reflected Argentina's position in relation to the trade embargoes imposed on it by the European Community and some other countries following the Falklands/Malvinas war with Britain.[8] This dispute in GATT, and later litigation between Nicaragua and the United States, have demonstrated how ineffectual the GATT is in dealing with trade disputes motivated by nontrade considerations.

The operational portion of the Ministerial Declaration set forth seventeen separate mandates for action. These made up the Work Program, most of it over two years, with instructions to report back to the contracting parties at their 1984 session. The mandates will be treated individually, since they provide a useful insight into the directions in which the GATT has headed in the 1980s and a fuller understanding of what is currently at stake in the international trading system.

The mandate on *safeguards* reflected the work of the Safeguards Committee since the Tokyo Round. While no progress had been made over the central question of selectivity in safeguards, some work had been done to tease out the elements that a decision on safeguards would have to address. The 1982 text called for a comprehensive understanding, to be drawn up for adoption by the Contracting Parties not later than their 1983 session. Based on the principles of GATT, the comprehensive understanding was to deal with transparency, coverage, objective criteria for action including the concept of serious injury or threat thereof, temporary nature, digressivity and structural adjustment, compensation and retaliation, notification, consultation, multilateral surveillance, and dispute settlement. In the event, the safeguards problem remained unresolved and was carried over as an important issue in the Uruguay Round.

In the text on GATT *rules and activities relating to developing countries*, a number of initiatives were put in motion. Among them was a program of consultations to examine how individual contracting parties had responded to the requirements of Part IV of the GATT. The provisions of Part IV, it will be recalled, concern policy actions, to be taken or resisted, in the light of the development and trade needs of the developing countries. Part IV calls for priority attention to be given to these needs but does not permit departures from the MFN principle. It also spells out the principle of nonreciprocity. At the insistence of the United States, developing countries were also to participate in the Part IV consultations, even though Part IV commitments applied overwhelmingly to developed countries.

The Ministerial Declaration contained a lengthy text on *dispute-settlement procedures*. These procedures had been modified in the Tokyo Round, and the 1982 text represented a further attempt to improve matters. That the dispute-settlement mechanism needed improvement was dramatized by the record number of cases brought to the GATT in 1981 and 1982. This was taken both as a sign of the times and as an affirmation of a willingness to use the multilateral route to settle differences, but it did show how the procedures could be further improved. Much attention was focused on what were seen as excessive delays and the need for greater transparency. Further improvements were provisionally made in the procedures early in the Uruguay Round. There has always been an awareness that, however good the dispute-settlement procedures, their effectiveness depends ultimately on the contracting parties' political willingness to submit to multilateral adjudication and act upon the results.

Since the end of the Tokyo Round, discussions on *trade in agriculture* had concentrated on "access and competition." Access was concerned with the range of import-inhibiting polices used by governments to reserve the domestic market for local producers. Competition dealt with subsidies, especially their effects on sales in third markets. Three other issues were also examined. These were access to supplies, GATT disciplines in agriculture, and the various means by which governments had exempted themselves from the application of these rules.

After protracted argument, it was agreed to establish a Committee on Trade in Agriculture to carry out an intensive two-year work program. The program was to lead to "appropriate recommendations" covering "all measures affecting trade, market access, and competition and supply in agricultural products. . . ." It is an indication of the sensitivity of the issue that the text also says that "full account shall be taken of the need for a balance of rights and obligations under the GATT . . . [and] of specific characteristics and problems in agriculture. . . ."

On November 27, two days before final agreement on the Ministerial Declaration, the European Community had sent a letter to the chairman of the meeting, setting out what it regarded as an acceptable text on agriculture. The declaration made by the Community at the end of the meeting referred to above, noted that not all EC suggestions had been adopted. Certain relevant portions of the earlier text were repeated, and the declaration also said:

[W]hile we accept and fully support a major work program on agriculture which will examine all measures on the same basis, we underline that this acceptance is on the understanding that this is not a commitment to any new negotiation or obligation in relation to agricultural products.

The Community clearly felt on the defensive in agriculture and has continued to maintain that its common agricultural policy is inviolable. The United States and other countries were pressing for some action or agreed language which would, more or less explicitly, signal a commitment to prepare for actual negotiations. This did not happen until the run-up to the Uruguay Round.

The mandate on *tropical products* called for "consultations and appropriate negotiations aimed at further liberalization of trade in tropical products." Tropical products have always been a sector symbolic of the trade interests of the developing countries in the GATT, and of the idea that industrial countries could do something concrete to benefit the developing countries. Successive attempts to secure trade liberalization in tropical products have always produced rancor, as industrial countries have been unwilling to go very far with a unilateral approach to liberalization, whereas this is what the developing countries have expected. For the first time, the issue came into the open in 1982. The reference to "appropriate negotiations" was industrial country code for the idea that any trade liberalization would have to be negotiated through an exchange of concessions involving at least some developing countries. In the event, the code words were not given the same interpretation by all countries. After extensive consultations, and some modest and desultory unilateral liberalization measures by some developed countries, the process foundered. The matter did not resurface until the Uruguay Round.

Quantitative restrictions and other nontariff measures were to be reviewed in terms of the grounds on which they were maintained and their conformity with the GATT. Quantitative trade restrictions are illegal under GATT except in carefully defined circumstances (chapter 7). This item was included in the work program because many countries were resorting to quantitative restrictions without having satisfied their trading partners that there was any GATT justification for them. The review was aimed at achieving the "elimination of quantitative restrictions which are not in conformity with the General Agreement or their being brought into conformity with the General Agreement. . . ."

A perennial problem has been the question whether or not existing restrictions are consistent with GATT. Related to this is the question whether such a determination can be made to identify what is and what is not negotiable. The EC declaration after the meeting states:

> [W]e recall that there is a long historical background to the few residual measures which still exist within the Community; and that, if we are to achieve further liberalization, this will have to take account of the fact that there is an imbalance in the level of commitments which Contracting Parties have accepted.

This issue was carried over to the Uruguay Round, although in 1985 the European Community did take some unilateral action on residual restrictions.

There was little to say about *tariffs* in the 1982 context. The Tokyo Round reductions were still being phased in, and tariffs usually do not become an issue until a negotiation is in prospect. Nevertheless, India and Brazil did raise the question of tariff escalation[9] in the Preparatory Committee, and it was agreed to give prompt attention to the issue "with a view to effective action toward the elimination or reduction of such escalation where it inhibits international trade. . . ."

The contracting parties decided to "review the operation of the *MTN Agreements and Arrangements*[10] . . . with a view to determining what action if any is called for, in terms of their decision of 1979." The review was to focus on the adequacy and effectiveness or the MTN codes and on obstacles to their acceptance by interested parties. There were essentially two issues here. One was the discriminatory application of some provisions of the codes, most notably the selective application by the United States of the injury test in countervailing-duty investigations. The other was a generalized complaint by the developing countries that their exclusion from meaningful participation in the design of the codes in the Tokyo Round had produced results that made signature of some codes difficult for them. An examination of this issue under the 1982 Work Program did not identify many concrete problems in this sense, and in any case, the codes were subject to fundamental reappraisal and some renegotiation in the Uruguay Round.

The mandate on *structural adjustment and trade policy* was carried over from the Tokyo Round Work Program. The basic objective of this exercise was to provide a context for discussing the relationship between open trade, protection, and the domestic adjustment consequences of trade liberalization. It was never intended as a negotiating exercise. The GATT discussion on structural adjustment and trade policy, which was carried out by a Working Party on the basis of submissions from contracting parties and GATT secretariat documentation, probably raised general awareness of the links between trade policy and other policies that might support or frustrate the objectives of trade policy.

The mandate on *trade in counterfeit goods* responded directly to U.S. initiatives in this area. The issue had been discussed around the margins of the Tokyo Round, and the United States had developed a draft code for dealing with trade in counterfeit goods. The code reflected a concern shared by certain countries that counterfeit goods were increasingly entering world trade. Support at that time had been inadequate to take the issue further, despite U.S. insistance, with some support from other countries, that counterfeiting was a serious and growing problem. The proponents of GATT action in this field insisted that the basic focus of the exercise was on trade actions to deal with trade problems. Developing countries questioned the GATT relevance of the issue, at least in the short term, and saw action here as potentially reducing their export earnings. For these reasons, a firm mandate for action could not be secured. Instead, the Contracting Parties instructed the GATT Council "to examine the question . . . with a view to determining the appropriateness of joint action in the GATT framework on the trade aspects of commercial counterfeiting and, if such joint action is found to be appropriate, the modalities for such action . . ." An Expert Group was established in 1984 to continue examining the issue. The narrower issue of counterfeiting was overtaken by the Uruguay Round negotiations on a range of other intellectual property issues.

The topic of *export of domestically prohibited goods* found its way onto the 1982 Work Program through a proposal by Sri Lanka and Nigeria. It responded to concern about the disposal of unwanted and possibly harmful goods in developing-country markets when they could not be sold domestically in industrial countries. It was agreed that contracting parties should, to the maximum extent feasible, notify to GATT any goods produced and exported that were banned for domestic sale. This matter is being pursued, but outside the framework of the Uruguay Round. Support for action on the issue has not been overwhelming, but it has increased as environmental concerns grow.

The question of *export credits for capital goods* was raised by members of the Association of South East Asian Nations (ASEAN). The developing countries have two conflicting concerns here, bearing in mind that government export credit for capital goods is almost universally available. As importers, developing countries want to acquire capital goods as cheaply as possible and are pleased to benefit from subsidized credit in exporting countries. As exporters, however, developing countries do not want to compete with richer countries on the terms of subsidized credits. Although the former concern was addressed in the 1982 context, the latter lurks in the background for some countries. Moreover, under the auspices of the Organization for Economic Cooperation and Development (OECD), the tendency in the last few years has been to look for reductions in this kind of subsidy. For these reasons, and because the issue was already fairly marginal for the countries that raised it, nothing has happened.

Textiles and clothing was made an issue in 1982 by many exporting developing countries. No fewer than twenty-five developing countries proposed some language that would effectively have been a commitment to the expeditious phase-out of the Multi-Fiber Arrangement (MFA). This position was somewhat weakened by the fact that MFA III had just entered into force at the end of 1981 and would run until the summer of 1986. In the end, agreement was reached to study trade in textiles, the effects of current restrictive regimes in the sector, and the trade effects of the removal or the maintenance of such regimes. An extensive study was completed, and following agreement on MFA IV in 1986, the Uruguay Round mandate brought the possibility of eliminating the MFA a little closer. Following the failure to complete the Uruguay Round on schedule, MFA IV was extended for seventeen months, until the end of 1992, and then again until the end of 1993.

The 1982 mandate on *problems of trade in certain natural resource products* covers a collection of sectoral issues raised in the Preparatory Committee. The sectors were nonferrous metals and minerals (Peru), forestry products (Chile), and fish and fisheries products (Canada). Largely on the basis of a Canadian initiative, a "sectoral approach" negotiation had been used in the Tokyo Round, but it did not come to anything. In 1982, the mandate merely called for an examination of trade problems and recommendations for their solution. As a direct offshoot of this exercise, an expanded list of sectors was examined in the Uruguay Round. A sectoral focus is problematic in that it is either special pleading for additional protection, in which case strong interests are probably behind the initiative, or it is a demand for priority trade liberalization. In the latter case, coordinated support is harder to marshall, particularly as the act of singling out a sector is likely to be taken by trading partners to imply that countries interested in the issue are willing to offer something extra in a negotiation. Generally, they are not. The choice of sectors is in any case invidious, because every contracting party could think of some sector in which accelerated trade liberalization would be particularly attractive.

Exchange rate fluctuations and their effect on trade was another EC issue. Some member governments had become frustrated with the effects of large speculative capital flows on exchange rates and wanted to make the case that volatile exchange rates had deleterious effects on trade and should be controlled.

Under the 1982 mandate, the International Monetary Fund (IMF) was to be invited to study the effects of exchange rate volatility on international trade. The IMF study did not provide strong support for the idea of a significant trade effect. In 1984 the Contracting Parties acknowledged that exchange rate fluctuations could in certain circumstances contribute to uncertainty and increased protectionist pressures, but they also said that protective trade action could not remedy the problem. It was also recognized that smaller traders with geographically concentrated import and export markets may have a harder time coping with erratic exchange rate movements than larger traders. The European Community returned to the matter toward the end of 1990, with the demand that the Uruguay Round results include a declaration on policy coherence containing a reference to the problem of exchange rate volatility.

The mandates on *dual pricing and rules of origin* simply called for studies, on the basis of which the issues were to be further considered. Rules of origin refers to the criteria that countries use to determine the origin of products entering trade. This determination is necessary under preferential trading arrangements and wherever any kind of discriminatory trade measure is applied. Such rules can act as a barrier to trade. Dual pricing refers to the practice of maintaining a price differential on the same product according to whether it is sold domestically or exported. Export restrictions, for example, can lower the domestic price of a good to the advantage of domestic users. The United States had raised the rules of origin question. The Community had raised dual pricing, with specific reference to this practice in the oil market, and also to export restrictions. In the 1982 Ministerial Declaration, there seemed to be an assumption that the entirely unrelated issues of rules of origin and dual pricing could be coupled so that they would cancel each other out. They were dropped, although rules-of-origin reappeared as an issue in the Uruguay Round. Export restrictions were not taken up in 1982, and neither had the work in this area come to anything in the Tokyo Round.

The decision in 1982 on *services* was considerably less than the United States had hoped for, but support for action in the GATT was limited at that time. Nevertheless, it was a first step in placing services on the international trade agenda. The 1982 mandate recommended to "each contracting party with an interest in services of different types to undertake, as far as it is able, national examination of the issues in this sector." It invited contracting parties to exchange information on such matters among themselves. The results of these activities were to be reviewed at the 1984 session of the Contracting Parties, when consideration would also be given to the question whether any multilateral action was appropriate or desirable. The phrasing of the mandate made it obvious that there was no joint commitment to pursue any action at all in GATT, not even of an exploratory nature.

The United States had hoped for a clearer and more positive mandate for the multilateral study of problems in the services area. The idea was to analyze the applicability of GATT principles, rules, and procedures to services, using an inventory of barriers to trade in services as a basis for the work. This would have led to a decision on what action to take within GATT. Even the modest mandate achieved proved difficult to work on within GATT in 1983 and 1984, largely because of opposition from developing countries. These countries resorted to procedural tactics to frustrate the exercise. When meetings were held in the GATT building among certain delegations, the developing countries protested that this was an illegitimate use of multilateral facilities. They supported this argument by claiming that the 1982 decision required national studies to be conducted before any exchange of information. Thus, until a representative number of contracting parties had undertaken national studies, there should be no meetings. The catch was that the national studies would not be representative if the developing countries did not participate in them.

The services issue was new. Not until the Trade Act of 1974 did a mandate exist for negotiations on services. In the legislation, which provided negotiating authority for the Tokyo Round, international trade is defined to include trade in both goods and services. In the event, the United States made some bilateral requests for trade liberalization in services, but it did not propose services as a negotiating issue in the Tokyo Round.

Although some industrial countries had initially not been convinced of the desirability or feasibility of dealing with trade in services in the GATT context, these concerns were largely dispelled within a year or two of the 1982 decision. The real opposition to the initiative came from the developing countries, and it was strong. The basic position was that the GATT was not competent to deal with trade in services, nor were the GATT's principles and objectives suited to such an undertaking. The competence argument was intrinsically weak, because the competence of the GATT is determined by the contracting parties, and implicit in such a determination is a judgment on the applicability or otherwise of the principles and objectives of the organization.

What was behind developing-country opposition to the inclusion of trade in services in the GATT? An adequate answer must take a number of diverse factors into consideration. To begin with, the enthusiasm and determination with which the United States embraced its services initiative gave rise to suspicion, and the classic doubt that what was good for the United States would serve developing-country interests. The situation was not helped by a lack of specificity on the part of the United States about what it wanted and why.[11] Basically, knowledge and understanding of the issue was scant. More substantially, developing countries were disillusioned with the pace of progress in GATT's traditional areas of competence, where they considered their real trade interests to lie. By branching off into new areas, the industrial countries would be less likely to attend to outstanding traditional issues, they thought, and the agenda was already crowded with unfinished business. Third, there was a feeling that incorporating services into GATT negotiations would give developed countries one more instrument to extract concessions from developing countries. The industrial countries would press for access to developing-country services markets in exchange for access to their goods markets.

On the substance of the services issue, many government officials were firmly of the view that services were too different from goods to be incorporated within the same framework. A particular concern was the effect of open services markets on sovereignty and on the capacity of governments to exercise control. In addition, many services seemed to require the physical proximity of the supplier and the consumer in order for a sale to be transacted. This meant that suppliers would want to establish production in the domestic market to reach consumers. It looked as if, in the name of liberalization of trade in services, countries would be opening their doors to foreign investment, which was yet another sensitive area of government policy control. Even if modern communications technology sometimes obviates the need for physical proximity, a substantial problem remained, controlling and measuring cross-border flows of services.

Returning to the procedural issues in the GATT in the early 1980s, the logjam over whether or not the GATT secretariat and building could be used for meetings on services was broken in 1984 by a Contracting Party decision. By that decision, the chairman of the contracting parties was to organize the exchange of information envisaged in the 1982 mandate and the GATT secretariat was to provide necessary support. Many developing countries still opposed the entire enterprise. The process of exchanging information continued throughout 1985, but against a background of heightened tension. In 1985 the issue took on a symbolic importance far beyond services-related considerations. It became the chosen battleground for the much wider debate about where the GATT system was going and whether or not the time was ripe for a new round of negotiations.

The Balance Sheet for the United States

For the United States, the results of the 1982 Ministerial Meeting were mixed. The objectives of the United States in 1982 could be summed up under three headings. First, it wanted to address certain long-standing problems.

Second, this was the first occasion on which the United States orchestrated a purposeful drive toward "modernizing" the GATT by extending it to new areas and redefining certain relationships within the institution. Third, though not explicitly stated, it seems that the United States would have liked the 1982 meeting to be the first step in preparing for a new round of negotiations.

In traditional areas of concern, agriculture takes pride of place. The resistance of the European Community prevented acceptance of the kind of commitment in principle to trade liberalization and improved discipline wanted by the United States. In retrospect, however, the 1982 Work Program did result in a significant amount of preparatory work that was later used to develop the Uruguay Round negotiating mandate. In other traditional areas, the United States was not the *demandeur*, although in view of protectionist pressures in the United States and elsewhere at the time, progress on safeguards and dispute-settlement procedures was a definite U.S. interest.

In the new areas, placing services on the multilateral agenda for the first time was an achievement, despite the somewhat tentative fashion in which it was done. On intellectual property issues, the situation was similar. The introduction of trade in counterfeit goods was the first step in a much broader and more ambitious enterprise, involving international standards and enforcement mechanisms for a wide range of intellectual property rights.

Two other issues raised by the United States in the Preparatory Committee were not included in the 1982 Work Program: aspects of trade in high-technology products and trade-related investment issues. The U.S. position regarding trade in high-technology products was that technological advances in such areas as electronics, telecommunications, fiber optics, robotics, and biotechnology were having an increasing impact on trade. At the same time, government support policies in these areas were exercising a significant influence on trade flows and the development of various industries. The United States recognized that these issues could be dealt with in the GATT in various contexts, but considered that a coordinated approach was called for.

Although the U.S. proposal was only for a study, on the basis of which subsequent decisions could be made, the initiative was seen as a proposal to control subsidies on research and development (R&D) expenditure. The European Community was set against this, partly because of some member states' interest in promoting advanced technology, but also because of the EC belief that the objectives of R&D spending in Europe were achieved more surreptitiously in the United States through defense spending. It was a matter of balanced competition. The issue was dropped at the last moment at the Ministerial Meeting, and it was agreed to take it up in the GATT Council. For the next two years, the United States sought agreement on a study of the issues, but was consistently blocked, principally by the Community. That the matter was not seriously pursued in the preparations for the Uruguay Round suggests that it was no longer a priority. It would seem that the United States preferred to fold the issue into the wider negotiations on subsidies. On the other hand, the prominence of the U.S.-EC airbus dispute in 1991 and 1992 indicated that the question of subsidies to high-technology industries is far from dead.

On trade-related investment measures, the United States was seeking recognition that investment policies could undermine and distort trade-liberalization efforts. Concern focused on the local content and export requirements that some countries linked to the authorization to invest. The 1982 proposal was for the establishment of an inventory of trade-distorting or restricting investment measures, an assessment of their impact, an analysis of the relevance of GATT articles to the issue, and an examination of ways GATT disciplines might be improved in this area. In view of the strength of the developing-country opposition to the inclusion of trade-related investment measures in the 1982 Work Program, the United States decided not to pursue the matter, considering all the other unresolved issues. This issue emerged again, in more far-reaching fashion, in the Uruguay Round.

The evolving policy of the United States, supported in some measure by other industrial countries, to question the assumptions underlying developing-country participation in the trading system also bears mention. The Tokyo Round had produced a series of texts codifying earlier practices exempting developing countries from certain GATT obligations. The impression after the Tokyo Round was that the developing countries were on the offensive, and part of the industrial countries' defensiveness derived from their unwillingness to take meaningful action in areas of particular interest to developing countries such as agriculture, textiles, and safeguards.

Under the trade pressures of the early 1980s, however, a deal built around exemptions for developing countries in exchange for noncompliance by industrial countries was too subtle and implicit to be sustainable. The contraction in import demand resulting from the debt crisis had highlighted the growing importance of some developing-country markets for countries like the United States. Added to this were the rising protectionist pressures of those years. The result was growing demands for higher levels of commitment and discipline within the trading system on the part of the more advanced and bigger developing countries. This only manifested itself in small ways in the 1982 Ministerial Declaration when, for example, the United States insisted that developing countries should also consult under Part IV and where tropical product negotiations were to have an explicit reciprocal element. However, by the time the debate about launching a new round of negotiations was underway, the graduation issue was a major underlying factor in some of the positions taken. The question became much more explicit in the Uruguay Round but has lost much of its sting as a result of the unilateral trade liberalization undertaken by so many developing countries starting in the mid-1980s.

Finally, although it is arguable that the United States had hoped that the 1982 Ministerial Meeting would create the conditions for launching a new round of trade negotiations, the Work Program that finally emerged from the meeting should have given some comfort. Just before, and during the meeting, there were grounds for doubting that agreement would be possible. The United States Trade Representative, Ambassador William Brock, had said just before the meeting that he was "convinced that the GATT system [was] in serious trouble."[12] The differences between the European Community and most of its trading partners over agriculture were the single most important reason initiatives for a new round were premature in 1982. On the other hand, if agriculture had not been the limiting factor, trade in services would have been.

In assessing the results of the Ministerial Meeting, Ambassador Brock said in congressional testimony that, in view of the economic climate, "perhaps our greatest achievement was in keeping the GATT system together and moving in a positive direction."[13] In important respects, the Work Program was a holding operation. In many areas, examinations of issues and studies were called for, and decisions were postponed. It would be simplistic to assume that the tension and disagreement, so manifest before the final deal was struck in 1982 and their rapid reemergence afterward, had not taken a toll on the credibility of the system. It would be surprising, for example, if the U.S. policy switch in the early 1980s toward the establishment of regional trading arrangements had not in part been motivated by doubts about the viability of multilateral processes. Indeed, the history of the development of Section 301 of the Trade Act of 1974 is a monument to the rejection of multilateral due process.

Yet, the United States has not tried, either then or since, to sabotage or withdraw from the multilateral trading system. It could well have done so but instead has preferred to play the game both ways. Whether the system can resist the pressure this puts on it is, of course, a basic question for this study. For the present purposes, a remark by Ambassador Brock in the same congressional testimony is worth recording. Noting that nothing had been achieved in respect of trade-related investment measures, he stated:

> The United States will move to protect its legitimate interests in this area. We will pursue our legitimate complaints, perhaps in a more

unilateral and confrontational manner than would have occurred if the GATT Ministerial had made more progress in this area.

NEGOTIATING THE LAUNCH OF THE URUGUAY ROUND

The years from 1983 to 1985 were among the most stressful in GATT history. The situation in 1985, in particular, was every bit as difficult as it had been in November 1982. The resilience of the GATT as an institution was once again tested to its limit. In mid-1983, even before the results of the 1982 Work Program could be judged, the idea of preparing for a new round of negotiations was floated. The initiative was taken by Prime Minister Nakasone of Japan, and in the June 1984 London Summit meeting, the seven major industrial powers agreed to consult among their trading partners about the objectives and timing of a new round. Considering where things were left in November 1982, and bearing in mind that by mid-1983 the first signs of economic recovery from the 1982 recession were appearing, the time seemed ripe to the major trading powers to start talking about a new round. Not all countries agreed, however. Some of the EC states were concerned about the implications of the initiative for agriculture. What might have been reservation in Europe was outright opposition in developing countries.

Some of the reasons for developing countries' reluctance to contemplate a new round have been touched upon. Many developing countries felt ignored when it came to their trading interests, and threatened when it came to those of their developing-country trading partners. If enough developing countries could have been convinced that their trade interests in areas like textiles and agriculture would receive serious attention, the opposition that built to the idea of a new round could have been diffused at the outset and not after a bitter battle of attrition. As it was, developing countries did not believe they would benefit at all from a new round, but they did see significant potential developments that they regarded as inimical to their interests. These related to the new areas and to the interpretation of developing-country status under the GATT.

Concerns about trade in services sprung from a lack of information on the issues and on the intentions of the United States, the fear that traditional trade issues would be ignored in a "modernized" GATT, and substantive concerns about such matters as the relation between trade in services and investment. In effect, these concerns were also relevant to some of the other new issues that the United States was promoting, particularly trade-related investment rights and intellectual property issues. These issues received so little attention in the debate prior to the decision to launch the Uruguay Round because of the essentially political component of developing-country opposition, which was conveniently encapsulated in the services discussions. Although more and more developing countries refrained from opposing the U.S. initiatives in these areas as time went on, the final settlement of the Uruguay Round negotiating agenda had to wait until the last stages of the Punta del Este meeting that launched the round, in September 1986. Informal discussion on new negotiations began in GATT in early 1985. In May, the European Community proposed a meeting of high officials to consider the issues involved in launching a new round.

Although voting procedures are clearly set out in the GATT, they have hardly ever been used to decide a contentious matter. The established practice is consensus, since the enforcement of unpopular decisions on contracting parties would normally be impossible. After bitter and inconclusive debate on the proposal during the summer, the United States called for a vote. In calling for the vote, the United States must have been reasonably confident of its ability to muster the necessary majority. The confidence was justified. A Special Session of the Contracting Parties was convened in early October. At that session, the Contracting Parties agreed that a preparatory process had been started on the proposed new round of multilateral trade negotiations, and that a group of senior officials would be established to further that process.

All the issues in the 1982 Work Program were discussed by the officials, and a few more besides. The additional issues raised included the state-trading provisions of the GATT, the rules on regional arrangements, procedures for renegotiating tariff concessions, various aspects of the functioning of the GATT system, countertrade, high technology, and investment. The GATT agenda had become even more wide-ranging, as old issues were revived and new ones introduced. It proved impossible for the senior officials' group to reach agreement on the terms of its report to the contracting parties, as the positions of key developing countries remained firm. However, before the contracting parties had to make a decision in November, an informal agreement was reached among the main protagonists on the issue of the new round, including the United States, the European Community, Brazil, and India. The precise content of this arrangement was never revealed, but it allowed the Contracting Parties in November 1985 to establish a preparatory committee by consensus. The preparatory committee was directed to prepare recommendations by mid-July 1986 for the program of negotiations for adoption at a ministerial meeting in September 1986.

CHAPTER 10

THE URUGUAY ROUND

I n the nine months before the September 1986 ministerial meeting in Punta del Este that launched the Uruguay Round, progress toward a consensus was painfully slow. Indeed, several key issues were left open until the Punta del Este meeting and had to be settled by ministers at the last moment.[1] Virtually nothing happened in the Preparatory Committee for most of the first half of 1986.

THE PREPARATORY PHASE

The committee worked mechanically and repetitiously through a long list of negotiating issues. Since the 1982 Ministerial Meeting, countries had felt free to raise just about any trade or allegedly trade-related issue for consideration. This behavior reflected the view that countries regarded the entire trading system as being in flux and in need of redefinition. The list of topics before the Preparatory Committee was as follows: standstill; rollback; treatment of developing countries; safeguards; trade in agriculture; dispute-settlement procedures; tropical products; quantitative restrictions and other nontariff measures; Multilateral Tariff Negotiation (MTN) Agreements and Arrangements; subsidies; structural adjustment and trade policy; trade in counterfeit goods and other aspects of intellectual property; exports of domestically prohibited goods; textiles and clothing; export credits for capital goods; problems of trade in natural resource products; exchange rate fluctuations and their effect on trade; trade in services; General Agreement on Tariffs and Trade (GATT) Article XVII (state trading); GATT Article XXIV (customs unions and free trade areas); renegotiation of tariff concessions; functioning of the GATT system; notification and surveillance procedures; compensatory trade; trade in high-technology goods; trade-related investment measures; restrictive business practices; relationship between the new round and monetary and financial developments; workers' rights; and commodity price fluctuations. In all, the list contained thirty-one subjects. Nineteen items became the subject of specific negotiating mandates in the Uruguay Round, and four others were referred to in a preambular context.

The "balance-of-benefits" issue should also be mentioned here. Like the United States, the European Community has frequently complained about a lack of reciprocal access to the Japanese market. The Community has felt uninhibited about making these kinds of complaints in the GATT, while the United States has relied more on bilateral discussions and negotiations.[2] The balance-of-benefits question was one aspect of the EC attack on Japan's alleged protectionism and unwillingness to open its domestic market to foreign competition, while making significant inroads into other countries' home markets. The Community had fired an earlier salvo in its broad-based campaign against Japan with a request, in 1983, that a GATT working party examine the charge that Japan's policies led to a "nullification or impairment of the benefits otherwise accruing to the European Community under the GATT, and [were] an impediment to the attainment of GATT's objectives."[3] The EC complaint charged that: visible and invisible trade barriers; excessively complicated approval; testing; customs procedures; and a concentration and interlinking of production, finance, and distribution structures created an imbalance in contracting parties' access to GATT benefits.

Much of the argumentation relied on the existence of increasingly large bilateral trade imbalances. This reasoning rests on the same kind of results-oriented, ex post reckoning of reciprocity that was criticized earlier in relation to recent U.S. attitudes about fair trade. The EC allegations were also too general to allow a GATT-type procedure to work effectively. This was why the European Community asked for a GATT working party, and not a quasi-legal dispute-settlement panel, which is the usual procedure in such a case. Not surprisingly, Japan resisted what it no doubt saw as a demand for a GATT forum for "Japan bashing."[4] After somewhat inconclusive bilateral discussions, the request for the working party was eventually dropped.

The same issue was raised again by the European Community in the Preparatory Committee. The balance-of-benefits argument was simply that Japan was not making a contribution to the GATT trading system commensurate with its benefits under the system. Once again, a lack of precision dogged the discussion, and led to an exchange of angry and accusatory statements between the Community and Japan. What the European Community expected from Japan was unclear. Toward mid-summer, when the Preparatory Committee was starting to wind up its proceedings, the issue was left in abeyance, but was resuscitated by the Community at the end of the Punta del Este meeting.

Apart from the stalemated discussions in the Preparatory Committee, individual countries and groups of like-minded countries started to formulate composite positions. From around April 1986, draft ministerial declarations began to circulate informally. Canada, Australia, and Japan were among the first countries to produce such texts. At the same time, two groups that would dominate the preparatory process began to form: the Group of Nine (G-9), comprising Australia, Canada, and New Zealand and the members of the European Free Trade Association (EFTA)[5] and the Group of Ten (G-10) developing countries,[6] largely inspired by Brazil and India.

The G-9 and G-10 draft ministerial texts—entirely incompatible—drew the battle lines for the rest of the preparatory process. The G-9 text was unequivocal about the objective of launching a new round of negotiations. The G-10 text displayed doubts even about this basic objective, articulating the opposition of certain developing countries to the entire negotiating exercise. Despite their efforts at compromise and recruitment, the G-10 did not attract additional supporters, and presented a minority text to the Preparatory Committee.

The G-9 was a group of small industrial countries alarmed by the degree of polarization that had emerged in the 1985 discussions on a new round, and which seemed to persist during the preparatory process. These countries felt threatened by a possible breakdown of multilateral processes. For its part, the United States was in no mood to compromise on its demands for multilateral action in the new areas. It knew it could count on support from some industrial countries and believed that most developing countries would not oppose the initiatives outright if that meant jeopardizing meaningful U.S. participation in the round. The G-9 countries had understood the stakes and wanted to offer a platform that would entice some developing countries into helping to formulate a negotiating agenda that would not alienate the United States.

In mid-summer 1986, the large industrial countries kept a low profile, not associating themselves too openly or explicitly with the G-9. There were elements of the G-9 proposal that they did not like, but the United States, Japan, and the European Community could happily have taken the text as a negotiating basis. The developing countries that were outside the G-10 confronted a difficult decision in June 1986. They had to choose sides. Soon after the G-9 and G-10 texts were circulated, a group of around twenty developing countries started to meet informally with the G-9. This was the beginning of what came to be known as the "EFTA process," so named because the enlarged group met at EFTA Headquarters in Geneva.

Often lasting well into the night, these "EFTA meetings" were long and difficult; many divergent positions had to be mediated. The process intensified as the July 31 deadline neared for the Preparatory Committee to complete its work, and the large industrial countries joined in the process. The negotiators wanted to come as close as possible to consensus positions before submitting a text to the Preparatory Committee. The formal text was presented to the committee on July 30 under the joint sponsorship of Colombia and Switzerland.[7] Outstanding issues included high-technology products, textiles and clothing, agriculture, intellectual property, services, and trade-related investment measures. All but the high-technology issue were agreed in the final Punta del Este Declaration.

THE PUNTA DEL ESTE DECLARATION

Securing agreement on a single negotiating text[8] was left to the chairman of the Punta del Este meeting, the foreign minister of Uruguay, Enrique Iglesias. Scheduled for Monday, September 15 through Friday, September 19, the meeting lasted into Saturday. Despite promoting rumors about the possibility of a failed meeting and about procedural maneuvers to push through majority decisions, the general feeling was that the stakes were too high for ministers to fail to agree on a new round of negotiations. The more pressing issue, however, was whether the negotiating mandate would permit the GATT to play a meaningful role in determining the future design and course of international trade relations. Multilateralism was on the line, not in the obvious and dramatic sense that the GATT might sink without trace, but rather in terms of the substance and quality of decisions that were to be taken.

In the event, the negotiating mandates were fine. They provided authority for wide-ranging negotiations on practically every subject that had been put forward. Negotiations were to be completed in four years.

But before the Declaration could be formally adopted, the balance-of-benefits issue between the European Community and Japan had to be settled. Eventually the meeting chairman read out an agreed statement, noting the EC proposal on the need to redress growing disequilibria in world trade and to achieve a greater mutuality of interest. It also recorded the primary Japanese response, that a proposal of this nature could undermine the principles of

GATT, including a guaranteed open, nondiscriminatory trading system. The statement acknowledged that growing trade disequilibria were a serious problem, to be tackled by the countries concerned through appropriate policy measures, including macroeconomic policy, exchange rates, structural reform, and trade policy. Finally, the statement recorded agreement that genuine efforts should be made to ensure that mutual advantages and increased benefits accrued to all parties, in accordance with the principles of the GATT. In practical terms, this accommodation served to calm a politically charged situation, but did nothing to address the underlying issue. It was a negotiated statement of perceptions of the problem.

The Punta del Este Declaration was divided into two sections, maintaining the distinction between services as a non-GATT subject of negotiation, and the rest of the negotiating agenda.[9] This separation had been agreed upon to placate developing-country opposition to including services. It was supposed to ensure that developing countries would not be forced to open up their service sectors, including liberalized investment regimes, in order to derive traditional GATT benefits in the areas that interested them. In practice, the separation was unlikely to affect the negotiations, since in the end there was bound to be considerable fungibility among issues.

The trade in goods section of the declaration contained traditional GATT desiderata on halting protectionism, preserving basic principles, furthering the objectives of GATT, and developing a more open, viable and durable multilateral trading system. Debt, finance, money, and development also received a mention. Some concerns that did not find their way into the blueprint for mainstream negotiations were folded into "objectives." There mentioned were difficulties in commodity markets and the growing importance of trade in high-technology products.

The "governing principles" section responded to a number of specific concerns: transparency in the conduct of negotiations and the need to ensure benefits for all participants (an obvious reference to the fear of small countries that they might be effectively excluded from the negotiations and forced to accept the results as presented to them). A statement to the effect that the negotiations should be treated as a single undertaking was supposed to forestall a situation where a few countries could push through agreements in their favored areas while ignoring issues important to other countries. The importance of "parallelism" among issues was a recurrent theme in the negotiations. Concessions were to be balanced within broad trading areas to avoid "unwarranted cross-sectoral demands." This was supposed to quiet developing countries' fears that they would derive benefits in the negotiations only if they were compliant on the services issue.

Developing-country issues were addressed toward the end of the Declaration. Language negotiated in the Tokyo Round, relating to nonreciprocity and graduation, was repeated. References were also made to the least developed countries' special situation. The repetition of old language on developing-country participation in the GATT system was indicative of the new circumstances. There were to be no more stand-alone negotiations on special treatment for developing countries.

Political commitments, reflecting a lack of mutual confidence about national commitments to respect the GATT, were made on standstill and rollback; any attempt to give them binding force would tend to generate more friction than action. Standstill required countries to pledge not to adopt any GATT-inconsistent measures, to exercise GATT rights with restraint and in a GATT-consistent manner, and to refrain from enacting any measures to improve their negotiating positions. Rollback required the phasing out of GATT-inconsistent measures by the end of the negotiations. No GATT concessions were to be sought in exchange. The Punta del Este commitments were the most elaborate to date. They were to be progressively implemented "on an equitable basis in consultations among participants concerned, including all affected participants."

Without a formal GATT dispute-settlement framework, however, it is hard to see what will induce countries to admit guilt or acquiesce to charges. A number of pending dispute-settlement findings could have been notified as rollback actions, and many countries felt they should be acted upon immediately. This did occur with respect to the U.S. cases on superfund and import fees, and the Japanese case involving certain agricultural products, but in other instances parties preferred to wait to see whether the Uruguay Round results might obviate the need for remedial action. One notable case falling into this category was the Japanese complaint against the European Community concerning the application of anticircumvention duties in an antidumping action.[10]

For goods, there were no fewer than fourteen separate negotiating mandates, several of them involving a range of unrelated issues. For convenience, the mandates can be categorized thematically into four groups: market access, rule-making, institutional reform, and the new issues. Despite some overlapping, these subdivisions capture the broad content of the Uruguay Round. In the area of market access, there were mandates on tariffs, nontariff measures, tropical products, and natural resource-based products. The mandates involving rule-making included textiles, agriculture, the review and revision of various GATT articles, safeguards, improvements in the Tokyo Round Agreements and Arrangements, and subsidies and countervailing duties.

Negotiations involving agriculture and textiles had a strong normative element, but were also directly concerned with improved market access.

The institutional issues covered dispute settlement and the functioning of the GATT system. The "functioning" mandate, a separate section in the Declaration, covered surveillance, GATT capacities as a decisionmaking institution, and relationships with other international agencies. The "new issues" were trade-related aspects of intellectual property rights and trade-related investment measures.

Adding the services mandate made fifteen negotiating mandates altogether in the Uruguay Round. The objective in services was to establish a multilateral framework of principles and rules for trade in services, with "a view to expansion of such trade under conditions of transparency and progressive liberalization and as a means of promoting economic growth of all trading partners and the development of developing countries." Language in the mandate about respecting the policy objectives of national laws and regulations applying to services was intended to placate developing-country concerns about the intrusiveness of international commitments in this area and to assure them that their development objectives would not be undermined. The implication that increasing trade and promoting development might be mutually hostile objectives was a notable feature of the services mandate and the negotiations. No previous GATT discussions of the development imperative or the need for growth in developing countries had ever challenged the idea that freer trade was ultimately beneficial. The matter had always been debated in purely temporal terms.

PROGRESS OF THE URUGUAY ROUND

The Uruguay Round can be divided into three separate phases. The first phase took the negotiations up to the Mid-Term Review, a ministerial meeting held in Montreal, Canada, in December 1988, when the round was supposedly at the half-way point. The second phase took the round up to its putative conclusion in December 1990. The third phase was not foreseen, and has been dominated by one artificial deadline after another, as governments have repeatedly asserted their determination to complete the negotiations but failed to do so.

The Mid-Term Review

Any euphoria that might have been felt after the successful Punta del Este meeting was quickly dissipated. In the first six months, there were no negotiations of substance, only wrangles over organizational questions. Even after procedural and organizational issues had been settled, and the requisite negotiating groups and plans formed, several more months passed as countries reiterated their positions and talked around the issues. Negotiations did not begin in earnest until 1988.

A mid-term review meeting of the Trade Negotiations Committee (TNC) was set at ministerial level in Montreal, on December 5–8, 1988. Hopes were that this near-term target might speed up the negotiations, provide an opportunity to assess progress, implement any early results, and give political impetus to the remainder of the Uruguay Round. All year, the fifteen negotiating groups had worked on texts for the ministers' approval. How far these texts went toward embodying results was settled in each group.

Six groups reported out clear texts for approval in Montreal. These texts covered nontariff measures, natural resource-based products, GATT articles, the Tokyo Round Agreements and Arrangements, subsidies, and trade-related investment measures. Most texts, however, merely reflected the participants' diverse interests and intentions of continuing the negotiations. The nine negotiating groups that left matters pending for Montreal covered tariffs, textiles and clothing, agriculture, tropical products, safeguards, trade-related aspects of intellectual property rights, dispute settlement, functioning of the GATT system, and services.

Not all these subjects were to be fought over in any serious way in Montreal, and some of them could be settled quickly, along the lines similar to the pre-Montreal texts. As ministers gathered in Montreal, the issues considered problematic were trade in services, trade-related intellectual property rights (TRIPS), and agriculture. As it turned out, safeguards and textiles joined the insoluble hard core, and services was settled.

Up to that point, negotiations on trade in services had been controversial, to the surprise of no one. Well over a hundred points of discord were brought to Montreal. The text presented to the ministers was a monument to disagreement. One of the big surprises, and indeed successes, of Montreal was that all those differences were negotiated away. At last, it seemed that the services negotiations would move forward.

Throughout the Uruguay Round, intellectual property remained one of the most intractable issues of all, dividing countries along North-South lines in many ways. Initiated and spearheaded by the United States, the major industrial country drive for better international protection of intellectual property rights provoked deep-seated opposition among developing countries. Not only have those countries resisted the idea of standardized intellectual property norms and regulations throughout the world, they have also fiercely opposed the adjudication and enforcement of intellectual property rights in a

GATT context. Having resisted the inclusion of trade in counterfeit goods on the GATT agenda, this became the only intellectual property issue that developing countries would negotiate in the early phases of the Uruguay Round. Any hopes they may have harbored that a change of position on counterfeit would head off the broader TRIPS exercise, however, were to be dashed. They have also pressed for recognition of social or public policy considerations in discussions on intellectual property issues. These were the issues in dispute at Montreal.

Trade in agriculture retained its pride of place as a long-standing source of contention, both at Montreal and subsequently. The United States and the European Community were, as usual, at the center of the dispute. The United States wanted a long-term commitment to the total eradication of all border measures and all trade-distorting subsidies in agriculture and agreement on some short-term reform measures, including a freeze on internal support, export subsidy, and import protection levels. The Community flatly refused to make a commitment to complete eradication. The United States had chosen Montreal to hold fast on its "zero-zero option" proposal involving free trade in agriculture, and refused any compromise whatsoever on what became a stance of principle.

The two other sticky issues, safeguards and textiles, had been mined by India and other developing countries as a kind of insurance policy for Montreal to help shore up resistance to any significant advance on intellectual property. On safeguards, nondiscrimination was proposed and the removal of all existing selective measures of protection. On textiles and clothing, the developing countries wanted to add a timetable, with positive steps, to the Punta del Este commitment to eradicate the Multi-Fiber Arrangement.

On the plus side at Montreal, agreement was reached to reduce trade barriers on certain tropical products. For developing countries, tropical products have always been a special concern and unreciprocated concessions on them, a traditional objective. The industrial country response had always been tepid, and the whole exercise was clouded with symbolism. It was an interesting reflection of the growing unwillingness among industrial countries to forgo reciprocity from developing countries that for the first time, several developing countries also announced trade liberalization measures on tropical products at Montreal.[11] The tropical product results, announced on the eve of the Montreal meeting, were clearly orchestrated as an attempt to launch the Montreal meeting in a positive and promising atmosphere. In this, the announced results were partly successful, although the effect was moderated by the modest trade coverage of the proposed measures,[12] by suspicion among developing countries that this symbolism would be used against them in other areas of discussion, and by the U.S. indication that its offer was conditional upon satisfactory progress in agriculture. The effect was further eroded later in the week, when the European Community and the United States indulged in a public squabble about whose offer on tropical products was the more generous.

The Montreal meeting ended inconclusively. The agriculture negotiations failed, which was probably inevitable in view of the purist U.S. position. The situation was not helped by the widespread conviction that the United States was not serious about the zero-zero option, which implied free trade— something that had not been fully achieved in any other sector of the economy, and which would hardly be acceptable to the U.S. dairy, meat, tobacco, and sugar industries. In any event, the zero-zero option was impossible for the European Community to accept, given the magnitude and political sensitivity of its common agricultural policy. The U.S. position was supported by the smaller agricultural exporters, many of whom had joined one of the most effective coalitions in the Uruguay Round—the Cairns Group.[13] But the EC countries were also troubled by U.S. insistence on a position to which the United States itself would be unable to subscribe.

The United States and the Community wished to adopt whatever results were available at Montreal, and to pursue work on the outstanding issues. Several developing countries strongly opposed this idea, insisting on parallelism. It was agreed all results would be put "on hold." At the same time, GATT Director-General Arthur Dunkel would pursue work on the four outstanding issues— agriculture, TRIPS, textiles and clothing, and safeguards—and report back to the TNC in April 1989. By the time of the April meeting, the basis for continuing negotiations had been established in the four outstanding subject areas.

In agriculture, the United States had at last dropped the zero-zero option, and reform was to lead instead to a substantial long-term reduction of agricultural support and protection and improvement in GATT disciplines. In the short term, domestic and export support levels were to be frozen, based on a 1987–88 benchmark. The freeze was to last until the end of 1990, when the final Uruguay Round commitments would take effect. A compromise was agreed in TRIPS whereby negotiations would proceed on all fronts—the scope and use of substantive intellectual property rights, and their enforcement—on the understanding that a decision would be made at the end of the Uruguay Round whether to incorporate these commitments in GATT or in another forum such as the World Intellectual Property Organization (WIPO). Many developing countries wished to keep TRIPS out of the GATT to avoid cross-conditionality in negotiations and the possibility of punitive trade action to enforce intellectual property rights. The texts on safeguards and textiles and clothing contained minor advances, but largely left open participants' negotiating options.

Failure at Brussels

After the April decisions, the Uruguay Round was once again on course, though with much ground left to cover. By the Brussels ministerial meeting, planned for December 3–7, 1990, it was all supposed to be over. To ensure comparable progress in all areas of the negotiations and to maintain momentum, two informal targets were set. The first was that the main elements of all national positions should be on the negotiating table by the end of 1989. The second target was set for July 1990, when the outlines of agreements in all areas would be due, leaving the rest of the year to finish up.

The December 1989 target was vague enough not to present much difficulty. All it required was that countries had said what they wanted. It did not call for substantive negotiations. The July 1990 deadline was a different matter. At the July meeting of the Trade Negotiations Committee, Chairman Dunkel registered a "very deep sense of concern,"[14] noting that many of the reports from negotiating groups were compendiums of positions, reflecting the competing interests of participants. He concluded that the negotiators were collectively behind schedule.

The market-access negotiations involving tariffs and nontariff measures had scarcely advanced at all by July. For negotiations on rules, institutional issues, and the new areas, the picture was mixed. For dispute settlement and functioning of the GATT system, there was only a progress report and no negotiating text. In other cases, there were draft texts (rules of origin, preshipment inspection, textiles, agriculture, GATT articles, MTN Agreements and Arrangements, safeguards, subsidies, trade-related investment measures [TRIMS], TRIPS, and services), but differences remained wide on many issues.

Discussion was delayed during the TNC meeting (July 23–26) because the European Community refused to accept the chairman's text on agriculture. This was finally settled by agreement that the text should be used as a "means to intensify the negotiations" rather than as a "basis for negotiations." This kind of linguistic squabble was a foretaste of the escalating battle over agriculture that would finally doom the Brussels meeting and put the entire Uruguay Round in jeopardy. At the end of the July TNC meeting, new deadlines were set, mostly for September and October. By then, differences were supposed to have been reduced to a small number of truly intractable problems requiring political decisions by ministers. These deadlines came and went, with little sign of progress in key areas. For the first time, there was open speculation about whether the Uruguay Round would finish on schedule.

What went to Brussels from the TNC was a 392-page document, entitled the "Draft Final Act Embodying the Results of the Uruguay Round of Multilateral Trade Negotiations." It contained little that could be described as final. Although in a few areas a text was available that could serve as a reasonable basis for negotiations (textiles, safeguards, some MTN codes, some GATT articles, dispute settlement, and TRIPS), other texts contained numerous formulations of alternative language. Four major areas were without any text—antidumping, TRIMS, agriculture, and the GATT's balance-of-payments provisions. In subsidies, the text was accompanied by dissenting statements from the European Community, Brazil, Mexico, and Pakistan.

This was hardly an auspicious beginning. Groups were established under particular ministers to deal with services, rules, TRIPS, TRIMS, agriculture, textiles, and market access. Some progress was made through informal negotiations in most of these areas from December 3–6. Since well before the Brussels meeting, however, it had been obvious that U.S. determination to see progress in agriculture (with strong support from the Cairns Group), and EC reluctance to make meaningful reforms (with largely unspoken support from Japan and others), would place agriculture at center stage in Brussels. At the very least, the major players expected a crisis on this issue.

And crisis came in Brussels toward the end of Thursday, December 6. Until the final hours, the United States had favored a 75 percent reduction in border restrictions and domestic support levels, and a 90 percent cut in export subsidies on agriculture. These reductions were to be staged over ten years starting from January 1991 and using 1990 as a base year. The EC proposal had been limited to a 30 percent reduction in domestic support levels over five years from a 1986 base level. The European Community maintained that the degree of domestic support determined the levels of import restrictions and export subsidies, and that commitments on these elements were therefore unnecessary. Other differences between the two positions were on the European Community "rebalancing" proposal, tariffication, and minimum market access commitments. Rebalancing referred to the EC demand that it should be permitted to raise barriers on cereal feed substitutes in exchange for liberalizing trade on other products. Tariffication would substitute tariffs for nontariff trade restrictions, such as quantitative restrictions and variable levies.

In an attempt to bridge the differences in agriculture, Swedish Agriculture Minister Mats Hellstrom, who had been presiding over the agricultural negotiations, made a compromise proposal. This called for 30 percent cuts in border restrictions, domestic support, and export subsidies over a five-year period from a 1990 base. The proposed compromise encompassed elements of both positions. The United States and the Cairns Group accepted the proposal as a basis for negotiations. The European Community had in the meanwhile been attempting to soften its own position, but against a background of considerable internal dissension. Soon after the release of the

Hellstrom proposal, it was clear that the European Community would reject it. The final attempt at reconciliation broke down on the Thursday night after brief exchanges in which the European Community, Japan, and Korea rejected the compromise effort, and some developing-country members of the Cairns Group walked out. The other informal groups that had been meeting were interrupted. The Brussels meeting had failed. The European Community had wanted to continue, in the hope of hammering out a compromise. None of the other participants had an appetite for it. At a formal session of the TNC on Friday morning, Arthur Dunkel was empowered to continue seeking a solution to the outstanding issues and to reconvene the TNC at his discretion.

The Uruguay Round had failed to meet its most important target, set at the very outset of the negotiations in Punta del Este four years earlier. Bitterness and recrimination accompanied the failure—and anger from the dozens of countries that had witnessed the world's two major trading entities play brinkmanship and talk past each other for many frustrating months. There is no shortage of explanations as to who was to blame for the events at Brussels and why the meeting failed. Agreement between the United States and the European Community would obviously have been a necessary, and in all probability a sufficient condition for a successful completion of the Uruguay Round at that time. But in the months just before the Brussels meeting, it was beginning to look as if any agreement would have been modest on virtually all fronts, falling well short of the hopes embodied in the broad and ambitious agenda set at Punta del Este.

Whether the United States and the European Community let the Brussels meeting fail simply because they did not care enough about a successful outcome, or whether the failure reflected miscalculation and shortcomings of a more procedural nature, is an important question. The truth probably lies somewhere between these two explanations. Political steps could have been taken to ensure a satisfactory result had the Uruguay Round been considered important enough. The avoidance of failure was not perceived as sufficiently crucial to the national interest of the European Community or the United States for them to settle. The returns from "hanging tough" were apparently greater than those accruing from completing the negotiations, and may even have been so considered before Brussels. There was certainly praise from Congress for Carla Hills, the United States trade representative, for refusing to settle for less than what the United States demanded. In Europe, too, political leaders would have had a hard time allowing the Uruguay Round define CAP reform instead of doing it in a domestic context.

Some participants felt that part of the crisis on agriculture had been stage-managed, with a view to settlement toward the end of the week in Brussels.

To the extent that a crisis-creating strategy existed, whoever thought it could be controlled and managed miscalculated. The extraordinary range of complex issues under negotiation added stress to the situation and has led some observers to question whether GATT-style negotiating rounds are a thing of the past. Whatever view is taken on these matters, the Brussels failure dealt a severe blow to GATT credibility and diminished the role of multilateralism in trade relations for some time to come. GATT credibility was further bruised by the aftermath of Brussels, a period combining intransigence and indifference on the part of the major traders.

Right after the Brussels breakdown, some observers thought the Uruguay Round might be wrapped up in early 1991. There was concern lest the U.S. administration lose its nontariff negotiating authority. The authority would lapse if the president did not secure an extension from Congress by March 1, 1991. The original negotiating authority in the Omnibus Trade and Competitiveness Act of 1988 had foreseen the possibility of a two-year extension, if justified by progress in negotiations. Soon after the Brussels meeting it was clear that December's differences could not be bridged by March. The administration therefore sought an extension, needed, in any event, for free trade agreement negotiations with Mexico and similar agreements with other Latin American countries envisaged in the Enterprise for the Americas Initiative.

In February, Chairman Dunkel announced at a TNC meeting called at short notice that he had concluded after consultations a basis existed for restarting negotiations in all areas of the Uruguay Round where differences remained. The announcement was accompanied by proposed work agendas in each negotiating area. This was a message to the U.S. Congress just before it received President Bush's request for fast-track extension, but a message with little substance. Although the European Community had made minimal concessions to ensure U.S. willingness to continue, it had not refuted talk of achieving specific binding commitments to reduce domestic support, increase market access, and reduce export subsidies for agricultural products.

By early 1991 the Community was beginning internal discussions on CAP reform, driven by the realization that, from a budgetary perspective, its support policies were unsustainable. The Community has continued to maintain, however, that internal discussions on reform are entirely independent of any multilateral commitments that might be negotiated. The lack of internal cohesion in the Community makes it difficult to accommodate multilateral processes, except in a passive and reactive fashion, directed fundamentally at preserving the status quo.

The Congress had ninety days to approve or deny the administration's request for an extension of the fast-track negotiating authority. In the event, much of the debate dwelled on the FTA negotiating authority and reflected opposition to bilateral negotiations with Mexico. The Uruguay Round took a back seat, perhaps a relief to proponents of continuing the multilateral process, but also revealing of congressional perceptions about the real and immediate trade interests of the United States. Opposition to fast-track extension focused on the environmental, wage, and employment effects of a North American Free Trade Agreement. To overcome a well-organized campaign by environmental and labor lobbies,[15] considerable efforts were required from business interests and the administration.

Nothing of substance could happen in the Uruguay Round until the congressional deadline had passed. In the meanwhile, Arthur Dunkel again convened the TNC in April 1991. This time he announced a streamlining of the negotiating structure from fifteen negotiating groups to seven groups. The seven groups were to deal with market access (tariffs, nontariff measures, natural resource-based products, tropical products); textiles and clothing; agriculture; rule-making (TRIMS, subsidies and countervailing duties, antidumping, safeguards, preshipment inspection, rules of origin, technical barriers to trade, import licensing procedures, customs valuation, government procurement, and a number of specific GATT articles); TRIPS; institutions (Final Act,[16] dispute settlement, and functioning of the GATT system) and services.

Negotiations continued throughout the rest of 1991. No formal deadlines were set, but Dunkel intimated in June that more and more governments were beginning to see December 1991 as a feasible and desirable target for completing the Uruguay Round. Too many deadlines had been missed for a new one to be believable. Moreover, it is dubious whether the political games and brinkmanship associated with trade negotiations would allow a deadline to be met if it was not tied to some overriding imperative such as the expiration of negotiating authority.

As the year wore on, however, deadlines again became more specific. Dunkel announced December 1991 as the deadline for a full set of Uruguay Round texts, and mid-November for negotiating groups to finalize their texts for TNC submission. Dunkel had become emboldened by successive high-level efforts by the United States and the European Community to break the agriculture deadlock. The Community had also made progress on defining CAP reform. The London summit of the G-7 in July had laid much emphasis on completing the Uruguay Round.

Once again, it was not to be. Dunkel issued a 440-page second version of the Draft Final Act on December 20, but it was not a consensus document. Key texts, including those on agriculture, antidumping, and subsidies had been put together as compromise positions by Dunkel's staff. This was reflected in reactions to the document. The European Community argued that the suggested compromise for agriculture went too far and threatened the foundations of the CAP. The United States thought the text did not go far enough. Assorted interest groups expressed opposition to various parts of the text, including agriculture, textiles and clothing, TRIPS, antidumping, subsidies, services, technical barriers to trade, and sanitary and phytosanitary measures. A TNC meeting in mid-January made it clear that there was no basis for agreement.

The new Dunkel target was mid-April 1992. Four working groups were established. One was to deal with market access, since negotiations to reduce tariff and nontariff barriers were far from complete. Another group was charged with access negotiations and other outstanding issues in services. A third group was to review the Uruguay Round texts for legal consistency and also address institutional issues such as the establishment of a Multilateral Trade Organization. The fourth group was to deal with everything else.

As the mid-April deadline approached, and progress on agriculture remained elusive despite multiple high-level efforts to break the deadlock, the focus of attention moved to the Munich summit of the G-7 scheduled for early July. But even before that meeting took place, officials from a number of the summit countries sought to lower expectations about an agreement in Munich. Whatever hopes there had been for completion of the Uruguay Round in 1992 began to look remote. Deadline fatigue, frustration at missed opportunities, and a sense that serious commitment to the GATT round was absent, all contributed to growing disillusionment with the Uruguay Round. Assurances from the summiteers in Munich that the round would be completed in 1992, and effusive affirmations of its importance, were given little attention and less credence. In the United States, the impending completion of NAFTA negotiations (which finally came through on August 12) further sapped interest in the Uruguay Round.

The administration's negotiating authority expired on June 1, 1993. Ninety days before that, Congress had to be notified of an intention to enter into Uruguay Round agreements. If the mulitlateral trade negotiations were to have stood a chance of being completed within the life of the fast-track authority, it would have required an extraordinary commitment of time and determination at the highest political level. Following the failure of the Bush administration to complete the negotiations (thanks in part to the French position on agriculture) President Clinton would have needed to place international trade relations near the top of his list of priorities. This was manifestly not the case, with so much attention focused on such matters as the budget and health care reform.

As to the longer-term prospects for concluding a multilateral trade negotiation, any renewed negotiating authority for the executive would likely entail new conditions on such issues as environmental policy and labor legislation. These are areas where some believe the GATT has been neglectful, but where international agreement may also prove elusive. A new grant of authority would give interest groups and Congress an opportunity to constrain the executive's room for maneuver in negotiations, thereby promoting outcomes that they would have liked to see in the Uruguay Round. More generally, emphasis on regional agreements, particularly when they are crafted around special deals in uncompetitive sectors, makes for growing incompatibility with a multilateral focus based on nondiscrimination.

The Draft Final Act

An important question to consider is what the Draft Final Act (DFA) of the Uruguay Round offers in terms of trade liberalization opportunities. This short review of the DFA seeks to identify the main elements of the package, emphasizing both its weak and strong points.

The DFA's *institutional provisions* would establish a new Multilateral Trade Organization (MTO) as a framework for adopting the Uruguay Round results. The MTO would become a new GATT, incorporating all its old functions, as well as taking on board the new issues. The DFA draft envisaged that the MTO would replace the provisional accession instruments through which countries joined GATT from 1947 onward (chapter 2). This implied elimination of the grandfather clause contained in the provisional accession protocols, under which countries could avoid any GATT discipline that contradicted preexisting mandatory legislation. Discussions on the DFA in 1990 and 1991 revealed U.S. opposition to the elimination of the grandfather clause. The United States was seeking a reservation that would allow it to maintain the discriminatory features of the Jones Act, dealing with coastal shipping. An important implication of the MTO is that all GATT agreements, notably the Tokyo Round codes, would be considered part of the same instrument,[17] which would eliminate the problem of multitiered rights and obligations that voluntary adherence to the codes has created (chapter 7).

The *market access* negotiations covered both tariffs and nontariff measures. These negotiations had proceeded slowly, partly because participants were unwilling to settle on their final positions until the completion of the negotiations was imminent, and partly because deadlock in agriculture meant that liberalization offers were not forthcoming for this sector. There was a commitment from the mid-term review in Montreal, however, that average tariff cuts would be at least as great as they were in the Tokyo Round, implying a 30 percent reduction. A reduction of this magnitude would bring significant trade benefits.[18] The United States took a position early in the negotiations against a harmonized tariff cut of the kind that had been used in the Tokyo Round to reduce the dispersion of tariff rates. On the other hand, the United States was pushing for free trade in those sectors where it was competitive. The United States also led the initiative, on the fringes of the Uruguay Round, for the Multilateral Steel Agreement to liberalize steel trade (chapter 5).

The text on *antidumping duties* contains a number of significant innovations, several of which run counter to current U.S. practice. Prominent among these are more stringent rules on calculating dumping margins (averaging procedures and the inclusion of sales below cost), the use of actual instead of imputed amounts for profits and sales margins when calculating constructed costs, the preconditions for an industry to file a petition (standing), *de minimis* criteria for calculating dumping and injury, and a "sunset" provision for the termination of cases. These changes would make for a less permissive use of antidumping remedies. On the other hand, current EC and U.S. practice on anticircumvention, allows antidumping action to be extended to sales or production arrangements in other countries if the original antidumping order is being circumvented.

The text on *subsidies and countervailing duties* has very similar provisions to antidumping on the subsidy-remedy side. The United States has long sought stronger disciplines on subsidy practices. As the dominant user of countervailing duties, the United States argues that subsidy practices need to be controlled if improved disciplines on countervailing duties are to be put in place. The U.S. objective of extending subsidy prohibitions beyond export subsidies on manufactured goods remains largely unfulfilled in the DFA. Consequently, EC efforts to develop a category of noncountervailable subsidies were also largely frustrated, although nonactionable, nonspecific subsidies are defined.[19] One feature of the draft agreement strongly promoted by the United States was the commitment by most developing countries to phase out their export subsidies on manufactures within a specified time frame. Previously, developing countries had been permitted to maintain these subsidies. Another positive feature of the text from the U.S. standpoint was the introduction of a presumption that any specific subsidy of more than 5 percent caused serious prejudice and should not be applied. But there are exceptions to this rule. The subsidies text generally reveals a lack of serious commitment on the part of some U.S. trading partners to discipline subsidies.

The DFA contains renegotiated agreements on *technical barriers to trade, import licensing procedures, customs valuation, and government procurement*. For the most part, these agreements are extended or improved. There has been some disagreement on the extent to which nonfederal authorities can be held responsible for commitments assumed at the federal level on technical standards, a point on which the United States is vulnerable because of state powers in these matters. The proposed language on this point has been strengthened to make central governments "fully responsible" for compliance with the agreement by local government bodies. The previous formulation merely entreated central authorities to take "reasonable measures" to ensure observance.

Environmental interests have expressed concern that the standards agreement (technical barriers to trade) might force the United States to lower some of its own product and process standards. The customs valuation code has been weakened, to make it easier for customs authorities to challenge transaction values, the methodological base of the code. Amendments to the procurement code seek to facilitate participation. The changes in the customs valuation code are designed to accommodate universal code membership under the MTO arrangements.

Of all the potential Uruguay Round results, *agriculture* is one of the most important. Not only have past attempts to address agriculture ended in failure, but prevailing distortions are also among the worst in any sector. Under the DFA, measures against imports, domestic supports, and export subsidies would all be reduced. Import quotas would be converted to tariffs, tariffs would be reduced by an average of 36 percent in 1993–99, and there would be minimum access commitments rising to 5 percent of the market by 1999. Special "snapback" provisions on market access would be triggered by certain price and quantity change thresholds. Domestic support levels would be reduced by 20 percent in 1993–99, calculated from a 1986–88 base. Export subsidies would be subject to budgetary outlay and quantity commitments, with reductions of 36 percent and 24 percent, respectively, in 1993–99, from a 1986–90 base.

These numbers were unacceptable to the European Community and the United States, but agricultural liberalization of any magnitude would mark progress. A potential danger of this kind of package, however, is that it would encourage the development of a quantity-based regime in agriculture, a first step toward de facto market sharing and discrimination. This problem could arise in relation to the snapback provisions and export-subsidy reduction commitments. The disagreements separating the United States and European Community turned on several factors, including the identification of policies that were to be subject to the domestic support-reduction commitments, the size of the export subsidy-reduction commitment, and the EC rebalancing demand. A further issue was the "peace clause," under which the United States and the Community would agree not to bring any dispute-settlement cases against each another for five years. Close observers of the negotiations have remarked that differences were not great between the parties in mid-1992. This gives some credence to the notion that the completion of the Uruguay Round was not considered a political priority at that time.

The draft *safeguards* agreement is a mixed blessing from a systemic perspective. The agreement tightens procedures in significant ways, making for greater accountability and discipline in the use of safeguard measures. It also introduces time limits for actions. A major element of the agreement is the commitment to eliminate voluntary export restraints (VERs) within four years. Each participant is allowed one exception to the VER elimination commitment, until the end of 1999. The European Community has already indicated that it would exempt its VER with Japan on motor vehicles. The U.S. choice could well be the same.

On the less positive side, the agreement weakens the obligation to provide compensatory liberalization if a safeguard measure is taken, which could lead to a less restrained use of safeguards. More seriously, it allows "quota modulation," which means that discriminatory safeguard measures can be taken in certain circumstances. Although selectivity is supposed to be carefully monitored and controlled, an important principle has been set aside. Done at the insistence of the European Community, it could have negative longer term effects on the trading system. Moreover, by allowing quota allocations under the safeguard arrangements to be agreed between the importing and supplying countries, a risk remains that concealed VER-type arrangements could be struck. Controls on quota modulation via the Safeguard Committee seem to become operative only if there has not been prior agreement on an allocation. If the safeguards text was ever applied, and VERs actually eliminated, an important question would be whether the disciplines on antidumping and countervailing-duty remedies are strong enough to prevent the de facto substitution of the VERs and other safeguard measures with unfair trade remedies. This is a legitimate concern.

Like agriculture, the draft agreement on *textiles and clothing* is a first, the return of textiles and clothing to mainstream GATT disciplines. Their reintegration within the GATT is to be achieved in three phases over ten years. The share of the sector to be integrated and the quota growth rates are stipulated, but the order in which the quantitative restraints are to be removed is left to importers. A special snapback provision is also available for items subject to restriction under the MFA during the transition. Developing countries whose exports are restricted under the MFA have criticized the agreement on the grounds that too many restrictions are left until the last phase for elimination. They fear that because there are so many, the MFA will not be fully eliminated.

The draft agreement on the GATT *balance-of-payments provisions* imposes new disciplines on the use of trade restrictions to conserve foreign exchange. A preannounced schedule must be drawn up for eliminating balance-of-payments restrictions. Price-based measures (surcharges or import deposits) rather than quantitative restrictions should be used, and across-the-board measures are preferred except for essential imports. This had been a contentious issue early in the Uruguay Round, when developing countries were resisting pressure for further discipline from the United States and other countries. The industrial countries had argued that restrictions ostensibly taken for balance-of-payments purposes were protecting some domestic industries. However, as more and more developing countries opted for liberal trade policies, and countries like Brazil and Korea declared that they would no longer use the balance-of-payments justification for trade restrictions (under Article XVIII:B of the GATT), the issue lost much of its sting.

The DFA contains two texts on *dispute-settlement procedures*. The first sets out detailed rules and procedures to be followed in disputes, building on pre-existing GATT practices, but extending them in significant ways. The rules provide for the automatic establishment of a dispute-settlement panel if bilateral consultations fail, strict time limits for each phase of a dispute, arbitration facilities, an appeals procedure, compensation or retaliation when an offending policy is not brought into compliance, and a system of ex post surveillance and follow-up of the implementation of dispute-settlement decisions. The draft text also establishes that central governments are responsible for the action of local authorities and must pay compensation or face retaliation in the event the latter violate any MTO provision. Most important of all, however, these arrangements virtually guarantee the adoption of panel findings, which can only be blocked by a consensus decision. An obligation to act on the findings follows from adoption. Another provision directly relevant to the United States is the undertaking not to make unilateral determinations of the GATT-consistency of other countries' policies. This is a direct assault on Section 301.

Once the principal protagonist for dispute-settlement reform, the United States has found itself increasingly on the defensive. The automatic panel adoption provisions have met with strong domestic opposition, especially from environmentalists, who fear that this is a surrender of sovereignty that will undermine environmental standards. An important factor in their opposition was the 1991 GATT finding against a U.S. tuna ban on Mexican exports under the Marine Mammal Protection Act, justified on grounds of excessive dolphin kills by Mexican tuna fisheries. A similar position on the automatic adoption of GATT rulings is likely to be taken by any interest group that fears a negative GATT ruling.

Unsurprisingly, the GATT attack on Section 301 has also encountered opposition. The U.S. administration has intimated that Section 301 will not be eliminated, since it will still allow private parties a right of complaint and could also be used on non-GATT issues.[20] The interpretation of the proposed GATT language referring to Section 301 would have to be stretched beyond credibility to argue that Section 301 would be under no new constraints as a result of the dispute-settlement text. This issue could complicate congressional consideration of the DFA.

The second text on dispute settlement seeks to bring all the various fora that have grown up over the years within a unified framework. This integrated system would seek to ensure procedural and interpretive consistency in dispute-settlement practices across all issues. Some developing countries strongly opposed this decision because it foresees the possibility of "cross-retaliation." This means that a country could retaliate in the field of goods trade, for example, because of an infringement in the area of services or intellectual property. The proposed MTO provides an umbrella for a three-legged institution, dealing, respectively, with goods, services, and TRIPS. The integrated dispute-settlement system undermines the separability implied by this structure. But the idea that cross-retaliation could be avoided is unrealistic, particularly in view of the strong U.S. position on the issue.

The DFA text on *Article XXIV (customs unions and free trade areas)* is of minimal significance, considering how prevalent regional trading arrangements have become, and the importance of maintaining consistency between these arrangements and countries' multilateral obligations. Apart from some minor clarifications and extensions of Article XXIV rules, the draft also seeks to improve transparency through notification and review procedures. Article XXIV provisions have never been clear enough or adequately enforced to guard against trade diversion and unwarranted discrimination within regional groups. A major challenge for the GATT or its successor organization in the years ahead will be to maintain some policy consistency at the multilateral level and to ensure that regional groupings do not build exclusive fortresses and engage in interregional trade warfare (chapter 7).

The draft TRIMS agreement is a far more modest document than had been sought by the United States, the principal protagonist for TRIMS. The United States wanted to discipline domestic content requirements, export performance requirements and a range of other performance requirements linked either with the right to invest or with particular investment incentives. Countries maintaining investment regimes that placed operating conditions on investors did not want to deal with this issue. But the United States also seemed to place less emphasis on the issue as the negotiations wore on, reflecting increased demand for foreign investment that was associated with more liberal economic and trade policies in many parts of the world. Moreover, the United States itself became a net importer of investment funds in the 1980s and might have speculated about its own use of TRIMS, such as equity requirements on Japanese investors and the Exon-Florio provision for foreign investment screening on national security grounds in the 1988 Omnibus Trade and Competitiveness Act.

The TRIMS text does little more than specify that local content requirements and trade-balancing requirements are contrary to GATT national treatment rules (Article III) and that trade balancing, foreign exchange balancing, and quantitative restrictions on exports contravene the GATT prohibition on quantitative trade restrictions (Article XI). Parties to the agreement are given specific time periods in which to eliminate prohibited TRIMS. There is some irony in this agreement because if the enumerated measures were already contrary to GATT, then the phase-out requirements amount to grace periods for illegal behavior. Modest as the TRIMS agreement was, a future GATT agenda may be expected to address investment issues more substantively, considering the growing importance of international capital flows.

The Uruguay Round work on TRIPS has been a consistent U.S. priority, although U.S. initiatives in the round were supplemented by active bilateral efforts, including Special 301. The DFA text is far-reaching. It covers substantive intellectual property rights and measures for their enforcement. It establishes that national treatment and MFN are to apply, except where there are specific indications to the contrary.[21] Intellectual property standards are set in the areas of copyright, trademarks, geographic indications, industrial designs, patents, layouts of integrated circuits, and trade secrets. While the TRIPS exercise was directed primarily at developing countries at the beginning of the round, the focus shifted to industrial country issues as time went on. This was aided by the fact that many developing countries undertook reforms, not entirely independently of the Special 301 process.

Several complaints about the draft TRIPS agreement were registered by industry interests in the United States. Some related to developing countries specifically, such as the length of phase-in periods for their TRIPS commitments. Other complaints were of more general concern, on such matters as the treatment of pipeline protection for pharmaceuticals, exclusions from patentability, and the nontreatment of the exhaustion of intellectual property rights. In some areas, the United States found itself on the defensive, rather than playing its customary role of *demandeur* in the TRIPS negotiation. The United States refused, for example, to change its legislation to accommodate moral rights (certain authors' rights under the Berne Convention). Reluctantly, the United States accepted the "first to file" standard over the "first to invent" standard for patents. The United States took a hard line on controlling compulsory licensing, while refusing to recognize similarities between U.S. government use provisions and compulsory licenses.

TRIPS is one area in the Uruguay Round where it is legitimate to question the welfare implications of the negotiating objectives. Unlike trade liberalization, where the benefits are clear (globally and nationally, except in very specific circumstances), extending intellectual property protection can be of questionable benefit. The justification for exclusionary rights under the TRIPS agreement is that they allow firms to recoup their research and development (R&D) expenditures. This means that, in the absence of intellectual property (IP) protection, R&D would be expected to fall and the benefits from innovation would be reduced. The question is whether the small markets typical of many developing countries are sufficiently large for the absence of IP protection to affect the supply of R&D. If they are not, then the additional costs to developing-country consumers of paying for IP protection represents a welfare loss that is not recouped through enhanced R&D benefits.

Arvind Subramanian has argued that this is likely to be the situation in the pharmaceuticals industry, where developing countries jointly account for only 10 percent to 15 percent of consumption.[22] Moreover, the additional argument that developing countries would starve themselves of investment and be denied the benefits of technology transfer is also weak in the pharmaceuticals sector, where reverse engineering can be undertaken with relative ease. The Uruguay Round was not a forum in which these issues were likely to be aired, but parts of the TRIPS agreement, as they relate to particular sectors, may have enhanced monopolistic power and raised profits without conferring any benefits except to firms holding IP rights.

Finally, the DFA text on *services* establishes a General Agreement on Trade in Services (GATS). Many GATS provisions are modelled on the GATT, although texts have not yet been developed on safeguards and subsidies. The GATS rests on the MFN and national treatment principles and relies on a concept of market access (which concerns market entry barriers and operating restrictions). In some earlier conceptions of GATS, MFN was to be a basic operating principle of general applicability. But agreement on this point proved impossible, and an annex of exceptions to MFN is envisaged, where signatories will record the sectors in which they will not grant MFN treatment. The United States has promoted this approach, largely with maritime and air transport in mind, as well as some telecommunications services.

For telecommunications, the United States wishes to bargain access to its market for preferential access to other markets. This is justified as an antidote to free-riding and illustrates the inherent conflict between strong reciprocity conditions and nondiscrimination. Under these kinds of arrangements, broad-based exchanges of liberalization measures are excluded because reciprocity can only be satisfied through within-sector deals. Market sharing will replace competition as the dominant mode for doing business in this sector. It is as yet unclear how many sectors will be treated in this fashion, but if discrimination based on a strict interpretation of reciprocity pervades the services agreement, there will not be much of a multilateral system to talk of, and opportunities for beneficial specialization will be severely curtailed.

The concept of national treatment is novel in GATS. The primary determinant of foreign access to the domestic market for services is often the degree to which national treatment is provided (where establishment rights or physical presence is required to supply a service), so in GATS national treatment is an objective, not a principle. Participants are to make sector-specific commitments that will specify the applicable national treatment and market access conditions. By mid-1992, many countries had produced lists of their sector-specific offers, but negotiations had not advanced sufficiently for a judgment to be possible on how effective the GATS will prove as an instrument of trade liberalization. The GATS foresees successive rounds of negotiations.

THE URUGUAY ROUND AND U.S. OBJECTIVES

As with all the earlier GATT rounds of negotiations, the United States was a prime mover behind the Uruguay Round, but launching the negotiations was not easy. It was a process of attrition, characterized by endless disagreements, procedural maneuvers, and blocking tactics. Multilateral approaches to trade relations looked unpromising in the first half of the 1980s. Faith in the system was severely strained. Regionalism and bilateral or unilateral approaches to trade relations were attracting increased attention. Right up until the closing stages of the Punta del Este meeting, it might have been reasonable to expect the negotiations to be launched with a much more limited agenda. Yet the Uruguay Round was successfully initiated with a wide-ranging and substantially unencumbered set of negotiating mandates. With hindsight, of course, initiating the negotiations looks like the easy part—it was agreement to talk, not to act.

From a U.S. perspective, the content of the Punta del Este Declaration must have been a source of satisfaction. With two fairly minor exceptions, involving high-technology products and workers' rights, everything that the United States had been fighting for was realized. Most noteworthy was the inclusion of negotiating mandates on trade in services, intellectual property rights, and trade-related investment measures. The determination of the United States to see these items on the negotiating agenda had been matched in intensity by opposition from developing countries during the preparatory process. Another notable U.S. success was the mandate on trade in agriculture. Efforts to engage in serious negotiations on agriculture had been frustrated by the European Community for well over a decade. The Tokyo Round results had been minimal, and the 1982 Ministerial Meeting had almost collapsed over the issue. Here for the first time was a mandate that could lead to agricultural reform.

The United States was also determined to redefine the terms of developing-country participation in the trading system, especially for the more economically advanced of the developing countries. The Punta del Este Declaration did little more than repeat language in existing texts, thereby emphasizing the sea change in attitudes toward the question of special and differential treatment for developing countries.

As for the two issues sponsored by the United States that did not find a place in the Uruguay Round negotiations—high-technology products and workers' rights—at least a part of the reason that the subjects were dropped was that the United States did not push them hard enough to overcome opposition. The question of workers' rights was not raised in the Preparatory Committee until June 1986, rather late in the process. In a paper proposing that workers' rights should be taken up in the negotiations, the United States argued that denying these rights could distort trade and was contrary to basic GATT objectives. Multilateral action was therefore necessary. Although the U.S. paper did not offer a definition of workers' rights, it did say that a consideration of the issue should concern not only workplace standards such as minimum wages and health and safety standards, but also broad political rights such as freedom of association and the right of collective bargaining. The U.S. interest in this issue was a response to pressure from labor and human rights groups. The denial of workers' rights had received specific mention in the 1988 Trade and Competitiveness Act as an actionable unfair trade practice under Section 301 of the 1974 Trade Act (chapter 3). The 1974 Act had provided that a country's failure to take steps toward affording internationally recognized worker rights was sufficient cause for the denial of benefits under the Generalized System of Preferences. Several countries have been subject to review for alleged violations of worker rights over the years, and Nicaragua, Romania, Burma, Paraguay, Chile, and the Central African Republic have seen their GSP benefits either suspended or removed at one time or another.

The reaction to U.S. attempts to multilateralize its approach to workers' rights issues was strongly negative among developing countries. In the Preparatory Committee, over twenty countries spoke against the U.S proposal, arguing that the issue had no place in GATT, and that it would be extremely difficult to agree on a universal definition of these rights, especially in a trade policy context. Some of the more emotive interventions in this debate questioned the sincerity of U.S. concerns about the welfare of foreign workers.[23] Others raised racial considerations. The underlying assumption was that a workers' rights agenda would be used to reduce wage differentials through government intervention, thereby undermining a vital developing-country source of comparative advantage. Protectionism, they argued, was masquerading as morality.

After failing to pursue the inclusion of workers' right on the Uruguay Round agenda, the United States has repeatedly proposed the establishment of a GATT working party to consider the relationship of internationally recognized workers' rights to international trade. The GATT Council agreed in November 1987 that informal consultations would be held on the U.S. proposal. The issue was raised at no fewer than a dozen council meetings in 1988 and 1989. Industrial countries generally supported the request for a working party, while the developing countries opposed it, but there was no support for the United States on the substance of the issue.

With strong industrial country opposition to the inclusion of high-technology products as a separate subject for negotiation, the United States did not insist. There was a view that this subject could be rolled into the broader mandate on subsidies. The high-technology issue was different from workers' rights, since in the latter case other industrial countries were not strongly opposed, but indifferent. It does appear that unless the United States can mobilize enough support, particularly from other industrial countries, it will have difficulty in securing GATT action on the issue. Whether such support is forthcoming depends on both the strength of U.S. convictions on an initiative and the degree to which other industrial countries see their interests involved.

How much of what the United States really wanted from the Uruguay Round was contained in the DFA is difficult to assess. U.S. priorities have shifted over time, and they have not been consistently spelled out. At any point, the U.S. negotiators would have been able to list their priorities, both among the topics for negotiation and on the substance of each issue, but the list changed in response to a variety of external pressures. Most other participants did not display great consistency either, but the system is more responsive to, and dependent upon, the United States because of its traditionally dominant role.

In several areas of the negotiations, mixed signals came from the United States. In TRIPS, the United States had ambitious objectives with respect to changes in other countries' IP regimes, but resisted suggestions that a few changes might be necessary in U.S. law as well. In services, a bold and forthright initial position was diluted to the point of raising questions about the desirability of a multilateral services agreement. In agriculture, a free trade posture for over two years blocked the serious negotiations that the United States had spent enormous effort promoting.

A list of U.S. priorities at the outset of the Uruguay Round would probably include: agriculture, TRIPS, services, TRIMS, fuller participation by the developing countries, dispute settlement, and subsidies. As discussed, the DFA text on agriculture charted new territory, even if it did not go as far as the United States would have liked. Doubts may persist about the welfare benefits accruing from a TRIPS agreement, but the DFA text contains most of what the United States wanted. The outcome of the services negotiations remains in doubt, on account of the absence of concrete liberalization commitments and the threat to the integrity of the agreement of special case pleading. The draft TRIMS agreement is an empty box, but the United States appeared to lose some of its enthusiasm for a far-reaching agreement as the negotiations wore on.

On the issue of developing-country participation, U.S. goals were largely achieved. Special and differential treatment no longer served as an irresistible rallying cry for exempting developing countries from GATT obligations, as it had done in the Tokyo Round, and from meaningful participation in the rights and obligations of the trading system. Some developing countries would probably argue that they are now long on obligations and short on rights. There could be something to this, if existing regimes in agriculture and textiles and clothing persist, alongside a permissive use of unfair trade remedies. But from the U.S. perspective, developing countries participated more meaningfully than ever before in the Uruguay Round, and many of them moved impressively toward more liberal economic and trade regimes in the latter half of the 1980s.

On dispute settlement, the United States achieved its objectives of tightening procedures and ensuring greater automaticity in dealing with panel reports and their conclusions. But the achievement has a sting in its tail because of its potential implications for Section 301, and in the light of strong domestic opposition to what is perceived as an unacceptable cession of sovereignty. The draft subsidies agreement is probably less than what the United States hoped for, but the presumption that any subsidy over 5 percent (unless completely nonspecific) causes serious prejudice and should be avoided is an advance.

Though not on the U.S. list of priorities, and perhaps seen as problematic by the United States, several other texts in the DFA would make a positive and significant contribution to the trading system. These include antidumping, technical barriers to trade, import licensing, safeguards, and textiles and clothing. This assumes, of course, that the DFA would be broadly accepted as it stands, and that participants would take their new commitments seriously. There are also the broad liberalization results that would be expected from cuts in tariffs and the removal of nontariff barriers. When the scope and content of the DFA is assessed, and the good parts of the package weighed against those that raise doubts, the conclusion is that completion of the Uruguay Round would on balance be beneficial to all participants. Completion has not happened so far because governments have focused on near-term horizons and have allowed themselves to be distracted. A lack of political will has more to do with an inconclusive result than the existence of substantive differences that cannot be bridged.

CONCLUSIONS

The Direction of U.S. Trade Policy

The trade policy of the United States has become less consistent and more reactive over the last decade. The propensity has been growing to cater to sectoral interests. A protectionist bias has permeated the trade policy statutes. Dealings with trading partners are more adversarial than before, both inside and outside the General Agreement on Tariffs and Trade (GATT). A historic commitment to nondiscriminatory multilateral trade arrangements has waned, taking some of the GATT's credibility and viability with it.

All this has occurred against a background of striking economic and political change. A relative decline in U.S. power has been mirrored in the gathering strength of the European Community (EC) and Japan as trading partners, and the growth of U.S. dependence on foreign markets. The redistribution of economic power has created an increasingly multipolar world. But the United States remains the chief political and military power, a leadership role accentuated by the dismemberment of the Soviet Union, and demonstrated by the Gulf War.

Much of the early U.S. embrace of multilateralism responded to strategic, geopolitical imperatives; the economic advantages to the United States of open, nondiscriminatory trading arrangements were a secondary consideration. Gradually, the geopolitical motivation has been replaced by a narrowing economic focus. The increasing dependence of the United States on trade as a source of income and growth has sharpened economic interests in the trading system, feeding a sense of vulnerability and a defensive articulation of the national interest.

These trends have been translated into heightened protectionism, especially in the Congress, where attitudes toward foreign trade and multilateral commitments were always equivocal and sometimes openly hostile. The pressures on Congress to respond to constituency pleas for action against imports, and against foreign governments for allegedly protectionist behavior, increased enormously in the early 1980s. Much of the pressure derived directly from the effects of the strong dollar on competitiveness, against a background of the ballooning twin deficits. Action against specific import flows became associated in the public imagination with patriotism, with saving America from deindustrialization. The economic folly of justifying industry-specific trade restrictions as a cure to the trade deficit was overlooked, and protectionist interests successfully bent policy outcomes in their favor.

The surge in protectionist pressures in the early 1980s accelerated preexisting tendencies. The pressure abated somewhat after 1985, when the dollar fell back to more sustainable levels against other currencies, but a new tone had taken hold in the policy debate, and new policy directions had become entrenched. There was a growing sense of grievance against the trading partners of the United States. Reciprocity and fairness became rallying cries for all those in favor of an activist stance by government in trade matters. It became conventional wisdom that various U.S. industries' problems of competitiveness were overwhelmingly attributable to the trade practices of foreign governments and corporations. Demands for a "level playing field" were increasingly strident. The attainment of a level playing field required an explicit and specific use of power on a discriminatory basis. The assumption that U.S. industries' problems were due to the behavior of foreigners was made too easily to permit serious reflection on the real sources of difficulty. Too often, the demands on foreigners set policy standards that the United States itself felt under no obligation to meet. None of this sat well with established multilateral rules and due process, nor with foreign governments.

From an open trade policy perspective, it has been argued that the fair trade rhetoric was a means to outmaneuver protectionists and avoid market closings. A primary objective of the fair traders, after all, is to prize open foreign markets, to strike a blow for free trade. The administration no doubt hoped that crowbar tactics would prove effective, but this basically flawed approach neutralizes a vital domestic source of pressure on protectionists—export interests that would exchange domestic trade liberalization for improved access to foreign markets. Exporters could look to aggressive unilateralism as a device for improving their market opportunities, while import-competing interests, crying foul, could simultaneously promote their interest in insulated domestic markets.

There may be some disagreement about how effective the crowbar politics of the Section 301 approach to fair trade and reciprocity has been. Here, it has been argued that its results have been geographically uneven and limited in terms of actual market opening. At the same time, crowbar politics have soured international trade relations, garbled the articulation of liberal trade objectives, and rendered agreement on common action around them elusive at the international level. Aggressive unilateralism cannot serve long as an instrument of stable international trade relations.

The Congress has increasingly seen delegation of authority to the executive branch as an obstacle to the conduct of good constituency politics and successful election campaigns. Congress has sought to weaken the executive, convinced that the president cannot be trusted to strike the right balance between protection and open trade. If left to their own devices, presidents are too liberal for the liking of Congress. Little by little, statutory and institutional changes have constrained the president, forcing the administration to act in ways that would ensure protectionist outcomes or prevent action that would promote more liberal outcomes. The statutes also became more and more friendly to protection seekers.

The shift in the locus of power over trade policy outcomes away from the administration and toward Congress did not oblige Congress to assume trade policy functions on a day to day basis. Members of Congress wanted trade policy outcomes more likely to placate their constituents and secure reelection, but they did not want to be branded protectionists, or be seen to care only about short-term sectoral interests when these were detrimental to the longer term national interest. A subtle manipulation of statutes, institutions, and processes has created a situation in which trade restrictions can take effect with no-one in particular seeming to be responsible for them. The politics of responsibility avoidance have operated through the rhetoric of fair trade and reciprocity, diverting the policy debate away from domestic failings and competitive difficulties, and focusing it instead on the trade policy behavior of foreign governments and firms. The Section 301 remedies and the imposition of antidumping and countervailing-duty statutes are predicated upon unfair behavior by foreigners. The antidumping and countervailing-duty statutes have developed a complexity and automaticity that gives them every appearance of being neutral, balanced, and immune to politics. A growing body of analysis demonstrates their inherent protectionist bias. Protectionist outcomes have been secured through voluntary export restraints (VERs), the "no hands" protection instrument. VERs are administered by exporters, and require no action on the part of the importing country. Both Congress and the executive branch have supported this expedient.

The politics of responsibility avoidance also allow members of Congress to play to their constituents, by submitting far-reaching legislative proposals in what has almost become a ritual of overstatement. Lawmakers know that their proposals will be pared down or eliminated through legislative procedures, but in the meanwhile such proposals meet with approval from sectoral interest groups, bringing little of the opprobrium that would result if these initiatives ever found their way into law. This behavior encourages escalation of protectionist demands, stretches credibility, and saps public confidence.

The GATT Trading System

Largely through U.S. initiatives, the seeds of what became the GATT were sown in the early 1940s. Although the GATT eventually came into being through a series of unplanned events, it contained a coherent set of trade rules. Those rules served as the backbone of the trading system for much of the postwar period. Besides being a set of rules, the GATT provided a dispute-settlement mechanism and an institutional context for trade negotiations. The system was given coherence, and a certain simplicity, through the most-favored-nation (MFN) principle, to which only controlled exceptions were permitted. The GATT sought to extend trade liberalization, to provide the means for consolidating existing levels of market access, and to ensure transparency in trade policy. Quantitative trade restrictions were to be used only under exceptional conditions and for a limited period of time.

The GATT had certain weaknesses from the outset, some of which assumed increasing importance as time passed. It relied heavily on a mercantilist notion of reciprocity, which was politically necessary then and probably still is now, but the concept has developed in ways that are hostile to the defense of nondiscrimination, and sometimes, to trade liberalization. The coverage of the system was incomplete from the outset, both in respect of sectors and policy disciplines. In the political and economic conditions of the late 1940s and early 1950s, something of a "conspiracy" of noncompliance developed as regards particular disciplines. The United States, as the leader in the system, was willing to overlook some legal disobedience by other countries for broader political reasons. These kinds of arrangements, and the exceptions from disciplines that the United States allowed itself, became a source of friction when national objectives and international power relations began to change.

To the early weaknesses must be added the sustained assault on principle from which the GATT suffered, starting around the early 1970s. This was a difficult period economically, and the GATT did not fully succeed in holding the line against growing protectionism and systemic decline. The gradual undermining of multilateral commitments, and widening differences of view over what the rules of the system should be, were never dramatic enough to threaten the GATT's existence. On the contrary, successive attempts were made to strengthen and extend the system. The GATT agenda became increasingly diverse and complex. The Uruguay Round was the most developed expression of the broadened GATT agenda. It was an ambitious attempt to settle difficult old issues and challenging new ones in a multilateral setting.

The failure of the Brussels ministerial meeting of December 1990 to complete the Uruguay Round as planned was a blow to the credibility of the system. What happened at Brussels followed a pattern of suspense and crisis that began with the near collapse of the 1982 ministerial meeting. A breakdown was avoided on that occasion through the establishment of a program of work and studies. Agreement to launch the Uruguay Round came at the last minute in September 1986, after bitter months of haggling. The December 1988 Montreal Mid-term Review of the Uruguay Round broke down, and negotiations could not be resumed until the next April. On each of these occasions, virtually no decisions implying firm policy commitments were required. It was largely a matter of agreement to negotiate. Viewed in this light, it might perhaps have been foretold that the Brussels meeting would fail, on the one occasion in the last ten years that hard commitments were called for. Attempts to jump-start the negotiations since Brussels have fizzled, further impugning the credibility of governments that ceaselessly reaffirm the importance of a successful Uruguay Round to their vital national interests and global welfare.

Despite negotiating disappointments, the GATT has continued to mediate trade disputes with reasonable success, although there is a lengthening list of dispute cases where governments have refused to act. The resolution of these disputes has been linked to the negotiations, yet another sign of the absence of agreement about the rules of the game. The GATT has found it increasingly difficult to address the fundamental differences that divide countries. This is apparent in relations between the three major trading powers, the United States, the European Community, and Japan. And just when the difficulties and tensions surrounding developing-country participation in the trading system had begun to dissipate, these countries feel acute disappointment at the deadlock and delay. They wonder what kind of system they have bought into, after years of hesitation and resistance to industrial country pressure.

What of the United States in the GATT? The story of the trading system in the 1980s shows some of the frustrations that the United States has encountered in its efforts to animate the GATT. It is a story of persistent efforts at persuasion. Until the Brussels failure, the United States usually achieved its objectives in the GATT. Increasingly, the United States has presented two contrasting faces of U.S. trade policy. One promises seemingly solid support for the GATT, as reflected in numerous multilateral initiatives and considerable negotiating efforts on the part of the U.S. administration. The GATT-supportive strand of trade policy has for the most part promoted open markets and nondiscrimination. The other face, with an aggressive and unilaterally defined set of trade policies tinged with protectionism, tends to dominate at home, with apparent disregard for the multilateral trading system.

Part of the explanation for an aggressively unilateral stance in U.S. trade policy may be that negotiators have tried to secure better cooperation from other governments in defense of the multilateral trading system by demonstrating the consequences of straying from the GATT path. This explanation presupposes firm commitment to multilateralism in the United States, and a strategy to defend the GATT. But doubts about such a commitment are raised by discriminatory U.S. policies of protection in certain sectors, and a growing fascination with regionalism. A more plausible explanation of unilateralism in U.S. trade policy is that the GATT's agenda no longer mirrors U.S. objectives.

The unilateral approach has also been used to influence the perceptions of trading partners about what the United States would do if it fails to achieve its negotiating goals in the GATT. In the intellectual property field, for example, Special 301 has been used to persuade countries to support IP negotiations in the Uruguay Round. More generally, Section 301 has provided a means of influencing the GATT dispute-settlement rules and procedures.

Aside from any strategic use the United States might make of the GATT to promote its trade policy goals, the defensive aspect of U.S. behavior in GATT has become more prominent. The United States has found itself under attack for the restrictive nature of its antidumping and countervailing-duty laws, for its reluctance to open up its textiles and apparel market, and for backpedaling on some of the new issues, such as services and trade-related investment measures put on the GATT agenda by the United States in the first place. This has weakened the U.S. leadership role, raising doubts about the country's commitment to GATT principles and objectives. Moreover, the administration has entertained departures from the GATT rules, most notably through its patronage of voluntary export restraints. Heightened emphasis on the unilateral facet of U.S. trade policy can be partly explained in terms of evolving relations between Congress and the executive. The executive branch has seen GATT as an instrument for staving off protectionist tendencies in the Congress. Leadership in the GATT, emphasizing trade liberalization and the promise of more open foreign markets, has been the administration's way of responding to congressional pressures and demands. This approach was moderately successful in the past, but it has proved increasingly difficult for the administration to deliver the goods. The strategy has not been supported by a well-functioning GATT.

It required a broad-based consensus in GATT, at least among the major trading partners. The consensus has weakened, as shown most dramatically by the disputes between the United States and the European Community over agriculture, and between Japan and its trading partners over a host of issues. Moreover, in the first half of the 1980s, the GATT was paralyzed, as drawn-out efforts to launch new trade negotiations met with stiff opposition from certain developing countries, and EC equivocation. The trading partners of the United States have become less willing to follow the U.S. script in the GATT. This has made the commitment to multilateralism less attractive, and less effective in terms of the administration's objectives in respect both of trade policy and of Congress.

For years, Congress has shackled the administration in ways that reduced negotiating flexibility. This was part-institutional, for example through the strengthened role of private sector advisory committees, and part-legal, through a closer definition of negotiating objectives. The GATT appeared ineffectual to Congress if it could not bring about changes in the trade policies of other countries. It did not matter whether the changes sought by Congress dovetailed with the objectives of GATT. For many in Congress, whose longstanding hostility to GATT was driven by the challenge that GATT posed to congressional authority, the weakening of the institution was seen as a vindication of that stance. Only Congress could be trusted to run trade policy, even if it chose to do so in ways that emphasized power without responsibility.

Other major players in the trading system have proven incapable or unwilling to exercise leadership in the GATT. The European Community is hampered by its internal structure, which gives rise to a continuing struggle for influence between the executive Commission and the member states, and among the member states. The absence of a consistent decisionmaking core means it is easier to be reactive than to take initiatives, and settle for lowest-common-denominator positions dominated by interests in the status quo. Looking back over the GATT's history, it is hard to identify any initiatives that the European Community has taken to promote and strengthen the multilateral trading system. EC participation has been largely defensive and, where possible, accommodating.

Until matters seemed to get out of hand in the Uruguay Round, the European Community had always done enough to ensure that the GATT stayed intact and credible. This has been important to the EC Commission as a way of maintaining control over the member states, and to the member states as a defense against possible divide-and-rule tactics by large trading partners. But so far the necessary political and economic cohesion has been lacking for a proactive EC stance. In their self-conscious search for a unified identity that would forever lay destructive historical rivalries to rest and give Europe a seat at the high table of world affairs, the Europeans have been acutely sensitive to any hint that their policy decisions are unduly influenced by interests beyond their shores. This inability to lead, combined with an unwillingness to be led, has produced paralysis.

It remains to be seen whether fuller EC integration as a result of "Europe 1992," and moves toward monetary union envisaged in the Maastricht Treaty, will permit Europe to play a leadership role in international trade relations commensurate with its economic power. Reform of the common agricultural policy and controls on surplus production behind enormous protectionist barriers would remove a major source of trade friction between the European Community and the rest of the world.

The staggering lack of parity between Japan's economic power and political influence is a source of instability in international relations. Until Japan assumes the political responsibilities that correspond to its economic strength, the current tensions will persist. Japan was a latecomer to the GATT, joining in 1955 under U.S. protection and in the face of a discriminatory response from many countries that persists to this day. Japan has never used the GATT actively to promote the multilateral trading system and has hardly ever used it to defend its trading interests in terms of GATT rules. The 1989 antidumping case brought and won in GATT by Japan against the European Community was unprecedented. This action, together with strong public reactions to the accusatory flavor of President Bush's 1992 Tokyo trip, suggests that Japan is becoming less passive in the face of criticism. Perhaps Japan will become more reluctant to restrict its exports and expand its imports by administrative fiat in order to stave off the threat of trade restrictions. This would be good for the trading system.

What would a higher political profile and more active participation in the multilateral trading system require of Japan in terms of changes in its own policies? Instead of doing as little as possible to comply with foreign demands to neutralize the threat of the moment, Japan could cooperate more fully in distinguishing between competitiveness on one hand, and government-supported advantages, predation, and barriers to entry on the other. This might encourage the United States to do the same, rather than jumping too readily to the conclusion that the inability of U.S. industry to meet foreign competition can only be explained by other parties' unfair trade practices. More active participation in GATT would mean a willingness to defend Japanese trade policies in that forum and a more active use of the institution to protect Japan's own trade interests. In the Uruguay Round, Japan was active in negotiations on TRIMs, antidumping, and Article XXIV (regional arrangements), but was inhibited from taking more broad-based positions in favor of completing the round because of its defensive position on agriculture, especially the rice market.

Prospects for the Trading System

If multilateralism is in disrepair, why bother to fix it? The GATT's decline results from the accumulated actions of governments, and perhaps governments are ready to try something else. The question must be answered in two parts: why has the GATT system ceased to function effectively, and what alternatives are out there? The creeping demise of GATT could stem from its lack of usefulness as a system of trade rules, or it could arise from the neglect of policymakers. Has the GATT system failed governments, or have governments failed themselves?

The weakening of a multilateral approach to trade relations has been gradual, by default through the accumulation of ad hoc sector-specific decisions. These decisions, when justified, have been defended as special cases, and often characterized as temporary. Once sectors have benefited from special case status, it is difficult to return them to the mainstream. Witness agriculture, textiles, and autos. The unwillingness of the Bush administration to renew the voluntary export restraints on steel, and failure to reach an international agreement on trade in these products, led in mid-1992 to dozens of filings of antidumping and countervailing-duty cases. The steel case shows how the unfair trade remedies can come to the rescue of an industry seeking protection even when the authorities decide against prolonging special case treatment. It remains to be seen whether the VERs introduced on machine tools in 1987 will be phased out by the end of 1993, as scheduled. The postwar commitment of the United States to the GATT was driven largely by geopolitical considerations. The economic case for open trade and nondiscrimination took a back seat. If appreciation of the nonstrategic, economic case for the GATT was limited at the outset, it is perhaps not surprising that enthusiasm for the institution has waned with the end of the cold war. The economic advantages to the world trading community of a rules-based system promoting open trade were taken for granted. The costs of ad hoc departures from these arrangements have been assumed little by little through special case treatment of individual industries. This, together with the fact that the costs tend to be widely distributed among consumers, has made them less noticeable. Moreover, even if the special case industries have multiplied over time, they are still the exception and not the rule. The conclusion, then, is that the GATT's diminished success as arbiter of international trade relations reflects accumulated neglect on the part of governments, and not obsolescence of the underlying GATT conception.

The second part of the question is whether alternative arrangements exist whereby the benefits of specialization and exchange across national frontiers can be captured without a GATT-like nondiscriminatory multilateral framework. It has been forcefully argued that the administrative, market-sharing approach to trade that underlies the special case treatment of sectors is no substitute, simply because it is almost always protectionist in intent. Administered trading arrangements built around market-sharing agreements have always amounted to rearguard actions aimed at preserving the status quo in the light of changed competitive realities. Their aim has been to avoid adjustment costs.

What if instead of drawing out the past, industrial policy looked to the future and diverted resources to new and promising industries? Might this not be an effective substitute for the GATT muddle? The political system of the United States precludes this option. The U.S. brand of democratic government lacks the necessary machinery for decisions favoring one industry over another to be based on technical rather than political grounds. Mechanisms do not exist for arbitrating among the claimants of government favors, and political capture is almost inevitable. Support that preserves the status quo and support that promotes innovation or modernization are hard to distinguish in practice. Moreover, the simple truth that supporting one industry means, by definition, penalizing another is sometimes overlooked by backers of industrial policy. If running an industrial policy were not fraught with such difficulties, why would all the subterfuges of responsibility avoidance traced in this study have been necessary in order to secure special case treatment for the politically powerful?

As fundamental as the difficulty of running a policy of measured and appropriate intervention under the U.S. political system is the question of bureaucratic capacity to read the market. Picking winners is not an exact science. Besides, political drag will make bureaucratic decisionmaking cumbersome, lacking the agility to act rapidly. As discussed earlier, both the extent of administrative intervention in industrial decisionmaking in Japan, and the success of such a strategy, have been exaggerated.

Regionalism is another potentially competing approach to the GATT conception of trade relations. Regional trading arrangements have looked increasingly attractive as the multilateral system has waned. They can, after all, cash in on the benefits of international specialization without all the encumbrances of multilateral due process. Small groups of like-minded countries can take trade-liberalizing action, avoiding the transaction costs and delays that have come to be associated with doing business in the GATT. There is no intrinsic reason why regionalism has to undermine a broader commitment to nondiscriminatory liberal trade arrangements, but this can easily occur. It is improbable that regional trade agreements will avoid trade diversion altogether, and uncertain whether third parties will be compensated for lost trade opportunities through the dynamic benefits of trade creation.

Regional arrangements might build on existing sectoral distortions, and make them harder to address in the future. They may become exclusive and discriminatory, in a manner that promotes market sharing and destroys trading opportunities. A number of features of existing regional arrangements demonstrate the downside—the European Community has thrived on one of the most comprehensive protectionist edifices ever constructed by market economies, the common agricultural policy. The draft North American Free Trade Agreement excludes textiles and clothing, agriculture, autos, and energy products from its mainstream liberalization commitments. To the extent that regional arrangements consolidate sectoral protectionist deals, they are hostile to the broader conception of open trading arrangements. Where they do not, they can legitimately be seen as staging posts on the way to a rejuvenated multilateral trading system. Whatever the outcome of the Uruguay Round, an important challenge for the GATT in the coming years is to establish rules and procedures that will hold in check the negative aspects of regional pacts, ensuring a transition to geographically broader-based arrangements in the future. A number of ground rules have been suggested in this study for ensuring that regionalism is a positive force in the trading system (chapter 7).

In summary, the United States has armed itself with a formidable array of weapons against trade. These instruments of policy have been used sparingly, maintaining intact a large part of the traditional open trading arrangements on which the United States has thrived. But legal and procedural restraints on protectionist action have been removed, leaving only the self-discipline of policymakers as a safeguard against the destruction of the trading system. The dangers of pork barrel politics and unrestrained protectionism, from which Congress insulated itself in the 1930s, have been allowed to creep back into the system. Trade policy is ripe for capture. This risk was demonstrated in a small way by President Bush's trip to Japan in early 1992. For a few short days, the demands of sectoral interest groups that they be awarded Japanese market share were allowed to define the foreign policy of the United States toward one of its closest allies.

As the Clinton administration starts to shape the details of economic policy, competing pressures will assert themselves, which could affect decisions on trade. President Clinton seeks on the one hand to invest more in physical infrastructure and in training and education, in order to restore competitiveness and more rapid productivity growth to the American economy. On the other, the amount of spending that will be possible in pursuit of these objectives is severely constrained. The federal budget deficit is forecast to exceed $300 billion in the next few years, and in his election campaign Bill Clinton promised to cut it by $145 billion within four years. How, if at all, will the twin objectives of investing in infrastructure, high technology and people, and bringing government spending under control, impact on trade policy in the Clinton administration?

Trade policy did not figure as a major issue in the 1992 election campaign. A tendency might develop, however, to associate a pro-competitiveness policy for industry with trade restrictions, particularly as such measures do not make demands on the federal budget, but rather act as implicit taxes on consumers. The temptation will be strong to harness the fair trade statutes, or allow spurious arguments based on national security, in order to justify trade measures. But trade restrictions imposed to benefit specific firms or industries would not be consistent with the objective of broad-based improvements in national competitiveness. The narrow focus of trade restrictions would benefit some industries and penalize others, and would not serve the declared intention of enhancing the competitiveness of the American economy at large. Moreover, there is a grave danger that government attempts to make detailed judgments about firms and industries deserving of support will be mistaken, leading to a costly misappropriation of public funds. If the government believes that technological enhancement and improved competitiveness require financial involvement by the state, then the best hope for success is to create the conditions under which firms can prosper, rather than trying to micro-manage the decisions that firms take.

Even assuming that some credible criteria were developed to justify making specific industries or firms the target of government favors, rather than providing generally available support, trade restrictions would be an inefficient and dubious intervention. They would tax consumers, and choke off competition. As discussed earlier, industries that have proved successful in persuading governments to accord them trade protection have been just as successful in maintaining the protection year after year. Some specific industry groups have been highly successful in bending trade policies in their favor, especially in the face of the poorly organized and diffuse consumer interests that pay for these privileges. A nation in search of rejuvenation and renewed competitiveness can ill-afford the economic costs of political capture. The Clinton campaign commitment to control the influence of lobbyists and special interest groups could play a useful role in ensuring that trade policy serves national, not parochial interests.

Renewed commitment to a rules-based set of multilateral trading arrangements, founded on nondiscrimination, is the surest way of reducing the risk that the system will degenerate into a web of special case deals, choking off the benefits of specialization through trade, stifling change, and accelerating economic decline. The enemies of progress are pervasive discretion in trade policymaking, combined with the protectionist bias of the trade-remedy statutes, and assiduous pursuit of the politics of responsibility avoidance.

Revised approaches to trade policy discussion and formulation are called for in several areas. First, there needs to be more explicit recognition that the advantages of stable rules under multilateral arrangements accrue to all the parties involved. The multilateral trading system is not a construct that the United States underwrote as part of the burden of world leadership. It was never a matter of self-sacrifice. Self-interest has always been central to the enterprise, and the economic benefits of GATT-type arrangements deserve fuller acknowledgment. The United States should therefore seek an early completion of the Uruguay Round and also implement the domestically unpopular parts of the package. It would also mean greater recognition of multilateral disciplines and procedures, and a willingness to accept multilateral accountability in respect of regional initiatives.

Second, the habit should be broken of assuming that domestic industry's only problems stem from unfair foreign trade practices. A proper assessment of the competitiveness of industries under import pressure is urgently needed. By overworking the notion of unfairness, the right questions are never asked, and industries can insulate themselves from competition for seemingly indefinite periods. If a political decision is made to give industry protection, this should be made explicit and transparent. This suggests a revitalization of the Section 201 safeguard mechanism, and reform of the unfair trade statutes, most notably antidumping and countervailing-duty provisions.

Third, a willingness by Congress once again to allow a more thorough-going delegation of trade policy authority to the president would permit the executive branch to weigh trade policy decisions more carefully in the national interest, and to take full responsibility for its decisions. At the same time, Congress would take responsibility for the general direction of trade policy, but would deflect constituency pressure that gives rise to special-case pleading. Such a move would reduce the temptation to subvert the statutes in the name of troubled industries, and reduce the sway of special interest influences in decisions that can affect the economy at large, and millions of consumers.

Fourth, instead of letting concern about worker displacement lead to an accumulation of uncompetitive industries, trade adjustment assistance (TAA) can ease the transition of workers out of shrinking firms and industries. Experience with TAA has been disappointing in the United States, in large measure because it has never received high priority. Adequate TAA would not only make the country more responsive to change, but it would also recognize that the adjustment costs falling on the few mean greater gains for society at large.

The greatest challenge of all in the trade sphere is not how to deal with the misbehavior of foreigners, nor how to revamp the GATT. It is how to confront the politics of responsibility avoidance at home, and to design and implement policy in the national interest.

NOTES

CHAPTER 1

1. Organization for Economic Cooperation and Development, *National Accounts, 1960–1988* (Paris: OECD, 1990). The numbers for imports and exports start to diverge significantly after 1980 with the growth in the U.S. trade deficit. This is discussed further below.

2. GATT, *International Trade* (Geneva: General Agreement on Tariffs and Trade), various years.

3. Angus Maddison, *The World Economy in the 20th Century* (Paris: OECD, 1989). For the United States, the 1980s were a period of fairly strong growth following the 1981–82 recession. Annual average real growth amounted to 3.9 percent from 1983 to 1989. See *Economic Report of the President, 1993* (Washington, D.C.: U.S. Government Printing Office), Table B–2, p. 351.

4. A good deal has been written on the controversy over the relationship between unemployment and protection. A short and readable account of the debate is found in Charles Collyns, *Can Protection Cure Unemployment?* Thames Essay No. 31 (London: Trade Policy Research Centre, 1982).

5. For example, comparable rates over the same period were 13 percent for Korea, 11 percent for Taiwan, 10 percent for Mexico, 7 percent for Japan, and 7 percent for Brazil. Maddison, *World Economy in the 20th Century,* pp. 139–40.

6. For some recent analyses of the process and implications of globalization, see William Brock and Robert Hormats, eds., *The Global Economy: America's Role in the Decade Ahead* (New York: W. W. Norton, 1990), and Raymond Vernon and Debora Spar, *Beyond Globalism: Remaking American Foreign Economic Policy* (New York: Free Press, 1989).

7. This section draws heavily on the excellent work done in this field by the Institute for International Economics. In particular, see Stephen Marris, *Deficits and*

the Dollar: The World Economy at Risk, Policy Analyses in International Economics, 14 (Washington, D.C.: Institute for International Economics, 1985); C. Fred Bergsten, *America in the World Economy: A Strategy for the 1990s* (Washington, D.C.: Institute for International Economics, 1988); and William R. Cline, *United States External Adjustment and the World Economy* (Washington, D.C.: Institute for International Economics, 1989).

8. *Economic Report of the President, January, 1989* (Washington, D.C.: U.S. Government Printing Office, 1989), Table B–58, p. 373.

9. Ibid., Table B–71, p. 390.

10. These figures are taken from OECD, *National Accounts, 1960–1988.*

11. Ibid.

12. *Economic Report of the President, 1989*, Table B–58, p. 373.

13. *Economic Report of the President, 1993*, Table B–1, p. 348.

14. Gross private savings on average were equal to about 17.5 percent of GDP in 1979, and despite some year-to-year variation in the intervening period, had dropped to 16 percent in 1986 and was below 16 percent in every year from 1987 to 1991. Ibid., Table B–1, p. 348, and Table B–26, p. 378.

15. Cline, *United States External Adjustment*, pp. 61–62.

16. OECD, *National Accounts, 1960–1988.*

17. A major exception to the "hands-off" approach to trade policy in President Reagan's first term was his 1981 decision to "facilitate" a Japanese export restraint undertaking on automobiles. The Reagan administration also concluded steel export restraint agreements in 1982 and 1984. See Chapter 5.

18. Cline, *United States External Adjustment*, pp. 66–70.

19. OECD, *National Accounts, 1960–1988.*

20. The works cited earlier by the economists of the Institute for International Economics, Bergsten and Cline, look at these prospects and contains detailed proposals on how to deal with the twin deficits, prominent among which are action to bring down the budget deficit and the value of the dollar. The central challenge is how to adjust toward equilibrium at an adequate pace without provoking recession.

21. This statement would obviously be qualified by a more careful examination of all the relationships involved. It is widely acknowledged, for example, that the growth in the trade deficit from 1982 onward was fueled by the relatively faster economic growth in the United States in those years, and also by the reduction of import demand in the developing countries following the 1982 debt crisis.

22. Strictly speaking, trade barriers could affect the trade balance in anything other than the short term only if they somehow changed domestic consumption and investment relationships.

23. Ernest H. Preeg, *The American Challenge in World Trade: U.S. Interests in the Multilateral Trading System*, Significant Issues Series, vol. 11, no. 7 (Washington, D.C.: Center for Strategic Studies, 1989).

24. Jagdish N. Bhagwati, *Protectionism* (Cambridge, Mass.: MIT Press, 1988).

25. Ibid., quoted from UNCTAD sources.

26. OECD, *National Accounts, 1960–1988.* At current prices and 1985 exchange rates, the GDP of the United States was US$ 4,818 billion, that of Japan US$ 1,528 billion, and that of the EC US$ 3,151 billion.

27. National Science Foundation study quoted by Preeg, *American Challenge in World Trade*, p. 15.

28. Quoted in Paul Kennedy, *The Rise and Fall of the Great Powers: Economic Change and Military Conflict from 1500 to 2000* (New York: Vintage Books, 1987), p. 525.

29. Brock and Hormats, *Global Economy*, p. 8.

30. In particular, Mancur Olson, *The Rise and Decline of Nations* (New Haven: Yale University Press, 1982). Also, the epic book by Kennedy, *Rise and Fall of the Great Powers*, is a highly readable study of changes in the relative power of nations over the past five centuries.

31. Vernon and Spar, *Beyond Globalism*, p. 15.

32. The experience of the Gulf War suggests that even in the military field, where U.S. power is overwhelming, there was a clear preference for cooperative action and consensus building, something that did not characterize earlier U.S. adventures in Grenada and Panama. While the scale and risks of the latter two encounters as compared with the Gulf War are part of the explanation, the United States clearly wanted to share political responsibility in the Gulf in a manner it may not have felt constrained to do some years earlier.

33. In C. Michael Aho and Jonathan D. Aronson, *Trade Talks: America Better Listen!* (New York: Council on Foreign Relations, 1985), it is noted (p. 61) that while one in fourteen jobs was directly or indirectly related to manufactured exports in 1964, the ratio had risen to one in seven by 1980. Moreover, exports as a percentage of final sales more than doubled during the 1970s.

34. The best single introduction to this debate is Stephen D. Krasner, ed., *International Regimes* (Ithaca, N.Y.: Cornell University Press, 1983). This is a collection of conference papers originally published in the journal *International Organization* in the spring of 1982. The papers cover a wide spectrum of views about the validity of regime theory and the conclusions that might be drawn from it.

35. Charles P. Kindleberger, *The World in Depression, 1929–1939* (Berkeley: University of California Press, rev. ed., 1986). Kindleberger argues that the United Kingdom could not and the United States would not play the hegemonic role that would have been required to stave off the economic disasters of the 1930s, and hence the international regime came apart.

36. Essentially, public goods are goods whose benefits are indivisible. In other words, they are jointly consumed. This means that individuals cannot be induced to reveal their preferences for, or pay for such goods, because their total supply remains unchanged by individual decisions. This situation, where supply and demand cannot be equated at an equilibrium price, is an example of what economists call "market failure," and it means that public goods must be provided independently of private demand decisions. A good example of a public good is national defense.

37. Robert O. Keohane, *After Hegemony: Cooperation and Discord in the World Political Economy* (Princeton: Princeton University Press, 1984). A strong critique of hegemonic stability theory is that of Isabelle Grunberg, "Exploring the 'Myth' of Hegemonic Stability," *International Organization*, vol. 44, no. 4 (Autumn 1990). The author challenges the role of "benevolence" in many versions of hegemonic stability theory and questions the validity of the assumption that public goods exist in international regimes. Several of the issues discussed above are also analyzed in John S.

Odell and Thomas D. Willet, eds., *International Trade Policies: Gains from Exchange between Economics and Political Science* (Ann Arbor: University of Michigan Press, 1990).

38. For a fuller discussion, see Charles Lipson, "The Transformation of Trade: The Source and Effects of Regime Change," in Stephen D. Krasner, ed., *International Regimes* (Ithaca, N.Y.: Cornell University Press), pp. 233–71. In the same volume, see also Jock A. Finlayson and Mark W. Zacher, "The GATT and the Regulation of Trade Barriers: Regime Dynamics and Functions," pp. 273–314.

39. A good survey of this literature is provided in Robert E. Baldwin, "The Political Economy of Protectionism," in Jagdish N. Bhagwati, ed., *Import Competition and Response* (Chicago: University of Chicago Press, 1982), pp. 245–86. See also Richard Blackhurst, Nicolas Marian, and Jan Tumlir, *Trade Liberalization, Protectionism and Interdependence*, GATT Studies in International Trade, no. 5 (Geneva: GATT, 1977). A good recent work, focusing on the United States is that of I. M. Destler, *American Trade Politics*, 2nd ed. (Washington, D.C., and New York: Institute for International Economics and the Twentieth Century Fund, 1992).

40. Robert E. Baldwin, "The Economics of the GATT," in Peter Oppenheimer, ed., *Issues in International Economics*, Oxford International Symposia, vol. 5 (London: Oriel Press, 1980), pp. 82–93.

41. Baldwin, "Economics of the GATT"; Blackhurst, Marian, and Tumlir, *Trade Liberalization*; and Destler, *American Trade Politics*.

42. There have always been economic arguments as to why this may not be true in every case. This is taken up below.

43. In some private correspondence with Jan Tumlir, James Meade asserted that this consideration weighed with the original signatories to GATT. It helps to explain how reciprocity gained its initial foothold in the ethos of GATT.

44. This issue will be taken up in Chapter 7, where the nature of the trading system is analyzed in more depth.

45. For an overview of agricultural issues, see Organization for Economic Cooperation and Development, *National Policies and Agricultural Trade* (Paris: OECD, 1987).

46. See William R. Cline, *The Future of World Trade in Textiles and Apparel* (Washington, D.C.: Institute for International Economics, 1987).

47. Interest in this idea is likely to be stronger in the context of regional arrangements, at least in the first instance, because of jurisdictional difficulties involved in the enforcement of antitrust law.

48. These arrangements do not exist for Czechoslovakia, which is an original signatory of the general agreement.

49. In the summer of 1990, the Soviet Union was granted observer status in the GATT.

50. This is true of agriculture and subsidies, but not of textiles.

51. One illustration of changes in this area is the citrus dispute brought to the GATT by the United States against the EC in 1982. The United States contended that preferential access for Mediterranean countries to the EC market for certain citrus products compromised U.S. GATT rights. The United States had not raised the issue when the arrangements were first introduced. The GATT legal ruling was not

as clear as it might have been, but the finding was essentially in favor of the United States. The matter was eventually settled bilaterally.

52. Among the earliest discussions of the metamorphosis of the reciprocity principle is that of William R. Cline, *"Reciprocity": A New Approach to World Trade Policy?* (Washington, D.C.: Institute for International Economics, 1982).

53. According to Meyer, the United States cut its tariffs disproportionately in 1947 and did so again, by a factor of two, in the mid-1950s to facilitate the entry of Japan into GATT. Apparently, the United States also persuaded Canada, Denmark, Finland, Italy, Norway, and Sweden to make trade concessions to Japan in return for U.S. concessions to them. This is reported in Lipson, "Transformation of Trade," pp. 235, 256. The reference is to F. V. Meyer, *International Trade Policy* (New York: St. Martin's Press, 1978).

54. Most notably, in the selective denial by the United States of the injury test to developing countries in certain countervailing-duty cases if these countries had not made a commitment to eliminate export subsides on manufactured goods. Strictly speaking, this was not a case where reciprocity in the sense discussed above was at stake. Rather, it was the use of leverage to persuade countries to do something that they were not committed to doing in the GATT.

55. For an extensive analysis of the issues involved, see Jeffrey J. Schott, ed., *Free Trade Areas and U.S. Trade Policy* (Washington, D.C.: Institute for International Economics, 1989).

56. The environmental debate was lively in the early 1970s. A major part of the debate at that time was about the limits to growth and the depletion of finite resources, although pollution and environmental degradation more generally were also issues. At the international level, environmental concerns found expression in the convening of the 1972 Stockholm Conference and the establishment of the United Nations Environment Program. A major source of analysis on the international aspects of environmental issues is the Organization for Cooperation and Development.

57. The meaning of fast-track legislative authority for international trade negotiations is fully explained in chapter 2.

58. For a full discussion of these issues, see Patrick Low, ed., *International Trade and the Environment*, Discussion Paper no. 159 (Washington, D.C.: World Bank, 1992).

59. See, for example, Gunter Schramm and Jeremy Warford, eds., *Environmental Management and Economic Development* (Baltimore: Johns Hopkins University Press for World Bank, 1989).

60. For textbook treatments, see William Baumol and Wallace Oates, *The Theory of Environmental Policy* (Englewood Cliffs, N.J.: Prentice Hall, 1975), and Horst Siebert, *Economics of the Environment* (Lexington, Mass.: Lexington Books, 1981).

61. In March 1991, Senator Lloyd Bensten (Chairman, Senate Finance Committee) and Congressman Dan Rostenkowski (Chairman, House Ways and Means Committee) wrote a letter to President Bush expressing concerns about the effects of an FTA with Mexico on such issues as the environment, worker rights, jobs, and wages. The letter requested an action plan from the administration, by May 1, 1991, indicating how these issues would be addressed. The action plan, *Response of the Administration to Issues Raised in Connection with the Negotiation of a North American Free Trade Agreement* (May 1, 1991), was a carefully argued document that dealt explicitly with economic impact issues, provisions on trade liberalization in the proposed FTA,

worker adjustment provisions in the United States, labor standards and worker rights in the context of the FTA, and environmental matters. The action plan contained commitments explicitly to address environmental issues with Mexico, particularly in relation to common border problems.

62. This, for example, was part of an April 1991 legislative proposal by Senator David L. Boren, which would change U.S. countervailing-duty laws to make international differences in costs of the pollution abatement and control countervailable.

63. Although most of the focus on these issues in the United States has centered on the proposed North American FTA, attention has also turned recently to whether the GATT adequately addresses environmental protection issues. This is discussed later in the study.

CHAPTER 2

1. Events in the 1930s and 1940s leading up to the birth of GATT are recorded in several works. Perhaps the most important studies are those of Richard N. Gardner, *Sterling Dollar Diplomacy* (Oxford: Clarendon Press, 1956); Clair Wilcox, *A Charter for World Trade* (New York: Arno Press, 1949); and W. Brown, *The United States and the Restoration of World Trade* (Washington, D.C.: Brookings Institution, 1950).

2. See Gerard Curzon, *Multilateral Commercial Diplomacy* (London: Michael Joseph, 1965), pp. 15–34.

3. Wilcox, *Charter for World Trade*, p. 8.

4. Charles P. Kindleberger, *The World in Depression, 1929–1939*, 2d ed. (Berkeley, Ca.: University of California Press, 1986), p. 170. On account of price effects, not all the reduction in trade flows measured in dollars represented decreases in the volume of trade. Likewise, not all the reduction is attributable to the effects of trade barriers on supply and demand, since the latter were subject to other influences as well. None of these observations, however, detract from the fact that trade-policy errors contributed in significant measure to the dramatic shrinkage of trade flows in the period immediately following the Great Crash.

5. The 1933 World Economic conference had ended in failure over gold and exchange-rate issues.

6. Kindleberger, *World in Depression*, p. 233.

7. Ibid., p. 235.

8. See John H. Jackson, *World Trade and the Law of GATT* (Indianapolis: Bobbs-Merrill, 1969), p. 37.

9. John H. Jackson, "The General Agreement on Tariffs and Trade in the Domestic Law of the United States," *Michigan Law Review*, vol. 66, no. 2 (1967): 249.

10. Gardner, *Sterling Dollar Diplomacy*, p. 48.

11. For a summary analysis of these bilateral issues, see Jay Culbert, "War-Time Anglo-American Talks and the Making of the GATT," *The World Economy*, vol. 10, no. 4 (December 1987): 381–407.

12. Robert E. Hudec, *The GATT Legal System and World Trade Diplomacy* (New York: Praeger, 1975), pp. 14–18.

13. In GATT parlance, national treatment is the requirement that imports receive identical treatment to their domestic equivalents once they have crossed the frontier. The national treatment rule was designed to ensure that border commitments relating to the maximum tariffs that could be charged on products were not subsequently neutralized through the discriminatory use of domestic charges, taxes, or regulations.

14. The balance-of-payments safeguards permitted countries to use quantitative import restrictions when faced with a reserve shortage. The use of quantitative trade restrictions is normally prohibited under GATT.

15. Ibid. This analysis contrasts with what Dam says about a basic U.S. goal with respect to the charter: "Oversimplified only slightly, it was that all nontariff barriers should be flatly prohibited within the framework of a comprehensive code governing world trade." See Kenneth W. Dam, *Law and the International Economic Organization* (Chicago: University of Chicago Press, Midway Reprint, 1977), p. 12. This implies a rather unrealistic scenario where all exceptions to the prohibition of nontariff measures were agreed over the opposition of the United States.

16. The MFN and tariff binding commitments (Articles I and II) appear in Part I of the General Agreement, and the exemption for existing legislation (also known as the "grandfather clause") applies to Part II. Part III is not covered by the exemption, and it contains the rules on customs duties and free trade areas, and deals with procedural and administrative matters. Although this is discussed later in the study, it may be noted here that a tariff "binding" in GATT is a commitment, usually undertaken in the context of negotiations involving reciprocal exchanges, not to raise a tariff above a specified level.

17. Jackson, *World Trade and the Law of GATT*, pp. 60–66.

18. In effect, it is difficult to imagine the GATT as not being an organization, considering the way it acts and the things it does.

19. This appeared in the 1951 extension. See John H. Jackson, "Multilateral and Bilateral Negotiating Approaches for the Conduct of US Trade Policies," in Robert M. Stern, *US Trade Policies in a Changing World Economy* (Cambridge, Mass.: MIT Press, 1987), pp. 377–401.

20. These changes, known as the "fast-track" procedures, are described in greater detail in Chapter 3.

21. The most notable area where this has occurred is in agriculture, with the result that the United States sought, and received, a GATT waiver for its agricultural support policies in 1955.

22. See William Diebold, Jr., *The End of the ITO*, Essays in International Finance, no. 16 (Department of Economics, Princeton University, 1952), for an account of the circumstances surrounding the demise of the ITO.

23. Jackson, *World Trade and the Law of GATT*, p. 51.

24. See Diebold, *End of the ITO*, pp. 6–37.

25. For a coherent, but rather extreme expression of these views, see P. Cortney, *The Economic Munich* (New York: Philosophical Library, 1949).

26. Diebold, *End of the ITO*, pp. 14–24.

27. The development, significance, and legacy of the Tokyo Round Agreements and Arrangements are taken up in detail in chapter 5. There were six major nontariff measure

agreements, covering technical barriers to trade, customs valuation, government procurement, import licensing procedures, subsidies and countervailing duties, and antidumping.

28. This section draws heavily on a careful legal analysis by Robert E. Hudec, "The Legal Status of GATT in the Domestic Law of the United States," in M. Hilf, F. G. Jacobs, and E.-U. Petersmann, *The European Community and GATT* (Deventer: Kluwer, 1986).

29. *United States v. Guy W. Capps, Inc.*, 204 F.2d 655 (1953).

30. The Congress always has the power to override any existing international obligation.

31. Section 350 of the Reciprocal Trade Agreements Act of 1934.

32. The Trade Act of 1974 and the Omnibus Trade and Competitiveness Act of 1988 did the same thing for the Tokyo Round and the Uruguay Round, respectively.

33. *United States v. Yoshida International, Inc.*, 526 F.2d 560 (1975). In this case, the president's authority to impose a surcharge on imports, as he did in 1971, was challenged. The final court ruling supported the claim that Section 350 gave authority to raise tariffs, but only to the extent that increases corresponded to the reductions that had previously been proclaimed. In this particular instance, however, it was held that the action was in any case justified under the Trading with the Enemy Act of 1917.

34. Jackson, "General Agreement on Tariffs and Trade, (1967)."

35. For a general treatment of some of the issues raised by the Tokyo Round results, see John H. Jackson, "The Birth of the GATT-MTN System: A Constitutional Appraisal," *Law and Policy in International Business*, vol. 12, no. 21 (1983): 21.

36. No domestic law was written for the Import Licensing Code, since commitments under the Code did not require any changes in U.S. federal law.

37. Section 3 of the Trade Agreements Act of 1979.

38. The conditional MFN issue is further discussed in chapter 6.

CHAPTER 3

1. These early trends in tariff policy are briefly discussed in I. M. Destler, *American Trade Politics*, 2nd ed. (Washington, D.C., and New York: Institute for International Eocnomics and Twentieth Century Fund, 1992), and also in Economic Report of the President, 1989.

2. I. M. Destler, "United States Trade Policy Making in the Uruguay Round," in Henry R. Nau, ed., *Domestic Trade Politics and the Uruguay Round* (New York: Columbia University Press, 1989).

3. For a detailed analysis of the relationship between the executive and Congress in trade-policy matters, see Robert E. Baldwin, *The Political Economy of U.S. Import Policy* (Cambridge, Mass.: MIT Press, 1985). This work also traces policy trends through the statutes, and a good part of this section is based on Baldwin's analysis.

4. The Tariff Acts of 1890 and 1897 provided the countervailing-duty authority and the Antidumping Act of 1921 did the same for antidumping duties.

5. Tariff Act of 1922.

6. Tariff Act of 1930.

7. The 1954 act only referred to the extension of the president's negotiating authority.

8. John H. Jackson, *World Trade and the Law of GATT* (Indianapolis: Bobbs-Merrill, 1969), p. 52. As discussed in Chapter 2, there was always doubt as to whether the 1945 negotiating authority had been exceeded when the United States signed the General Agreement on Tariffs and Trade in 1947.

9. The authority was to cut rates above 5 percent by up to 50 percent and those below 5 percent could be eliminated.

10. Section 337 of the Tariff Act of 1930 is a statute dealing with unfair trade practices that is administered by the USITC. Most of the cases brought under this provision have dealt with patent, copyright, or trademark infringements.

11. This list is taken from Shirley A. Coffield, "Section 310 of the Trade Act of 1974: New Life in the Old Dog," *Federal Bar News and Journal,* vol. 33, no. 6 (July-August 1986): 248–51.

12. The GATT safeguard mechanism allows countries to renegotiate previous trade policy commitments in order temporarily to protect particular industries facing harmful import competition.

13. For a full legislative history of safeguards in the United States, see Christopher W. Derrick, "The Evolution of the Escape Clause: The United States' Quest for Effective Relief from Fairly Traded Imports," *North Carolina Journal of International Law and Commercial Regulation,* vol. 13, no. 2 (Spring 1988): 347–71.

14. According to Derrick, "The Evolution Escape Clause," there was only a 13 percent success rate among petitioners between 1951 and 1962, and an 11 percent success rate between 1962 and 1974. Changes in the safeguards provisions under the 1962 Trade Expansion Act had made the burden of proof of injury from imports more stringent than previously.

15. Most notably, by relaxing the causal link between a prior concession and the alleged injury, and by establishing that imports need only be "substantial cause" of injury, rather than a "major factor."

16. To approximately 35 percent of all petitions, according to Derrick, "Evolution of the Escape Clause."

17. Ibid., p. 358.

18. See figures from the Organization for Economic Cooperation and Development quoted in Chapter 4.

19. On this point, and for a thorough analysis of subsidies as a trade issue, see Gary Clyde Hufbauer and Joanna Shelton Erb, *Subsidies in International Trade* (Washington, D.C.: Institute for International Economics, 1984).

20. As discussed in chapter 6, this initiative met with little success.

21. See Joan E.Twiggs, *The Tokyo Round of Multilateral Trade Negotiations: A Case Study in Building Support for Diplomacy* (Lanham, Md.: University Press of America, 1987). This is an account of how well the fast-track system functioned for the Tokyo Round.

22. This modified legislation predating the GATT, which had not foreseen the injury test in antisubsidy cases involving dutiable imports. The injury test was extended selectively, however, basically only to GATT-member signatories of the Subsidies Code who had foresworn use of export subsidies on manufactured goods. The United States has always applied an injury test in antidumping cases.

23. Congress made explicit in 1979 that these undertakings were to be accepted only in exceptional circumstances.

24. As, for example, those applied on steel and motor vehicles.

25. For a detailed analysis of the context and content of this Act, see Stephen L. Lande and Craig VanGrasstek, *The Trade and Tariff Act of 1984: Trade Policy in the Reagan Administration* (Lexington, Mass.: Lexington Books, 1986).

26. The United States had agreed, reluctantly, to a GSP program authorized under the Trade Act of 1974 and renewed under the 1984 Act. The Caribbean Basin Initiative was introduced in 1983, largely for strategic reasons.

27. The terms had previously been defined in the legislative history of the 1974 act.

28. The steel arrangements will be discussed in chapter 5. The reciprocity legislation on wine required the USTR to examine all foreign barriers to U.S. wine, and then consult with Congress and the industry on ways of removing them. Retaliation is not mandated, nor negotiations authorized.

29. In the way that the 1962 and 1974 Acts were for the Kennedy and Tokyo Rounds.

30. Judith Hippler Bello and Alan F. Holmer, "The Heart of the 1988 Trade Act: A Legislative History of Amendments to Section 301," *Stanford Journal of International Law* (Fall 1988): 1–44.

31. Under the 1988 Act an "unjustifiable" practices is defined as a violation of the legal rights of the United States under a trade agreement or any practice that is unjustifiable and burdens and restricts the commerce of the United States. "Commerce" is defined to include goods, services, and investment.

32. The European Airbus is an obvious target of this provision.

33. Raymond J. Ahearn and Alfred Reifman, "Trade Legislation in 1987: Congress Takes Charge," in Robert E. Baldwin and J. David Richardson, eds., *Issues in the Uruguay Round*, NBER Conference Report (Cambridge, Mass.: 1986), p. 75.

CHAPTER 4

1. Apart from the standard arguments relating to dynamic externalities, recent theoretical developments in international economics have argued that the existence of market imperfections may mean that trade restrictions raise national welfare.

2. Voluntary export restraints are, of course, nontariff trade barriers. They are counted as such in the estimates given below of nontariff barriers, but are given a separate section as well because of their importance, quantitatively and systemically, as a modern instrument of protection.

3. These numbers conceal significant differences among countries. Following the 1934 Reciprocal Trade Agreements program in the United States, many U.S. tariffs were lower than the rates prevailing in Europe in the immediate aftermath of the war.

4. Jaime de Melo and David Tarr, *A General Equilibrium Analysis of U.S. Foreign Trade Policy* (Cambridge, Mass.: MIT Press, 1992).

5. There is no reason to suppose that the picture would change much for later years up to 1990.

6. Joint Ministerial Committee of the Board of Governors of the World Bank and the International Monetary Fund on the Transfer of Real Resources to Developing Countries (Development Committee), *The Impact of Industrial Countries' Trade, Agricultural and Industrial Policies on Developing Countries* (Washington, D.C.: Development Committee, 1991).

7. Jan Tumlir, *Protectionism: Trade Policy in Democratic Societies* (Washington, D.C.: American Enterprise Institute for Public Policy Research, 1985), p. 39. This monograph contains an excellent analysis of economic, political, and legal aspects of voluntary export restraints.

8. Michel Kostecki, "Export-Restraint Arrangements and Trade Liberalization," *The World Economy*, vol. 10, no. 4 (December 1987): 425–53.

9. General Agreement on Tariffs and Trade Secretariat, *Review of Developments in the Trading System: September 1988–February 1989* (Geneva: GATT, 1989).

10. All the VERs reported in the sample that affect agricultural products are protecting the EC market.

11. This will be seen from some of the sectoral cases examined in the next chapter.

12. Kostecki, "Export-Restraint Arrangements."

13. There is a view that the GATT Antidumping Code only foresees price undertakings, but it is not shared by the EC.

14. The Committee on Antidumping and the Committee on Subsidies and Countervailing Duties. These data are tabulated below.

15. These involved steel fork arms, certain knives, and cameras, respectively.

16. Eight cases led to the granting of adjustment assistance.

17. For a thorough recent treatment of these, see John H. Jackson, *The World Trading System: Law and Policy of International Economic Relations* (Cambridge, Mass.: MIT Press, 1989), chaps. 10–11. There is a useful tabulation of the sequence of steps involved in antidumping and countervailing-duty cases in J. M. Finger and Tracy Murray, *Policing Unfair Imports: The U.S. Example*, World Bank Working Papers no. WPS 401 (Washington, D.C.: World Bank, March 1990), p. 5. Basically, there are preliminary and final stages in the process when determinations are made. The USITC is responsible for the injury investigation (in all antidumping cases and in countervailing-duty cases where the injury test is granted—this excludes certain developing countries) and the Department of Commerce for the dumping or subsidy determination. The procedures foresee the possibility of applying provisional measures while at the preliminary stage of investigations.

18. It is important to bear in mind that from an economic perspective, even if reasonable definitions of dumping and subsidization can be agreed upon, and the practices can be shown to occur, it is not clear that the imposition of antidumping and countervailing duties is an appropriate response because of the advantages that accrue as a result of lower import prices. The price benefits fall to consumers and do not generally enter the reckoning because of the way the unfair trade statutes are designed.

19. The discussion that follows has been heavily influenced by the insightful work of J. Michael Finger, Patrick Messerlin, and others on these issues. See, in particular, J. M. Finger, H. Keith Hall, and Douglas R. Nelson, "The Political Economy of Administered Protection," *American Economic Review*, vol. 72, no. 1 (June 1982): 452–66, and Finger and Murray, *Policing Unfair Imports*. See also Patrick Messerlin,

"The EC Antidumping Regulations: A First Economic Appraisal (1980–85),"
Weltwirschaftliches Archiv, Band 125, Heft 3. An excellent recent work is Richard
Boltuck and Robert E. Litan, eds., *Down in the Dumps: Administration of the Unfair
Trade Laws* (Washington, D.C.: Brookings Institution, 1991).

20. Finger and Murray, *Policing Unfair Imports*.

21. In the EC, around 50 percent of antidumping complaints are rejected.

22. These were final determinations. Preliminary determinations showed a much
higher level of affirmative findings.

23. Petitions might be rejected if they are badly prepared or the case seems particularly weak. In practice, rejected petitions are not a large share of total petitions.

24. See United States General Accounting Office, *International Trade: Observations
on the Operations of the International Trade Commission*, GAO/NSIAD-87–80 (February
1987), and Alan M. Rugman and Andrew D. M. Anderson, *Administered Protection in
America* (London: Croom Helm, 1987), esp. chap. 3.

25. See in particular, Boltuck and Litan, eds., *Down in the Dumps*. See also Michael
S. Knoll, *Dump Our Antidumping Law*, Foreign Policy Briefing no. 11 (Washington,
D.C.: Cato Institute, July 1991).

26. The injury test is dispensed with in some countervailing-duty cases involving
developing countries.

27. Assuming, of course, the existence of subsidization or dumping.

28. See J. Michael Finger and Julio Nogués, "International Control of Subsidies and
Countervailing Duties," *World Bank Economic Review*, vol. 1, no. 4 (September 1987):
707–25.

29. For a discussion of these issues, see Organization for Economic Cooperation and
Development, *Competition and Trade Policies: Their Interaction* (Paris: OECD, 1984).

30. As discussed later, GATT's dispute-settlement machinery has been significantly
improved in recent years, and this is probably attributable in part to pressure exerted
by Section 301.

31. Outcomes are recorded in the year the case was initiated, although outcomes
might have occurred a year or more later.

32. The possibility of self-initiation was introduced in the Trade Act of 1984.

33. A more thorough and sophisticated analysis of the use of Section 301 is being
undertaken in Kimberley Ann Elliott and Thomas Bayard, *Reciprocity and Retaliation:
Does Might Make Right in U.S. Trade Policy?* (Washington, D.C.: Institute for International Economics, forthcoming). This study argues that the success of Section 301
was greater after 1985, when some two-thirds of the cases led to outcomes that coincided with U.S. objectives, compared to only one-third in the previous period. Again,
there is some subjectivity in the analysis.

34. These estimates are lower than those of Elliott and Bayard, mainly because the
outcome of more cases is treated as uncertain.

35. See, for example, Richard N. Cooper, "Industrial Policy and Trade
Distortion," in Dominick Salvatore, ed., *The New Protectionist Threat to World
Welfare* (New York: North Holland, 1987), pp. 233–65, and Avinash Dixit, "How
Should the United States Respond to Other Countries' Trade Policies?" in Robert
M. Stern, ed., *U.S. Trade Policies in a Changing World Economy* (Cambridge, Mass.:
MIT Press, 1987), pp. 245–82. Both these papers also look at economic arguments

which generally militate against support for retaliation or threats of it as a viable policy mode.

36. The EC cases involved citrus, Portuguese accession to the EC, and animal growth hormones; the Japanese cases leather and semiconductors; Canada's was advertising, Argentina's hides, and Brazil's patent protection of pharmaceuticals.

37. Counterretaliation measures were taken by the EC in the cases involving citrus and pasta, and the Spain and Portugal EC enlargement. The hormones case almost provoked counterretaliation.

38. This discussion does not, of course, weigh the amount of trade involved in all these different cases.

39. These were Brazil, India, Mexico, China, Korea, Saudi Arabia, Taiwan, and Thailand.

40. These were Argentina, Canada, Chile, Colombia, Egypt, Greece, Indonesia, Italy, Japan, Malaysia, Pakistan, Philippines, Portugal, Spain, Turkey, Venezuela, and Yugoslavia.

41. The SII is discussed further in chapter 5.

42. These were Saudi Arabia, Korea, and Taiwan.

43. This was Portugal.

44. Argentina, Canada, Chile, China, Colombia, Cyprus, Ecuador, El Salvador, Germany, Greece, Guatemala, Indonesia, Italy, Hungary, Japan, New Zealand, Pakistan, Paraguay, Peru, Saudi Arabia, Spain, United Arab Emirates, and Venezuela.

45. Australia, Brazil, Egypt, European Community, Hungary, Philippines, Poland, Republic of Korea, and Turkey.

46. S 1850 (October 22), by Baucus (D.-Mont.) and Danforth (R.-Mo.); HR 787 (October 23), approved by a House subcommittee; and HR 3702 (November 4) by Gephardt (D.-Mo.) and Levin (D.-Mich.). No action was taken on these bills before the end of congressional sessions in 1992, which means that the bills die. But they provide a flavor of what is likley to come in the next Congress.

47. A special GATT meeting was convened to hear complaints against the United States because of its Section 301 policy in March 1989.

48. Robert E. Hudec, "Thinking About the New Section 301: Beyond Good and Evil," in Jagdish N. Bhagwati and Hugh T. Patrick, eds., *Aggressive Unilateralism: America's 301 Trade Policy and the World Trading System* (Ann Arbor: University of Michigan Press, 1990).

49. An argument could be constructed around the idea that threats of retaliation can have a comparable effect to actual trade measures, but the case would be difficult to prove.

50. Hudec, "Thinking about the New Section 301."

51. J. Michael Finger, "That Old GATT Magic No More Cast Its Spell (How the Uruguay Round Failed)," *Journal of World Trade*, vol. 25, no. 2 (April 1991): 19–22.

CHAPTER 5

1. Among these are the sectors discussed in chapter 4 in relation to the increased use of VERs. Besides steel, textiles and clothing, autos, and semiconductors, these include a range of agricultural products, other transport equipment, other electronic products, footwear, machine tools, leather, and lumber.

2. For an interesting discussion of trade frictions with Japan, and an explanation how protagonists in the U.S. debate on the issue have been divided, see the May/June 1990 issue of *The International Economy*, pp. 26–45. The best generally available writings that aim to bring a little more balance to the discussion of the "Japan problem" in the United States are those of Jagdish Bhagwati. See Jagdish Bhagwati, "Aggressive Unilateralism: An Overview," in Jagdish Bhagwati and Hugh T. Patrick, eds., *Aggressive Unilateralism: America's 301 Trade Policy and the World Trading System* (Ann Arbor: University of Michigan Press, 1990). See also Jagdish N. Bhagwati, *The World Trading System at Risk* (Princeton: Princeton University Press, 1991). For a recent defense of the use of aggressive bilateral trade policy against Japan, see Rudiger Dornbusch, "Policy Options for Freer Trade: The Case for Bilateralism," in Robert Z. Lawrence and Charles L. Schultze, eds., *An American Trade Strategy: Options for the 1990s* (Washington, D.C.: Brookings Institution, 1990).

3. Yoshi Tsurumi, "U.S.-Japanese Relations: From Brinkmanship to Statesmanship," *World Policy Journal* (Winter 1989–90): 2–3.

4. The European Community has had an active and fractious bilateral dialogue with Japan, but has also brought the general issue to GATT, as will be discussed in the later part of this study.

5. There have, of course, been other sectoral disputes in recent years on such issues as beef, citrus, tobacco, and supercomputers.

6. For one evaluation of the MOSS talks, see United States General Accounting Office, *Evaluation of the Market-Oriented Sector-Selective Talks*, GAO/NSIAD-88-205 (July 1988).

7. In this context, these are arrangements whereby firms hold each other's stocks and therefore obviously have a collusive approach to business.

8. Bureau of National Affairs, *International Trade Reporter: Current Reports*, vol. 9, no. 12 (March 18, 1992): 494–95.

9. There have been other important non-agricultural sources of disagreement, such as the question of European airbus subsidies. Also, the EC's 1992 program for fuller integration has led to some differences in such areas as financial services, telecommunications, government procurement, and quantitative restrictions applied by member states.

10. Robert E. Hudec, "Legal Issues in US-EC Trade Policy: GATT Litigation 1960–1985," in Robert E. Baldwin, Carl B. Hamilton, and André Sapir, *Issues in US-EC Trade Relations* (Chicago: University of Chicago Press, 1988), pp. 17–64.

11. William T. Hogan, "Protectionism in the Steel Industry: A Historical Perspective," in Dominick Salvatore, ed., *The New Protectionist Threat to World Welfare* (New York: North-Holland, 1987), pp. 352–64.

12. Stephen L. Lande and Craig VanGrasstek, *The Trade and Tariff Act of 1984: Trade Policy in the Reagan Administration* (Lexington, Mass.: Lexington Books, 1986), p. 143.

13. The details for this section are taken mainly from Hogan, "Protectionism in the Steel Industry"; Organization for Economic Cooperation and Development, *Costs and Benefits of Protection* (Paris:OECD, 1985); Kent Jones, *Impasse and Crisis in Steel Trade Policy*, Thames Essay no. 35 (London: Trade Policy Research Centre, 1983); Thomas R. Howell, William A. Noellert, Jesse G. Kreier, and Alan Wm. Wolff, *Steel and the*

State: Government Intervention and Steel's Structural Crisis (Boulder, Colo.: Westview Press, 1988); and Alan F. Holmer and Judith Hippler Bello, "Section 201 of the Trade Act of 1974: The Reagan Record," *North Carolina Journal of International Law and Commercial Regulation*, vol. 13, no. 2 (Spring 1988): 185–223.

14. Howell et al., *Steel and the State*.

15. Ibid.

16. Andrew Anderson and Alan Rugman, "Subsidies in the U.S. Steel Industry: A New Conceptual Framework and Literature Review," *Journal of World Trade*, vol. 23, no. 6 (December 1989): 59–83.

17. Jaime de Melo and David Tarr, *A General Equilibrium Analysis of U.S. Foreign Trade Policy* (Cambridge, Mass.: MIT Press, 1992).

18. The United States had, nevertheless, negotiated orderly marketing arrangements in 1983 on stainless steel bar, rod, and alloy tool steel exports from Sweden, Austria, Japan, Canada, Poland, Argentina, and Spain.

19. Quoted in Martin Wolf, "Why Voluntary Export Restraints? An Historical Analysis," *The World Economy*, vol. 12, no. 3 (September 1989): 273–91.

20. 49 *Federal Register* 36,813 (1984).

21. For an interesting and innovative study of industry opposition to protection, and the way it can develop to counter-balance protection seekers, see I. M. Destler and John S. Odell, *Anti-Protection: Changing Forces in United States Trade Politics*, Policy Analyses in International Economics, 21 (Washington, D.C.: Institute for International Economics, 1987). This study demonstrates mixed results from the actions of anti-protection interest groups, and suggests ways that these interests might be more adequately represented.

22. Bureau of National Affairs, *International Trade Reporter: Current Reports*, vol. 9, no. 28 (July 8, 1992): 1164.

23. Ibid., p. 1162.

24. This is not true of some segments of the high fashion clothing market, where product differentiation through brand names is important.

25. The material in this section is drawn largely from William R. Cline, *The Future of World Trade in Textiles and Apparel* (Washington, D.C.: Institute for International Economics, 1987), and Ying-Pik Choi, Hwa Soo Chung, and Nicolas Marian, *The Multi-Fibre Arrangement in Theory and Practice* (London: Frances Pinter, 1985).

26. Certain European countries also extended textile import restraints to some developing countries during the 1950s.

27. Changes in the arrangements are tabulated in Vincent Cable, "Textiles and Clothing," in J. Michael Finger and Andrzej Olechowski, *The Uruguay Round: A Handbook on the Multilateral Trade Negotiations* (Washington, D.C: World Bank, November 1987), pp. 171–90.

28. See Martin Wolf, Hans Hinrich Glismann, Joseph Pelzman, and Dean Spinanger, *Costs of Protecting Jobs in Textiles and Clothing*, Thames Essay no. 37 (London: Trade Policy Research Centre, 1984). In OECD, *Costs and Benefits of Protection*, p. 106, it is reported that the earliest cotton textiles VER, between the United States and Japan in 1956 caused substantial trade diversion. From 1956–57 to 1960–61, U.S. imports of cotton textiles increased by 60 percent, but Japan's share fell from 52 percent to 30 percent, while that of Hong Kong rose from 1 percent to 25 percent.

29. Not necessarily by the same amount if imports and domestic goods are not perfect substitutes.

30. Cline, *Future of World Trade*, p. 15.

31. Irene Trela and John Whalley, "Unraveling the Threads of the MFA," in Carl B. Hamilton, ed., *Textiles Trade and the Developing Countries: Eliminating the Multi-Fibre Arrangement in the 1990s* (Washington, D.C.: World Bank, 1990).

32. De Melo and Tarr, *General Equilibrium Analysis*.

33. General Agreement on Tariffs and Trade, *Arrangement Regarding International Trade in Textiles* (Geneva: GATT, 1974).

34. Wolf et al., *Costs of Protecting Jobs*, p. 136.

35. The one exception to this was the successful retaliation by China in 1983 to a unilateral U.S. import quota. China retaliated against agricultural products, thus pitting two powerful lobbies against each other and forcing the textiles interests to retreat. See Destler and Odell, *Anti-Protection*, p. 16.

36. This story is reported by James Bovard, "The Mother of All Import Charades," *Wall Street Journal*, August 15, 1991.

37. Destler and Odell, *Anti-Protection*, pp. 20–21.

38. Some importing industrial countries, including Australia, New Zealand, Norway Sweden, and Japan are not members of the MFA, or else they maintain few, if any, MFA-type restrictions.

39. See draft of the North American Free Trade Agreement (September, 1992).

40. See Geoffrey Bannister and Patrick Low, *North American Free Trade in Textiles and Apparel: A Case of Constrained Liberalization*, PRE Working Paper no. 994, (Washington D.C.: World Bank, 1992).

41. Countries in the Organization for Economic Cooperation and Development.

42. OECD, *Costs and Benefits of Protection*, p. 131.

43. See Stephen D. Cohen, *The Making of United States International Economic Policy*, 3rd. ed. (New York: Praeger, 1988).

44. I. M. Destler, *American Trade Politics*, 2d ed. (Washington, D.C., and New York: Institute for International Economics and Twentieth Century Fund, 1992), p. 78.

45. It is also suggested that there was a bureaucratic interest on the part of Japan's Ministry of International Trade and Industry (MITI) to exert some influence over the domestic auto industry, and this situation presented a good opportunity to do so. See Cohen, *Making of United States International Eocnomic Policy*, p. 171.

46. Advisory Committee for Trade Policy and Negotiations (ACTPN), *Analysis of the U.S.-Japan Trade Problem*, Report to the United States Trade Representative (Washington, D.C., February, 1989), p. 85.

47. Ibid., p. 87.

48. As discussed below, the VER has been maintained.

49. Ronald Reagan, *An American Life* (New York: Simon & Schuster, 1990).

50. Ibid., pp. 253–55. Italics in original.

51. Quoted in Cohen, *Making of United States International Economic Policy*, p. 170.

52. Quoted in Destler, *American Trade Politics*, p. 79.

53. Bureau of National Affairs, *International Trade Reporter: Current Reports* (January 16, 1991).

54. HR 4100 was announced in December 1991 and formally introduced on January 22, 1992. A similar legislative proposal was introduced in the Senate the same day by Senator Donald Riegle, Jr. (D.-Mich.), and others. See Bureau of National Affairs, *International Trade Reporter: Current Reports*, vol. 9, no. 28 (July 8, 1992): 28, 183.

55. Robert W. Crandall, "Import Quotas in the Automobile Industry: The Costs of Protectionism," *The Brookings Review*, no. 4 (Summer 1984).

56. De Melo and Tarr, *General Equilibrium Analysis*.

57. Some would argue that the space program and defense spending amount to de facto industrial policy. To the extent that firms receiving subsidies of various kinds as a result of research or production arrangements involving space and defense activities can be regarded as beneficiaries of industrial policy, such policy has been demand led and largely uncoordinated. What has happened in the semiconductor industry is a supply based strategy aimed at supporting and strengthening the market position of an entire industry.

58. The textiles and clothing industry does not fit this comparison very well because it was already floundering in the 1950s.

59. The material for this section comes mainly from Clyde V. Prestowitz, Jr., *Trading Places: How We Allowed Japan to Take the Lead* (New York:Basic Books, 1988), chap. 2, pp. 26–70; the background paper by Gary Clyde Hufbauer in Twentieth Century Fund Task Force on the Future of American Trade Policy, *The Free Trade Debate* (New York: Priority Press Publications, 1989), chap. 4; the ACTPN Report (1989); United States General Accounting Office, *Observations on the U.S.-Japan Semiconductor Arrangement*, GAO/NSIAD-87–134BR (April 1987); and for more recent developments, various issues of Bureau of National Affairs, *International Trade Reporter: Current Reports*.

60. Prestowitz, *Trading Places*, p. 45.

61. This design would certainly be clearer in the case of the Section 301 and antidumping cases than for the antitrust and intellectual property ones.

62. Bureau of National Affairs, *International Trade Reporter: Current Reports*, vol. 6, no. 10 (March 1989).

63. Jagdish N. Bhagwati, "VERS, Quid Pro Quo DFI and VIEs: Political-Economy-Theoretical Analysis," *International Economic Journal*, vol. 1 (1987): 1–12.

64. Jagdish N. Bhagwati, *Protectionism* (Cambridge, Mass.: MIT Press, 1988), pp. 82–84.

65. There was no antidumping investigation of any kind to back up the allegation.

66. The only other such case occurred in respect of leather in March 1986, when tariffs were raised on Japanese leather and leather goods imports valued at US$ 24 million.

67. Bureau of National Affairs, *International Trade Reporter: Current Reports*, vol. 8, no. 23 (June 5, 1991): 845–6.

68. See, for example, Bureau of National Affairs, *International Trade Reporter: Current Reports*, vol. 9, no. 15 (April 1992): 650.

69. This is no less true when final goods are involved, but in that case the immediate costs of protection fall directly on consumers, who with their only allies, importers and retailers, do not often make effective lobbies.

70. Destler and Odell, *Anti-Protection*, chap. 6.

CHAPTER 6

1. I. M. Destler, *American Trade Politics*, 2d ed. (Washington, D.C., and New York: Institute for International Economics and Twentieth Century Fund, 1992), chap. 1.

2. Ibid.

3. This has been well understood by political scientists for a long time. See for example, Destler's discussion of E. E. Schattschneider's analysis of the problem in the 1930s, in ibid.

4. For a systematic analysis of this phenomenon, see I. M. Destler and John Odell, *Anti-Protection: Changing Forces in United States Trade Politics*, Policy Analyses in International Economics, 21 (Washington, D.C.: Institute for International Economics, 1987).

5. The interpretation presented here of trends in the trade policy-making process owe a good deal to the work of Pietro Nivola. For Nivola's insightful and original analysis of the dynamics of trade policy-making, see Pietro S. Nivola, "Trade Policy: Refereeing the Playing Field," in Thomas E. Mann, *A Question of Balance: The President, the Congress, and Foreign Policy* (Washington, D.C.: Brookings Institution, 1990), pp. 201–53. Yoffie provides an analysis along similar lines, which emphasizes the institutional nature of deficiencies in trade policy-making. See David B. Yoffie, "American Trade Policy: An Obsolete Bargain?" in John E. Chubb and Paul E. Peterson, eds., *Can the Government Govern?* (Washington, D.C.: Brookings Institution, 1989), pp. 100–138.

6. This was, in essence, a reference price system for determining the dutiable value of imports.

7. Destler, *American Trade Politics*, p. 71.

8. This was the trade matter in which the legislative veto was an issue after the Trade Act of 1984, as discussed above.

9. Martin Wolf, "Why Voluntary Export Restraints? An Historical Analysis," *The World Economy*, vol. 12, no. 3 (September 1989).

10. Nivola, "Trade Policy."

11. This "game" is described and analyzed in Robert Pastor, "The Cry-and-Sigh Syndrome: Congress and Trade Policy," in Allen Schick, ed., *Making Economic Policy in Congress* (Washington, D.C.: American Enterprise Institute, 1983), pp. 157–95.

12. This was demonstrated by Mondale in 1984 and Gephardt in 1988.

13. Alan F. Holmer and Judith Hippler Bello, "The 1988 Trade Bill: Is It Protectionist?" *International Trade Reporter: Current Reports*, vol. 5, no. 39 (October 5, 1988): 1347–52.

14. This is not to say that the sponsors of the proposal are economically illiterate. Gephardt is on record as acknowledging that no more than 20 percent of the trade deficit is attributable to foreign trade practices. See Raymond J. Ahearn and Alfred Reifman, "Trade Legislation in 1987: Congress Takes Charge," in Robert E. Baldwin and J. David Richardson, eds., *Issues in the Uruguay Round*, NBER Conference Report (Cambridge, Mass.: 1986), p. 92. This is probably a guess. Most estimates put the figure very much lower than 20 percent. Hufbauer in Twentieth Century Fund Task Force on the Future of American Trade Policy, *The Free Trade Debate* (1989), table

2.10, p. 174, estimates that about 6 percent of the deterioration in the trade deficit between 1980 and 1988 was attributable to new foreign nontariff barriers, whereas equivalent U.S. barriers made a negative contribution of about 17 percent to the deficit. This means that new foreign trade barriers did not come near to matching the trade-restricting effects of the United States' own new trade restrictions in the 1980s.

15. I. M. Destler, *American Trade Politics: System Under Stress* (Washington, D.C., and New York: Institute for International Economics and Twentieth Century Fund, 1986), Appendix A, pp. 223–37. The appendix was not repeated in the second edition of this book.

CHAPTER 7

1. It is arguable that even if there are recidivist trade policy tendencies, the GATT may score a partial success by moderating the trend toward deterioration.

2. The notion that trade liberalization is concessional, and must be rewarded by off-setting action, is difficult to justify in a gains from trade framework, unless it could be shown that by delaying trade liberalization a country will secure, through negotiation, additional benefits from comparable action by a trading partner. At best, this would be a short-term argument for delaying unilateral action.

3. For a full discussion of this branch of theoretical literature, see W. M. Corden, *Trade Policy and Economic Welfare* (Oxford: Clarendon Press, 1974).

4. This is the well-known optimum tariff argument for intervention.

5. These include the possibility of taking antidumping measures, the use of subsidies and countervailing duties, and trade restrictions to protect the balance of payments.

6. For a good, largely nontechnical introduction to this literature, see Paul Krugman, ed., *Strategic Trade Policy and the New International Economics* (Cambridge, Mass.: MIT Press, 1986). See also Gene M. Grossman and J. David Richardson, *Strategic Trade Policy: A Survey of Issues and Early Analysis*, Special Papers in International Economics, no. 15 (Princeton: Princeton University Press, 1985). For a survey of empirical work that uses models that incorporate imperfect competition, see J. David Richardson, "Empirical Research on Trade Liberalization with Imperfect Competition: A Survey," *OECD Economic Studies*, no. 12 (Spring 1989): 7–50.

7. In developing countries seeking to establish an industrial base, the situation is somewhat different, since there the issue is more generally between one sector, the nascent manufacturing sector, and another, usually the agricultural sector. It is, at least in theory, less a question of favoring one industry or firm over another. Most countries have used this kind of strategy in the industrialization process, and the successful ones have not protected industries for too long or too excessively, and have emphasized export competitiveness as much as protection from imports in the domestic market. The industrialization debate has concentrated more on the nature and duration of intervention than on the principle.

8. As previously discussed, this literature looks at the political market for protection, and focuses on imperfections in that market that allow producer interests favoring

protection to win out over consumer interests, despite the fact that the protectionist outcome is socially costly. Useful references to this literature include Robert E. Baldwin, "The Political Economy of Protectionism," in Jagdish N. Bhagwati, ed., *Import Competition and Response* (Chicago: University of Chicago Press, 1982), and Richard Blackhurst, Nicolas Marian, and Jan Tumlir, *Trade Liberalization, Protectionism and Interdependence,* GATT Studies in International Trade, no. 5 (Geneva: GATT, 1977). A good short survey is also provided in Bruno Frey, "The Political Economy of Protection," in David Greenaway, ed., *Current Issues in International Trade: Theory and Policy* (London: Macmillan, 1985), pp. 139–57. There is a lively analysis of how to redress imbalances in the political market for protection in J. M. Finger, "Incorporating the Gains from Trade into Policy," *The World Economy,* vol. 5, no. 4 (December 1982): 376–77.

9. See, for example, Paul R. Krugman, "The U.S. Response to Foreign Industrial Targeting," *Brookings Papers on Economic Activity,* no. 1 (1984): 101–04.

10. Paul R. Krugman, "Is Free Trade Passé?" *Economic Perspectives,* vol. 1, no. 2 (Fall 1987): 144.

11. Nondiscrimination and MFN are sometimes distinguished from each other by suggesting that MFN refers to a narrower range of policies and practices involving tariffs and charges, whereas nondiscrimination covers all manner of trade policies. For these purposes, such a distinction is not useful and the terms are used interchangeably.

12. The standard works on the GATT are the following: Gerard Curzon, *Multilateral Commercial Diplomacy* (London: Michael Joseph, 1965); John H. Jackson, *World Trade and the Law of GATT* (Indianapolis: Bobbs-Merrill, 1969); Robert E. Hudec, *The GATT Legal System and World Trade Diplomacy* (New York: Praeger, 1975); Kenneth W. Dam, *The GATT: Law and the International Economic Organization* (Chicago: University of Chicago Press, Midway Reprint, 1977); Edmond McGovern, *International Trade Regulation* (Exeter: Globefield Press, 1986); and John H. Jackson, *The World Trading System: Law and Policy of International Economic Relations* (Cambridge, Mass.: MIT Press, 1989). All these works provide a detailed analysis of the GATT, its origins and its functioning. The 1989 book by Jackson contains a good deal of recent material, incorporating changes in the GATT system that have occurred in the 1970s and 1980s.

13. As discussed elsewhere, the Article VI rules on antidumping and countervailing duties have been supplemented by agreements, known as codes, which were negotiated in the Tokyo Round.

14. The national security exception has been the subject of some dispute, since it has been invoked on occasion to justify politically motivated trade embargoes, such as that of the United States on Nicaragua, and of several countries on Argentina. Some of the Article XX exceptions are likely to received more attention as environmental issues linked to trade assume greater importance.

15. General Agreement on Tariffs and Trade, "Protocol Relating to Trade Negotiations among Developing Countries," *Basic Instruments and Selected Documents,* BISD 18/S, 11, 18th suppl. (Geneva: GATT, 1970–71), p. 11.

16. Formally entitled the Decision on Differential and More Favourable Treatment, Reciprocity and Fuller Participation of Developing Countries. This decision, of 28 November 28, 1979, contained a number of other provisions in favor of developing countries, which are referred to below.

17. The African, Caribbean, and Pacific (ACP) states covered by the Lomé Convention.

18. Prior to the 1979 Enabling Clause, GSP had been covered by an Article XXV waiver.

19. As discussed elsewhere, and particularly in chapters 7 and 10, the Tokyo Round of Multilateral Trade Negotiations (1973–79) was largely concerned with a range of nontariff measures. Among the Agreements and Arrangements that emerged from the Tokyo Round, the most important concerned technical barriers to trade, government procurement, subsidies and countervailing duties, customs valuation, import licensing procedures, and anti-dumping. The agreements are often referred to as codes.

20. The least developed countries are a group of some thirty-five countries designated by the United Nations as the world's poorest countries. They are located in Africa, Asia, and the Pacific.

21. This is a standard argument about the inability of governments to insulate themselves from political pressures and ensure an optimal outcome, even if the desired outcome is different to that which the market would produce. For an analysis of rent-seeking behavior, see Anne O. Krueger, "The Political Economy of the Rent-Seeking Society," *American Economic Review*, vol. 64 (1974): 291–303. For a more general analysis of the differences and similarities between quotas and tariffs see W. M. Corden, *The Theory of Protection* (Oxford: Clarendon Press, 1971), esp. chap. 9.

22. The only minor exceptions are those of Articles XXI and XX, dealing with national security and a range of other special exceptions, as discussed above.

23. Declaration on Trade Measures Taken for Balance of Payments Purposes of November 28, 1979.

24. Italy, Greece, Hungary, and Poland had temporary recourse to Article XII in the 1980s.

25. Developed countries can use Article XXVIII provisions to do the same thing, but this provision only permits the negotiated unbinding of previously consolidated tariffs, and not the use of quantitative restrictions.

26. Developing countries are exempted from this prohibition, but have increasingly undertaken to eliminate such subsidies.

27. The MFN principle alone will not ensure the best possible sourcing, because there may be barriers against imports entering the domestic market.

28. For a brief discussion of the history of the MFN principle, see William Diebold, Jr., "The History and the Issues," in William Diebold Jr., ed., *Bilateralism, Multilateralism and Canada in U.S. Trade Policy* (Cambridge, Mass.: Ballinger, 1988), pp. 1–36.

29. There is a good discussion of some of these issues in Richard H. Snape, "Is Non-Discrimination Really Dead?" *The World Economy*, vol. 11, no. 1 (March 1988): 1–17.

30. Many of the innovations in anti-dumping and countervailing-duty law cannot be said to infringe GATT rules. This is a reflection of a need for improvements in the GATT rules, but also an indication of the real difficulties involved in making technically sound, objectively based rules and regulations where many complex variables are involved. Even the most sincere efforts to attain objectivity would not eliminate administrative discretion and the potential for protectionist abuses.

31. See, in particular, Jan Tumlir, *Protectionsim: Trade Policy in Democratic Societies* (Washington, D.C.: American Enterprise Institute for Public Policy Research, 1985), and Jagdish N. Bhagwati, *Protectionism* (Cambridge, Mass.: MIT Press, 1988). See also the discussion in Michel Kostecki, "Export-Restraint Arrangements and Trade Liberalization, *The World Economy*, vol. 10, no. 4 (December 1987):425–454, and Martin Wolf, "Why Voluntary Export Restraints? An Historical Analysis," *The World Economy*, vol. 12, no. 3 (September 1989).

32. See John H. Jackson, "Consistency of Export-Restraint Arrangements with the GATT," *The World Economy*, vol. 11, no. 4 (December 1988): 485–500.

33. The two provisions most relevant here are Article XI, which outlaws quantitative trade restrictions (with specified exceptions), and Article XII, which says that any permitted quantitative restrictions must be applied on a nondiscriminatory basis. On both counts, the exporting country administering the restriction, in other words the victim, is the guilty party.

34. C. Fred Bergsten, Kimberly Ann Elliot, Jeffrey J. Schott, and Wendy E. Takacs, *Auction Quotas and United States Trade Policy*, Policy Analyses in International Economics, 19 (Washington, D.C.: Institute for International Economics, September 1987).

35. Laura Megna Baughman, "Auctioning of Quotas: Lots of Pain for Little Gain," *The World Economy*, vol. 11, no. 3 (September 1988): 397–415. The arguments about GATT violations do not hold up well. A GATT-consistent Article XIX safeguard action could involve auctioned quotas. However, unlike VERs, an Article XIX action would be quite visible and may involve the payment of compensation through alternative trade liberalization measures.

36. See the tabulated summary in Wolf, "Why Voluntary Export Restraints?" p. 285.

37. That does not happen by definition, but since the basic motivation for VERs is to facilitate the maintenance of higher levels of protection, a consequence is usually that the most dynamic and efficient exporting countries are the ones that provoke the restraints.

38. Jagdish N. Bhagwati, "VERs, Quid Pro Quo DFI and VIEs: Political-Economy-Theoretical Analysis," *International Economic Journal*, vol. 1 (1987):1–12.

39. A country accepting a VIE commitment is likely to concentrate on placating the *demandeurs* for the action, quite possibly leading to a discriminatory outcome in practice.

40. I. M. Destler and John S. Odell, *Anti-Protection: Changing Forces in United States Trade Politics*, Policy Analyses in International Economics, 21 (Washington, D.C.: Institute for International Economics, 1987).

41. Bhagwati, *Protectionism*, chap. 3.

42. The exclusion is from the national treatment provision of Article III. There is, however, a mild nondiscrimination provision in the rules dealing with state trading enterprises (Article XVII).

43. The MFN requirement with respect to the codes is derived from a 1979 decision, which adopts the codes as part of the GATT system. In that decision, it is clear that existing benefits under GATT, including the right to nondiscriminatory treatment, should not be compromised in respect of nonmembers of the codes by virtue of the existence of the codes.

44. G. C. Hufbauer, J. Shelton Erb, and H. P. Starr, "The GATT Codes and the Unconditional Most-Favored-Nation Principle," *Law and Policy in International Business*, vol. 12, no. 1 (1980): 59–93.

45. The injury test must establish that subsidization or dumping is causing or threatening material injury to a domestic industry before an antidumping or countervailing duty can be applied.

46. When the GATT was drawn up, it was agreed that countries could retain certain preexisting legislation even though it was not consistent with the requirements of the GATT. This became known as the Grandfather Clause.

47. India took the United States to the GATT over this issues in the early 1980s, but a settlement was reached whereby India received the injury test in exchange for an undertaking, the content of which amounted to considerably less than a full commitment to eliminate export subsidies on manufactures.

48. See, for example, Gary Clyde Hufbauer and Jeffrey J. Schott, *Trading for Growth: The Next Round of Trade Negotiations*, Policy Analyses in International Economics, 11 (Washington, D.C.: Institute for International Economics, September 1985).

49. Ibid., p. 20.

50. It is arguable that the threat of conditional MFN is sufficient to deal with the foot dragging problem, which is really only an issue between the United States, the European Community, and Japan.

51. See commentary by Martin Wolf to Paul Wonnacott and Mark Lutz, "Is There a Case for Free Trade Areas?" in Jeffrey J. Schott, ed., *Free Trade Areas and U.S. Trade Policy* (Washington, D.C.: Institute for International Economics, 1989), pp. 89–95.

52. James Baker, "The Geopolitical Implications of the U.S.-Canada Trade Pact," *The International Economy* (January/February 1988): 35.

53. Ibid., p. 41.

54. That is not to say that geographically limited arrangements could necessarily be controlled with respect to trade distortions and their damaging effects on third parties.

55. The problem goes further than just the intrinsic complexity of new areas of regulation. It is also the coverage of the system that must be determined. It is obvious, for example, why developing countries might resent rapid progress toward new multilateral disciplines on investment and intellectual property rights, when the protagonists of these initiatives cannot summon the political will do anything about discrimination and protectionism in such traditional areas as textiles and clothing.

56. Ernest H. Preeg, *The American Challenge in World Trade: U.S. Interests in the Multilateral Trading System*, Significant Issues Series, vol. 11, no. 7 (Washington, D.C.: Center for Strategic Studies, 1989).

57. See Hufbauer in Twentieth Century Fund Task Force on the Future of American Trade Policy, *The Free Trade Debate* (1989).

58. As Aho and Ostry point out, weakness in the GATT might have contributed to an interest in regionalism, but the GATT has in turn been affected by this reaction. See C. Michael Aho and Sylvia Ostry, "Regional Trading Blocs: Pragmatic or Problematic Policy?" in William Brock and Robert Hormats, eds., *The Global Economy: America's Role in the Decade Ahead* (New York: Norton, 1990), pp. 147–73. These authors also stress the "down-side" of regionalism, and the likelihood that regional arrangements will be unstable, generate friction, and politicize trade.

59. Martin Wolf, in comments on Paul Wonnacott and Mark Latz, "Is There a Case for Free Trade Areas?" in Jeffrey J. Schott, ed., *Free Trade Areas and U.S. Trade Policy* (Washington, D.C.: Institute for International Economics, 1989), p. 93.

60. Atlantic Council of the United States, *GATT Plus—A Proposal for Trade Reform* (New York: Praeger, 1976).

61. A possibility would be to attach an accession clause to the NAFTA, comparable to that of the GATT. This could have the additional advantage of making it unnecessary for the administration to seek approval from Congress every time a new country became involved in a free trade arrangement with the United States. This was not the approach adopted in NAFTA, where the agreement merely foresees that countries may apply to join.

62. Ronald J. Wonnacott, "U.S. Hub-and-Spoke Bilaterals and the Multilateral Trading System," *Commentary* (Toronto: C.D. Howe Institute, October 1990).

63. Ibid.

64. At present notification and consultation requirements vary between different kinds of arrangements, and are not always taken seriously.

65. See Jeffrey J. Schott, "More Free Trade Areas?" in Schott, ed., *Free Trade Areas and U.S. Trade Policy* (Washington, D.C.: Institute for International Economics, 1989), pp. 1–58.

66. For an excellent account of developing countries in the GATT system, see Robert E. Hudec, *Developing Countries in the GATT System,* Thames Essay no. 50 (Aldershot, U.K.: Gower for the Trade Policy Research Centre, 1987). For a clear, well argued analysis of the issues from a developing country perspective, see Diana Tussie, *The Less Developed Countries and the World Trading System: A Challenge to the GATT* (New York: St. Martin's Press, 1987).

67. For documentary evidence of this, and a general discussion of the issues, see John Whalley, *The Uruguay Round and Beyond: The Final Report from the Ford Foundation Supported Project on Developing Countries and the Global Trading System* (London: Macmillan, 1989).

68. See ibid.

69. This is not to say that certain GATT rules could not be interpreted as relevant to disciplines in these areas, but rather that the rules were not designed to deal with cross-border flows of labor and capital, and the issue was at most peripheral.

CHAPTER 8

1. Starting with the first tariff negotiation in Geneva in 1947, when the GATT came into being, subsequent rounds were held in Annecy, France (1949), Torquay, England (1951), Geneva (1956), Geneva (1960–61, the Dillon Round), Geneva (1964–67, the Kennedy Round), and Geneva (1973–79, the Tokyo Round).

2. See John H. Jackson, Jean-Victor Louis, and Mitsuo Matsushita, "Implementing the Tokyo Round: Legal Aspects of Changing Economic Rules," *Michigan Law Review,* vol. 81 (December 1982): 267.

3. The Antidumping Act of 1921 (as amended). For a discussion of this, and the most complete and authoritative analysis available of the Tokyo Round, see Gilbert R.

Winham, *International Trade and the Tokyo Round Negotiation* (Princeton: Princeton University Press, 1986).

4. Section 201(a) of the Renegotiation Amendments Act of 1968.

5. Winham, *International Trade and the Tokyo Round Negotiation*, p. 74.

6. The basic principle of negotiations in these fields was enunciated by the Rey group in the early 1970s.

7. Ad Article XXXVI:8.

8. United States, Canada, Japan, European Community, Austria, Finland, Norway, Sweden, Switzerland.

9. See General Agreement on Tariffs and Trade, *The Tokyo Round of Multilateral Trade Negotiations*, Report by the Director-General of GATT, Geneva, April 1979. See also Volume II of this report, dated January 1980.

CHAPTER 9

1. For a full account of the emergence of the new issues that eventually became part of the Uruguay Round negotiations, see A. Jane Bradley, "Intellectual Property Rights, Investment, and Trade in Services in the Uruguay Round: Laying the Foundations," *Stanford Journal of International Law*, vol. 23, no. 1 (Spring 1987): 57–87.

2. The CG–18, established in July 1975, is a restricted but representative high-level group of officials of contracting parties that meets under the chairmanship of the Director-General of the GATT to discuss existing and emerging trade policy issues on an informal and confidential basis. Its membership was originally 18 contracting parties. The CG–18 makes recommendations to the Contracting Parties. During its ten years of active existence, between 1975 and 1985, the CG–18 has been a very important GATT organ, acting as the conduit for introducing new ideas and initiatives into GATT processes, and for facilitating discussions of contentious issues in the more formal setting of other GATT bodies. The CG–18 has been largely moribund since 1985, in part because there were growing difficulties over keeping the size of the Group within reasonable proportions, and partly because the Uruguay Round mandate involved negotiations on institutional arrangements directly relevant to the existence of a body like the CG–18.

3. Reported in General Agreement on Tariffs and Trade, *GATT Activities in 1981* (Geneva: GATT, 1982), p. 7.

4. Included on the list were safeguards, agriculture, dispute settlement, participation of developing countries in the trading system, tropical products, quantitative import restrictions, nontariff measures, tariffs, structural adjustment, and trade policy, Tokyo Round Agreements and Arrangements, exports of domestically prohibited goods, trade in counterfeit goods, export credits on capital goods, textiles and clothing, trade in fish and fish products, trade in non-ferrous metals, trade in forestry products, trade in services, rules of origin, dual pricing, exchange rate fluctuations, aspects of trade in high technology products, export restrictions, trade-related investment measures, and trade practices of transnational corporations.

5. Statement by Australia, delivered to the ministerial meeting by Mr. Colin Teese, Deputy Secretary, Australian Department of Trade and Resources.

6. Internal GATT document L/5424, November 29, 1982.

7. "Declaration by the Commission of the European Communities on Behalf of the European Communities Concerning Certain Points of the GATT Ministerial Declaration at the 38th Session of the Contracting Parties," mimeo (n.d.).

8. It will be recalled that the military government of General Galtieri occupied the islands in April 1982 and that Britain repossessed them six weeks later.

9. Tariff escalation refers to a situation in which tariff levels rise along the processing chain, thereby making it easier for developing countries to export products in their raw state rather than in processed form. Tariff negotiations under GATT are based on nominal, not effective, tariffs. The effect of these negotiations on tariff escalation cannot be predicted, which is one reason why some tariff negotiations have been based on a harmonizing formula.

10. Those are the Tokyo Round codes on antidumping, subsidies, and countervailing duties, technical barriers, customs valuation, import licensing, and government procurement.

11. This was a common criticism at the time. One of the earliest extensive statements was that of the United States Trade Representative, published at the end of 1982. See William E. Brock, "A Simple Plan for Negotiating on Trade in Services," *The World Economy*, vol. 5, no. 3 (November 1982): 229–240.

12. Statement made at a news conference in Geneva on November 24, 1982.

13. This was in a prepared statement before the Senate Finance Committee on January 25, 1983 on "An Assessment of the GATT Ministerial Meeting."

CHAPTER 10

1. An excellent account of the Uruguay Round, in its preparatory and early phases, has recently been written by Alan Oxley, who was Australia's Ambassador to the GATT from 1985 to 1989. See Alan Oxley, *The Challenge of Free Trade* (New York: St. Martin's Press, 1990).

2. Both the United States and the European Community have used the GATT's dispute-settlement machinery quite extensively against Japan. The difference is that the European Community has brought its broad, fundamental complaints about Japanese economic and trade policies into GATT discussions, whereas the United States has not.

3. GATT Document L/5479 of 8 April, 1983.

4. The GATT secretariat came to refer informally to this case as the EC complaint against "the Japanese way of life."

5. EFTA members are Austria, Finland, Iceland, Norway, Sweden, and Switzerland.

6. The G-10 included Argentina, Brazil, Cuba, Egypt, India, Nicaragua, Nigeria, Peru, Tanzania, and Yugoslavia.

7. PREP.COM(86)W/47, also known as the "café au lait" text after its sponsors.

8. In the final days of the Geneva process, Argentina had submitted a third draft declaration, in the hope of mediating the differences between the G–10 (of which it was a member) and the majority position. But the initiative was largely ignored.

9. Section I was launched by the Contracting Parties to GATT meeting at ministerial level and Section II, dealing with services alone, was launched by Ministers.

10. This case was also notable as the first one ever brought by Japan under the dispute-settlement procedures of the GATT.

11. These offers were not significant in terms of trade coverage, but did represent a new departure. In effect, the only developing countries that came up with anything were Brazil, certain Central American countries, Colombia, Malaysia, Mexico, the Philippines, and Thailand.

12. Current trade coverage was estimated at between US$ 25 billion to US$30 billion. This number gives little indication of the likely trade effects of the liberalization.

13. This was a group of fourteen industrial and developing countries — Australia, Argentina, Brazil, Canada, Chile, Colombia, Fiji, Hungary, Indonesia, Malaysia, New Zealand, the Philippines, Thailand, and Uruguay—that met in Cairns, Australia, in 1986 and drew up a position in support of far-reaching liberalization of agricultural trade. This group is to be contrasted with the net importers, led by Egypt, Jamaica, Morocco, and Peru, who feared that trade liberalization in agriculture would raise world prices and lead to a deterioration in their terms of trade. These countries sought compensation for any income losses they would suffer as a result of liberalized trade.

14. *News of the Uruguay Round*, NUR 039 (July 30, 1990).

15. For a fuller account of the fast-track extension debate, see I. M. Destler, *American Trade Politics*, 2d ed. (Washington, D.C., and New York: Institute for International Economics and Twentieth Century Fund, 1992), pp. 97–102.

16. The discussions on the Final Act are concerned with institutional arrangements for the final adoption of Uruguay Round results.

17. With minor exceptions, including the Agreement on Trade in Civil Aircraft, the Agreement on Government Procurement, and the dairy and bovine meat arrangements.

18. For developing countries alone, it has been calculated that a 50 percent tariff reduction on the part of the European Community, Japan, and the United States would lead to an increase of $50 billion in exports. The gains to industrial countries would be significantly greater than this amount. See World Bank, *Global Economic Prospects and the Developing Countries* (Washington, D.C.: World Bank, 1992).

19. Apart from nonspecific subsidies as defined in the text, certain subsidies to R&D and certain regional development subsidies are considered nonactionable.

20. This in a letter from Deputy U.S. Trade Representative Julius Katz to the American Association of Exporters and Importers, dated April 16, 1992.

21. Many of these exceptions refer to preexisting intellectual property agreements, including the Paris Convention, the Berne Convention, and the Rome Convention.

22. See Arvind Subramanian, "TRIPS and the Paradigm of the GATT: A Tropical Temperate View," *The World Economy*, vol. 13, no. 4 (December 1990): 509–21. See also Arvind Subramanian, "Social Costs and Benefits of Increased Patent Protection for Pharmaceuticals," mimeo available from the author (1991).

23. There is a literature on this question largely arguing that in trade policy discussions the worker rights issue often amounts to a negation of comparative advantage. The complaint is essentially based on the fact that wage costs are lower in some countries than others, and the apparent concern for the welfare of workers is a smoke-screen for protectionism. See Deepak Lal, *Resurrection of the Pauper-Labour Argument*, Thames Essay no. 28 (London: Trade Policy Research Centre, 1981).

GLOSSARY

ACTPN	Advisory Committee for Trade Policy and Negotiations
ASP	American Selling Price
ASEAN	Association of South-East Asian Nations
CAP	EC common agricultural policy
CG-18	Consultative Group of Eighteen, GATT
CVD	Countervailing duty
DFA	Draft final act of the Uruguay Round
Dillon Round	Round of multilateral trade negotiations in GATT, 1960–61
DRAMs	Dynamic random access memories
EAI	Enterprise for the Americas Initiative
EC	European Community
EEC	European Economic Community
EFTA	European Free Trade Association
EPROMs	Erasable programmable read-only memories
FTA	Free trade area/agreement
GAO	General Accounting Office
GATS	General Agreement on Trade in Services
GATT	General Agreement on Tariffs and Trade
GDP	Gross Domestic Product
GSP	Generalized System of Preferences
IMF	International Monetary Fund
ITO	International Trade Organization

Kennedy Round	Round of multilateral trade negotiations in GATT, 1964–67
LTA	Long-Term Arrangement Regarding International Trade in Textiles
MFA	Multi-Fiber Arrangement
MFN	Most-favored-nation
MITI	Japanese Ministry of International Trade and Industry
Montant de soutien	Agricultural support price
MOSS	Market-Oriented Sector-Selective talks
MTN	Multilateral trade negotiation
MTO	Multilateral trade organization
NAFTA	North American Free Trade Agreement
NIC	Newly industrializing country
NTB	Nontariff barrier to trade
OECD	Organization for Economic Cooperation and Development
OMA	Orderly marketing arrangement
QR	Quantitative trade restriction
R&D	Research and development
SIA	Semiconductor Industry Association
SII	Structural Impediments Initiative
STA	Short-Term Arrangement Regarding International Trade in Textiles
STR	Special Trade Representative
TAA	Trade Adjustment Assistance
TNC	Trade Negotiations Committee
Tokyo Round	Round of multilateral trade negotiations in GATT, 1973–79
TPM	Trigger price mechanism
TRIPS	Trade-related intellectual property rights
TRIMS	Trade-related investment measures
UAW	United Auto Workers
UNCTAD	United Nations Conference on Trade and Development
Uruguay Round	Round of multilateral trade negotiations in GATT, 1986–
USITC	U.S. International Trade Commission
USTR	United States Trade Representative
VER	Voluntary export restraint
VIE	Voluntary import expansion
WIPO	World Intellectual Property Organization

INDEX

283

ABOUT THE AUTHOR

Patrick Low worked in the GATT secretariat in Geneva from 1980 to 1988. Currently on the staff of the World Bank, he has served as a visiting scholar at El Colegio de México in Mexico City and has worked as a consultant for several governments and international organizations. Dr. Low, who holds a doctorate in economics from the University of Sussex, England, has published a number of papers on trade and policy issues.